Mailer's Last Days

New and Selected Remembrances of a Life in Literature

Also By J. Michael Lennon

Norman Mailer: The Sixties (editor)

Norman Mailer: Works and Days

(with Donna Pedro Lennon and Gerald R. Lucas)

Selected Letters of Norman Mailer (editor)

Norman Mailer: A Double Life

On God: An Uncommon Conversation (with Norman Mailer)

The Spooky Art by Norman Mailer (editor)

The James Jones Reader (editor, with James R. Giles)

Conversations with Norman Mailer (editor)

Critical Essays on Norman Mailer (editor)

Pieces and Pontifications by Norman Mailer (editor)

Lively, informative, by turns analytical and poignant, J. Michael Lennon's omnium gatherum opens a wide window on the post-war American literary scene, framed by Mailer's astonishing career. Baldwin, Bishop, Didion, Jones, Lowell, McCarthy, Stone, and Vidal are among those who appear in this rich collection. And beneath it all, beats the book's true heart: Lennon's pursuit of his own distant father and his "adopted father"—Norman Mailer.

—Robert J. Begiebing, *Norman Mailer at 100: Conversations, Correlations, Confrontations*

One would be hard pressed to find a more eloquent gentleman than J. Michael Lennon—scholar, raconteur, devourer of books and connoisseur of the stories behind them. That Lennon has come out from behind the scenes of literary legend Norman Mailer's life and oeuvre is a gift not only to the first-rate literature of which he writes but to anyone who loves good stories with a dash of sass, a dose of philosophy and big gulpfuls of heart. A hybrid of biography, memoir, and criticism, this book is so compelling I wanted more Lennon long after the last page. I cannot praise this book enough.

—Beverly Donofrio, *Riding in Cars with Boys* and *Astonished*

I loved this book, and not simply because I have an endless appetite for Mailer, but because Lennon has satisfied a craving I didn't know I had: for a collection that packs the emotion of a memoir and the insight of literary criticism. It's a candid, original, beautifully written collection that provides moving portraits of two powerful writers and the intersection of their lives.

—Jonathan Eig, *Ali: A Life*

Thoughtful and erudite with surprising twists of humor, J. Michael Lennon's *Mailer's Last Days* is an exciting blend of literary genres. It is a master class in American and English Literature with poignant episodes of his own life as a boy, as a novice professor, as Mailer's biographer, archivist and close friend. The book takes us on a journey to the work of writers such as Joan Didion, Don DeLillo, James Jones, Graham Greene, Elizabeth Bishop and Ezra Pound. In a nutshell, it's an immersion into the American cultural and literary life of the Twentieth Century.

—Susan Mailer, *In Another Place:*
With and Without My Father Norman Mailer

By turns deeply personal and remarkably selfless in its attention to others, this uniquely devised memoir is also a moving love letter to literature. Each essay is eloquent, erudite, and engaging, an inspiring testament to the value of Lennon's literary life, and the abiding and meaningful friendship it yielded.

—Maggie McKinley, *Understanding Norman Mailer*

J. Michael Lennon elevates literary sensibilities as he seamlessly blends memoir, essays, and reviews in his innovative collection. With adroit storytelling marked by wit, honesty, and awareness, Lennon crafts arresting tales that create the portrait of a biographer. Lennon's enthralling prose is a joy to read.

—Nancy McKinley, *St. Christopher on Pluto*

J. Michael Lennon is a robust critic and biographer who, in these lively pieces, summons a whole world of great American writers and thinkers in their time. Not incidentally, he offers an astute and compelling portrait of himself as well—an unexpected tale of immersion in life stories. This is one of those books one calls "delicious." It's not easy to stop eating once you start.

—Jay Parini, *The Last Station* and *Borges and Me*

J. Michael Lennon accompanies us on a journey through American literary life, introducing us to the greats he's known, and pointing out, with sympathy unusual among distinguished critics, that perhaps the worst thing that can happen to a creative soul is to become famous.

—Charles J. Shields, *Lorraine Hansberry:*
The Life Behind A Raisin in the Sun

Mailer's Last Days

New and Selected Remembrances of a Life in Literature

J. Michael Lennon

Etruscan Press

Etruscan Press
Wilkes University
84 West South Street
Wilkes-Barre, PA 18766
(570) 408-4546

www.etruscanpress.org

Published 2022 by Etruscan Press
Printed in the United States of America
Cover design by Lisa Reynolds
Cover photo: Petra Lukoschek
Interior design and typesetting by Aaron Petrovitch
The text of this book is set in Goudy Old Style.

First Edition

17 18 19 20 5 4 3 2 1

Library of Congress Cataloging-in-Publication Data

Names: Lennon, Michael, author.
Title: Mailer's last days: new and selected remembrances of a life in
    literature / J. Michael Lennon.
Description: First edition. | Wilkes Barre : Etruscan Press, 2022. |
    Summary: "Lennon's remembrances in this collection are linked by his
    attempt to understand his relationship with his putative parent, Norman
    Mailer, a need intensified by his decades-long confusion about his
    relationship to his actual father. The literary essays and reviews that
    take up the middle of this collection are about people, writers for the
    most part, whose work Mailer admired, or were his literary colleagues
    and/or rivals"~ Provided by publisher.
Identifiers: LCCN 2021044047 | ISBN 9781736494653 (paperback)
Subjects: LCSH: Mailer, Norman~Friends and associates. | Lennon,
    Michael~Friends and associates. | Authors, American~20th
    century~Biography. | Biographers~United States~Biography.
Classification: LCC PS3525.A4152 Z7355 2022 | DDC 813/.51
    [B]~dc23/eng/2021-11-15
LC record available at https://lccn.loc.gov/2021044047

Please turn to the back of this book for a list of the sustaining funders of Etruscan Press.

This book is printed on recycled, acid-free paper.

For My Grandchildren:

Liam Anthony Lennon
Nicholas Anthony Lennon
Rory Catherine Lennon
Sean Allen Lennon

Contents

Acknowledgments

All of the essays and reviews and four of the eleven memoir pieces in this collection have appeared, sometimes in a slightly different form, in various journals and newspapers: "The Archivist's Apprentice," *Lifewriting Annual: Biographical and Autobiographical Studies* 5 (2021); "Mailer's Library," *Times Literary Supplement* (March 9, 2018); "Feathered with Forbearance: Shirley Hazzard on Graham Greene," *Provincetown Arts* (2001); "Bishop, Pound, and Prospero in Buzzards Bay," *Ocean State Review* (2016); "The Touchdown Twins: James Jones and Norman Mailer," *Mailer Review* (2020); "With the Goddess of the Night: John Bowers's Memoir," *Springfield, IL State Journal-Register* (June 25, 1984); "Lowney Handy and Her Improbable Writers Colony," *Blue Cross-Blue Shield Life Times of Illinois*, September 1989; "To Fame from Obscurity: The Letters of James Jones," *Chicago Tribune Books* (May 14, 1989); "James Jones's World War II Trilogy," *James Jones Journal* (Spring 2009); "Gore Vidal, American Iconoclast," *TLS* (October 16, 2015); "Gore and Norman in Provincetown," *Mailer Review* (2012); "Triumph at the Biltmore: John F. Kennedy's Nomination," Introduction to *JFK: Superman Comes to the Supermarket* by Norman Mailer, ed. Nina Weiner (Taschen, 2014); "A Meeting of Giants: Ali and Foreman," Introduction to *The Fight* by Norman Mailer, ed. J. Michael Lennon (Taschen, 2018); "Craftsman of Violence: Muhammad Ali," *TLS* (November 24, 2017); "She Is Her Own Most Memorable Character: Joan Didion," *Washington Post* (November 7, 2019); "Motion Slowed into Choreography: Didion Drives South," *TLS* (February 24, 2017); "Tom Wolfe, Upstart, R.I.P.," *Chicago Tribune*

(May 16, 2018); "Crafted Confession: Re-reading Mary McCarthy's *Memories of a Catholic Childhood*," *TLS* (July 10, 2020); "James Baldwin: Preacher vs. Writer," *Mailer Review* (2021); "Drenched in Dread: Don DeLillo's *Moribundi*," *TLS*, (May 6, 2016); "Dread Persists: DeLillo's Digital Disaster," *TLS* (October 23, 2020); "A Mistake 10,000 Miles Long: Robert Stone," *TLS* (March 12, 2021); "A Magnificent Keening: Philip Brady," *Hippocampus* (April 1, 2019), Internet; "Murder, Sex, and the Writing Life: An Interview with Mailer's Biographer," by Ronald K. Fried, *The Daily Beast* (November 19, 2013); "Norman Mailer: Novelist, Journalist, or Historian?" *Journal of Modern Literature* 30 (Fall 2006); "Hitler on My Mind: The Roots of *The Castle in the Forest*," *Provincetown Arts* (2008).

My thanks to the publications where these pieces appeared, and to my editors, in whom I have been quite fortunate: Phillip Sipiora, *Mailer Review*; Elizabeth Winston and the late Christopher Busa at *Provincetown Arts*; James Campbell and Toby Lichtig at *Times Literary Supplement*; Charles Kell at *Ocean State Review*; Nina Weiner at Taschen Books; Carol DeBoer-Langworthy at *Lifewriting Annual*; John Whalen-Bridge at *Journal of Modern Literature*; Nora Krug at *Washington Post*; Angela Eckhardt and Donna Talarico at *Hippocampus*; and Thomas J. Wood at *James Jones Journal*. I would also like to thank the talented staff at Etruscan Press: Robert Mooney, Bill Schneider, Pamela Turchin, Janine Dubik, and Executive Director Philip Brady.

Appreciations

The idea for this collection emerged slowly. The seed was first planted when, after the publication of my 2013 biography, *Norman Mailer: A Double Life*, I read a haunting memoir, *A Berkshire Boyhood: Confessions and Reflections of a Baby Boomer* published that same year by my friend, Bob Begiebing. We are contemporaries and founding board members of the Norman Mailer Society, and share the same passion for explaining and celebrating Mailer's life and work. We also share New England backgrounds, and fathers who were World War II veterans. Two years later, Bob published *The Territory Around Us*, a rich and learned collection of previously published essays focused in part on "transformative moments" in the lives of some major writers. The two volumes resonate with each other, crisscrossing in suggestive ways that started me thinking about collecting some of my own literary essays and reviews about Mailer and his contemporaries, along with a series of memoir pieces that I had begun writing.

I was simmering, simmering and then in 2017, another friend and colleague, Philip Brady, like me a founding faculty member of Wilkes University's Maslow Graduate Creative Writing Program, asked me to read his manuscript, the operative definition of which seemed to be "mixed bag." I liked it a lot (my review of it is included here), and two years later, when this generically unclassifiable, but magically coherent collection, *Phantom Signs: The Muse in Universe City*, was published, the desire to assemble my own collection came to a boil. Brady uses a panoply of rhetorical and poetic modalities, some of them intensely personal, some forensic, some poetic, some archival, some ostensibly (but not really) whimsical, all of them infused with the energies and accomplishments of his 40 years as a poet, memoirist, editor, and professor, and twenty as a publisher.

But there was a problem. My material, about 45 separate pieces, fell naturally into three categories: reviews, essays, and memoirs. Presenting these in three chronological enclaves looked to be, as far as reader response is concerned, the equivalent of three rows of potted plants. My Etruscan editor, friend, and Wilkes colleague, Robert Mooney, rolled up his editorial sleeves and gave me a way to introduce and arrange the pieces in what I hope is a comely sequence, one that follows my own development as a writer, and is entwined with my relationship with my father and Norman Mailer. At his urging, I added a good deal more memoir material, and dropped several reviews and essays, so that now the book in your hands is roughly half literary commentary and half memoir, laced together with cross-references and other ligatures of congruence.

I am indebted to these three gentlemen; the editors named in "Acknowledgments;" my keen and formidable agent, John T. (Ike) Williams; and several individuals who read my entire manuscript and provided detailed and astute commentary and correction: Donna Pedro, my wife and first reader, my eldest son Stephen, my brother Peter, Barbara Wasserman, Norman's sister and family historian, and Jack Galvin, novelist and graduate school friend.

For information, suggestions, encouragement, and other generous acts, I am also grateful to: Allen Ahearn, Rene Allen, Peter Alson, Kathleen Arruda, Madison Smartt Bell, Mashey Bernstein, Greg Bestick, John Bowers, Larsen Bowker, Philip Bufithis, Tom Bushar, Suzanna Calev, Maureen Corrigan, Bonnie Culver, John Dalziel, Carla Dane, Essy Davidowitz, Don DeLillo, Nicole DePolo, Patrick Dickson, the late Morris Dickstein, Maureen Hinchcliffe Donahue, Beverly Donofrio, Jim Engster, Judith Everson, Jaclyn Fowler, Jeanne Fuchs, Erika Funke, the late Melody Grell, Margaret Hall, the late George Hendrick, David Hicks, Howard Hymes, Kaylie

Jones, Ross Klavan, James Lennon, Joseph Lennon (with gratitude for late-inning assistance), Laurie Loewenstein, Mary Elizabeth Logan, Bill Lowenburg, Gerald R. Lucas, Carol MacAllister, Maureen Macedo, Danielle Mailer and Peter McEachern, John Buffalo Mailer, Michael Mailer, Susan Mailer, Warren and Annette Mason, Vicki Mayk, Colum McCann, Peter McGowan, Maggie McKinley, Nancy McKinley, Steve Mielke, Lynn Mitchell, Jason Mosser, Michael A. Nixon, Kevin Oderman, Mark Olshaker, Barry and Jane O'Neill, the late Dean Pappas, Denise Pappas, Sara Pisak, Taylor Polites, Nancy Potter, Frances Reilly, Max Rudin, Brian Sacolic, Lawrence Schiller, Larry Shiner, Joan Sibley, John C. Stachacz, Charles B. Strozier, Enid Stubin, Andrea Talarico, Jeff Talarigo, Angela Thorpe, Khachig Tölölyan, Chris Tomasino, David Wilson, Robert Wilson, Veronica Windholz, and John J. Winters.

Prologue:
In the "I" of the Storm

The rising action of my life in literature led to a friendship with one of the greatest American writers of the time I came of age. I met Norman Mailer in 1972, and for thirty-five years we grew ever closer in aesthetic interests and fervor for the same philosophical entanglements. For the last five years of his life—he died in 2007—we lived down the street from him in Provincetown, the historic town at the tip of Cape Cod where writers and artists have congregated for over a century. If I had a question for him, I'd bring it up at our daily morning meetings or the evening meals my wife Donna and I had with him and his wife, Norris, a few times a week. This was a boon because I was working on an edition of his letters and, later, his biography. My access wasn't exclusive; Mailer was close to promiscuous in this regard; knock on his door and he'd invite you in for a drink. He'd chat with people about football on Commercial Street in P-town, or discuss Kierkegaard with New York subway philosophers. Gay Talese, his longtime friend, said he was the most accessible major writer in the country.

What never occurred to me when writing the biography is that when I reached the time in his life when we became close, the early '80s, I had become, willy-nilly, a character in his story— that is, the epic sweep of his life. I was one of a large cast, but in some instances important enough that my participation in Cause

(2021)

Mailer as his editor and archivist and friend required expatiation in the biography. How to accomplish this was the problem. I don't know that I solved it by referring to myself in the third person as "J. Michael Lennon, a young professor at the University of Illinois-Springfield." The fact that Mailer used the third-person personal in several of his best books gave me a sliver of sanction, but I was never completely satisfied with the oddness of the perspective, nor my presumption in using it. In writing the memoir pieces in this collection, including the title essay, I was relieved to recreate some of the interactions I had with Mailer over the years using a more befitting pronoun: I.

Of course, I knew him before I met him, in the sense of the avid reader's attraction to the work of a particular writer who has succeeded in creating an unshakable admiration. As with many, my first encounter with Mailer was reading his bestselling war novel set on a fictional island in the Pacific, circa early 1944. I finished it in January 1965 when I was serving as gunnery officer on the USS *Uvalde* (AKA-88). The ship was tied up in Genoa for the Christmas holidays after three months at sea. Half the crew was on shore leave, and for the other half with duty on the ship, it was a quiet, tedious time of writing letters, reading, following the news from Vietnam, playing chess and Acey-deucey, and watching old and new James Bond films—*Thunderball* had just been released. Our ship's doctor concluded that prescribing some medicinal brandy from his sick bay pharmacy (alcohol for drinking on naval vessels is otherwise prohibited) might dissipate the melancholy mood of the wardroom, but the tiny bottles he distributed barely lifted the gloom. It was my first Christmas away from home. But it wasn't all bad. One night on liberty, I went to the Genoa Post Office to make a late-night, semi-drunken trunk call via a chain of three or four international operators to Newport, R.I. The call was to my girlfriend, Donna Pedro, and to my joy and surprise, she accepted my marriage proposal.

I spent a lot of my spare time on the *Uvalde* reading. After I finished a book, I added the title to a list I kept in a notebook, which I still have. Some of the other titles I read during the cruise are *The Sand Pebbles* by Richard McKenna, *Fifty Great Short Stories*, edited by Milton Crane, *The Third Man* by Graham Greene, *Dubliners* by Joyce, five James Bond novels, and Conrad's *Lord Jim*. On St. Patrick's Day, when we were underway for homeport in Norfolk, I finished, after several false starts, Joyce's *Ulysses*. If a book struck me, I often added a note. Here is what I recorded about *Naked*:

> Mailer is a horrible pessimist. He is cynical in a frightening way. Makes you wonder if anything is worthwhile; a protest against everything but the most elemental pleasures—but he writes almost as well as James Jones—stark, raw, vital, an odyssey of pain, fear and frustration. He lets no one off the hook.

I'd read *From Here to Eternity* in college, and until I discovered Joyce nothing had moved me as profoundly as Jones's depiction of his mulishly principled bugler and boxer, Pvt. Robert E. Lee Prewitt. But then Joyce overtook Jones, and in May of 1968, Mailer supplanted Joyce. This was occasioned by reading *The Armies of the Night*, Mailer's account of the October 1967 anti-war March on the Pentagon. I wrote this in my notebook:

> It is, as Alfred Kazin has said [in a *New York Times* review], a new form; Mailer has given us an essay-journal-diary-tract type book that deals with the state of the Union. Filled with "infernally shrewd" portraits of Robert Lowell, Dwight Macdonald, and a mélange of hippies, New Leftists, ban-the-bomb-ers, Wm. Sloan Coffin (now on trial for aiding draft resisters) and Americans of every color and determination on the political and social spectrum. Mailer cannot be tied down; he has plenty of edges by which we

Lt. (j.g.) Lennon and Donna Pedro, New York City, summer 1965. *Photo by W. Patrick Dickson*

might criticize him, but 10 exceptional attributes for each drawback. Could be the Pepys diary of the 60s.

By this time, Donna and I were married and parents of our first son, Stephen—two more would follow, Joseph in 1968, and James in 1969. We were living in Newport, where I was stationed as an instructor of military law at the U.S. Navy's Officer Candidate School. After two years of night classes, I was about to finish my M.A. at the University of Rhode Island, and was scheduled for discharge in November 1968. When I began my doctoral work the following fall, I joined the Vietnam Veterans Against the War. *Armies* was instrumental in my decision to join the protests, which were growing at the time.

Mailer's announced purpose in the book was to reveal a nation so deeply stressed that it looked to be on the path to a second civil war. It is brilliantly effective in depicting the conflict, but it was his prickly, obscene, and self-aware voice that impressed me the most. The only one like it I'd encountered before was Whitman's. This echo eventually led me to Mailer's 1959 collection, *Advertisements for Myself*, a title obviously intended to resonate with Whitman's break-out poem, "Song of Myself." The autobiographical episodes, or "advertisements," in Mailer's omnibus were, by turns, as brazen, hesitant, shrewd, over-stuffed, and sex-suffused as Whitman's *Leaves of Grass*, which I'd devoured in my first graduate course.

I recall with vivid clarity the moment on Labor Day weekend in 1969 when I finished reading *Advertisements*. I was sitting on a bench in Newport's Touro Park, a short walk from our third-floor apartment and across the street from the Redwood Library. Before me was a round, six-legged stone structure that the locals said was built by the Vikings. Longfellow had a poem, "The Skeleton in Armor," that advances the claim that a Norse warrior had built this "lofty tower" for his Indian bride. This was later shown to be false— it was probably a grain silo or a windmill—but at the time it was comforting to believe I was reading in the shadow of a thousand-year-old tower.

Leaving the U.S. Navy after five years to embark on a multi-year effort to become an English professor, I had given up my lieutenant's pay, commissary privileges, housing allowance, and free health care. I had a wife, three sons in diapers, and no income save the GI Bill. Besides these worries, there was a darker cloud: my father's drinking. His alcoholism had forced him into early retirement. His younger brother, Hughie, and I had recently delivered him to the VA hospital for treatment, but he checked himself out the next day. The family was still hopeful, but worried. Dad, stubborn as Prewitt, was manacled by Mr. Alcohol, and making no discernible effort to free himself. That fall I was betwixt and between.

It was just the right moment to read *Advertisements*, Mailer's fourth book and the first in which he opened up about his self-doubts and large ambitions. He was at slack tide in the mid-50s, gathering his energies to write a novel that he claimed would create "a revolution in the consciousness of our time." Up to then, his avowed stance had been that it was "much better when people who have read your book didn't know anything about you." It's hard to believe now, but in 1959, Mailer had only just begun writing about himself—his 1956 columns in the *Village Voice* were the first, tentative attempt—and collapsing together his personal and artistic worlds in *Advertisements* sent his style through a circus of variations and postures.

In his opening "Note to the Reader," he says that the collection has two tables of contents: one is a chronological list of his previous work: novel excerpts, short stories, poems, interviews, and journalism. The second is a list of the "advertisements" that preface (and sometimes also follow) these pieces, where he explored his "present tastes, preferences, apologies, prides, and occasional confessions." The purpose of this list, titled "Biography of a Style," was to encourage readers to swallow the advertisements whole, read them apart from the selections that they frame, for the purpose of meeting the new kind of writer he was becoming. He also wanted the agonies of creating the book to bleed through, yet sparingly, in the manner of Yeats, who wanted his readers to know, as one critic put it, "about the intense and unremitting labor required to create an apparently spontaneous line." For example, Mailer concludes one of his advertisements with this tease: "The confession is over—I sense that to give any more of what happened to me in the last few years might make for five thousand good words, but could also strip me of fifty thousand better ones." But the revelations are far from over; subsequent advertisements continue to offer glimpses of his writerly life. Many long passages are suffused with the rhetoric of revealing and then shrouding the advances and setbacks of his compositional process. In addition to being a genre-conflating work—part confession, part tirade, part visionary testament—*Advertisements* is a great work because Mailer is adept at what we might call confession interruptus. Again and again he bares his battered psyche, and then breaks off, only to return with more revelations, laced with witty revilements and cranky pontifications.

During these years I was looking for a new father, but didn't realize it. Changing my filial allegiance from John C. Lennon to Norman K. Mailer happened over time, which I only dimly understood until I began writing about my childhood and the dissociation caused by my father's alcoholism. I wrote about my early life in the three opening pieces in this collection as a way of coming to grips with this slow conveyance. At first unconsciously and later on, obviously, Mailer began to supplant my original father. I couldn't completely grasp how this transition occurred without examining my father's early life, especially his relationship with his father, Hugh H. Lennon, which I explore in the final essay of the collection, "Fathers and Sons." I'd repressed much that happened in Dad's last years, but with the help of my siblings, I've tried to recreate my dwindling relationship with him, and the chasm—no less—between him and his father that opened in 1933.

The majority of the 11 memoir pieces in this collection deal with both my father and/or Norman Mailer, culminating in the final two, "Mailer's Last Days," and "Fathers and Sons." Mailer is also referred to in most of the other 21 pieces in the collection, sometimes only glancingly. My friendship with Mailer, and our collaboration on several books as well as the organization of his archive (undertaken in partnership with my wife), created my abiding, obsessive interest in everything Mailerian: his works, his cosmology, his life, his friends, family, enemies, collaborators, colleagues, and literary heroes. Every review and essay and interview collected here is directly or obliquely linked by my need to understand Mailer, my adopted father, a need intensified by my decades-long confusion about my relationship to my actual one.

Mailer told me once that he had met four geniuses in his life: Charlie Chaplin, Ezra Pound, Fidel Castro, and Muhammad Ali. He never said much about Chaplin, but wrote about the other three— more about Ali, who became a good friend, than the other two. There are essays about Pound and Ali included here, and Castro is cited in the essay on President Kennedy, who stands in the annex to Mailer's genius pantheon. No public figure garnered more of his attention than JFK although Ali came close. The literary essays and reviews that take up the middle of this collection are about people, writers for the most part, whose work Mailer admired, or were his literary colleagues and/or rivals. Here are their names, which my biographer's training dictates that I give in the order Mailer first met them, as best I can determine: Robert Lowell (1949), Mary McCarthy (1949), James Jones (1951), Gore Vidal (1952), John Bowers (1953), Lowney Handy (1953), Robert F. Lucid (1958), John F. Kennedy (1960), Muhammad Ali (1963), Joan Didion (c. 1967), Tom Wolfe (late 60s), Ezra Pound (1970), Graham Greene (1983), Don DeLillo (c. 1985), and Philip Brady (2004). My headnotes to most of these essays fill in essential details about Mailer's relations with the figures discussed, and—with Lucid, Bowers, Vidal, Ali, DeLillo, Didion, and Brady—my own.

So these pieces look both ways: backwards from the time I met Mailer in 1972 to my childhood and early relations with my father, and forward to my deeper and deeper involvement with Mailer up to his death in 2007. The essays attempt to explain why and how I became Mailer's putative son, and how I became, for a time, less of a son to my actual father. Now, however, I feel closer to Dad than at any other time since he died of alcoholism in 1975.

Many of Norman's friends thought of themselves as his best friend, and several of these, the younger ones, thought of him as a father figure. I resolved early on never to utter my own filial feelings, both out the fear of being presumptuous, or being rejected, or both. I also wanted to maintain a sliver of professional distance. But once I slipped. It was after a poker game at Mailer's house a few months before he died. He and I were talking over a nightcap about a friend and neighbor, Chris Busa. I commented on how restrained Busa had been during the game earlier that night. At a previous game a few days before, Norman had chastised him fairly harshly for excessive maundering while deciding whether to bet or fold. Several of us clapped in agreement. Chastened, Chris said very little during our just-concluded game. Norman said, "He probably thinks of me as a father figure." I agreed, immediately adding that I did as well and had for many years. He seemed surprised at first, but then saw the truth of it and nodded slowly, gravely.

The Dark Closet:
A Fall River Memoir

I was ensconced in utero on the day the Japanese bombed Pearl Harbor, and not long after my birth in June 1942, my father went off to war. I lived with my mother, the former Mary Mitchell, and her parents at 44 Bark Street in Fall River, Massachusetts, until my father's return. While he was away, I was the little king, the hub of the familial wheel, especially for my maiden aunts and grandparents—I'm the eldest of 33 first cousins. At family gatherings, right up to the present, the same story of my spoiled early life is trotted out by one or another relative. Over the mantel in my Grandmother Lennon's home (she was a widow) hung Charles Chambers's painting of the Christ child, "The Light of the World," which during the first half of the twentieth century was the most popular religious print in the U.S., especially among Catholics. When I was around two, as my mother told it, "Jesus came down and Michael went up." My photograph hung there for decades. Taken by a photographer uncle, the color photo shows a freckle-faced, pug-nosed me holding a toy gun, and one strap of my overalls down. I still have the holster that my grandfather Mitchell later made for my pistol, one that he fashioned out of a piece of soft gray leather, held together with now-rusty brads. I knew that I could get him to make it for me.

John A. "Jack" Mitchell was a dour man, but gentle and loving with me. At age 65, just before I was born, he was diagnosed with

(2018)

colon cancer, and had a sigmoid colostomy, one of the first in the country. He wore a colostomy bag that my grandmother emptied and cleaned every day. When I sat on his lap, I could feel the bump it made under his blue wool cardigan sweater. Gram told me not to touch it.

Except for my large head, the rest of me could have been constructed of Popsicle sticks and glue. I was puny, but game, and walked unattended from my grandparents' home to visit Lafayette Park, about a quarter of a mile away on the main drag, Eastern Avenue. This wide thoroughfare, which fronted the park and a French parochial school, the Dominican Academy, was my turf. I knew several French families along the way—Nadeau, Boiseneau, and Pelletier—and often visited them, knocking on their doors and inviting myself in. I was also friendly in a formal sort of way with the General's equestrian statue at the entrance to the eponymous park and, across the avenue at the intersection of County Street, with an object that dominated my imaginative life as fully as Stonehenge did that of the Druids: Rolling Rock, a 140-ton, pudding-stone boulder deposited by melting glacial ice on a granite pedestal some 10,000 years ago. Before it was stabilized in 1861, the egg-shaped stone rock, known to geologists as a glacial erratic, could actually be moved by two hands, causing it to oscillate about two inches at the top. Neighborhood children were told that the local Indians used to place the hands of traitors beneath the edge of the rock, and then roll it slowly over their digits until they were as flat as a sheet of paper, although I can find no corroboration for this racist tale. When Gram sent me to Coriaty's Variety or Dagnall's Market, I would salute the General ("the hero of two worlds," as I would learn), touch the fabled rock, and then, my pockets bulging with rusty screws and other bits of junk I'd plucked from the gutter, return home to help Grandpa.

My grandfather was the head pipefitter at one of the cotton mills in Fall River, then known as "The Spindle City." The many-windowed (built before electricity) textile mills, four to eight stories high, and hundreds of feet long, were constructed from granite blasted out of local quarries. They employed the greater part of the city's workers for over a century, and all of my family, the Lennons and the Grants on my father's side, and the Mitchells and the Lynns on my mother's, worked in them. The mills were complicated steam-punk operations that required an army of loom fixers, bobbin boys, and pipe fitters to run and maintain the looms. As a teenager, my brother Peter delivered coffee and snacks to the mills. He told me that the din of the looms in the mills was so tremendous that hand signals were necessary to communicate. Until 1938 when national child labor laws were enacted, children from the age of 12 toiled 10 hours a day in the industry, including my grandmother, Lizzy Lynn. Shortly after she began work after completing eighth grade, she lost the index finger of her right hand in the relentless machinery of the enormous Weave Room of the Sagamore Mill, where Peter sold coffee and donuts 60 years later. Her compensation: $12 and a day off. She continued thereafter in the mills (her middle finger filling in just fine for the lost one), until the age of 28 when she married Jack Mitchell. He was 38, an Irish bachelor. She told the story of her digital loss many times to me, and it got mixed up in my head with the crushed fingers of the Indians. My siblings and I, and then our children, would rub the stump, a family ritual. Gram wasn't even a tiny bit nostalgic about her severed finger—it was gone and that was that.

Grandpa Mitchell housed his pipefitting tools in a garage workshop behind the house. It was Ali Baba's cave for me—gloomy, cluttered, and treasure-laden. He had dozens of hammers and mauls, and every variety of wrench, some three feet long, some with wooden handles. He named them all for me, but I only remember my favorite, the eagle beak wrench. Hooks and racks held chain falls, stump pullers, pipe threaders; bins brimmed with flanges, joints, and fittings; pipe lengths abounded. Grandpa carried his tools back and forth to work in the trunk of his Buick sedan, and also plied them in that dimly lit garage on a blackened workbench anchored by two massive vises and covered with rows of rasps and files (I remember the rat tail file) and pots of grease. His pipefitting prowess insured that his home was one of the first in the neighborhood to have a second bathroom, a tiny cubicle off the kitchen at the top of the cellar stairs. To flush, you pulled a chain to release water from the gravity tank above. The muted rush of those waters still resonates.

As far back as I can remember, helping Grandpa with his chores was my great pleasure. He had a large Victory Garden, as did everyone in the war years. In the summer, we picked beans, corn, squash, tomatoes, cukes, and reddish-green stalks of rhubarb, which I savored. Gram would give me a stalk after adding sugar to the groove to cut the tartness. My grandparents also kept chickens and turkeys, and let me toss feed into their cages. I was fascinated by the way the turkeys rotated their heads and the red flaps of flesh on their undulant necks. To my eyes, the Bark Street yard, with its garden, two garages (one was my uncles' clubhouse), and a two-story coop for the fowl, was a vast amphitheater of marvels—driving by the old house now, I see that the lot is no more than 100 feet wide and perhaps 150 feet deep. There were apple trees too, maybe a pear, and the stump of a massive cherry that went down in the great hurricane of 1938.

The chickens had their cage on the first floor of the coop; the turkeys, about a half dozen of them, were on the second. Every day Grandpa and I fed the birds. I carried an empty water bucket, and he had a larger one filled with feed. I threw the mixture of corn kernels and other seeds into the cages, while he filled my bucket from a faucet in the coop. The male turkey was Tom, but I've forgotten the names of the females. When they heard our feet on the stairs, they gobbled with ravenous excitement. The turkeys were immeasurably more interesting than the quotidian chickens, whose eggs Gram collected in the morning. I asked Grandpa many questions about the turkeys, and he told me what a wattle was. He didn't say much else about them. He liked to linger in the coop and watch the turkeys scarf and strut. I realize now that he knew his days were numbered, and was therefore, at times, morose.

After the war, when my father and my three uncles—my mother's brothers—would talk and drink Caribous (half whiskey, half Flame Tokay) while they played darts or watched the Friday night fights, I lurked and listened to them joke about the fate of the birds. As the story went, one spring Grandpa bought a rafter of birds, several poults and a tom, with the idea of fattening them for holiday meals. Grandma always cooked a turkey dinner on holidays, eaten around the big kitchen table under the Tiffany lamp. When it came time to slaughter a bird for Thanksgiving, Grandpa decided to wait. He'd do it just before Christmas. But Christmas passed, and the turkeys remained. My uncles chuckled when Joe, the youngest, finished the story: "All those birds died of old age."

"Your father's coming home," my mother announced to me one day in April 1946. Late in the afternoon, he walked through the French doors into my grandparents' parlor in his first lieutenant's army uniform. He was tall, thin, and had black hair. Black Irish, it was said. When he picked me up, his stubble scratched my cheek. He gave me packages of Wrigley's chewing gum, and I immediately swallowed several sticks and got sick. After his return, he and my mother rented an apartment at 57 Eastern Avenue, just around the corner from my grandparent's home. My parents pointed it out to me when I was older. But I have no memory of it and almost none of my father in those years. While he was away, I had established a happy routine, and when Dad returned, he didn't fit into it as he worked long days as a meter reader for the Fall River Electric Light Company. My mother and I spent most of the day at my grandparents' house, and usually ate the evening meal there, supper, as we called it, before he came home. But the larger reason, I believe, that I have no memory of our Eastern Avenue apartment is that 44 Bark Street—with its garden, its Stygian garage, the turkeys, the cherry tree stump, the mysterious third-floor attic, and the black bird (my grandmother's crow)—held sway over my days and dreams.

One day Gram found an injured bird in the yard. Martha, as she named her, was fairly large, with shiny, almost iridescent feathers (she might have been a grackle), and a broken wing. Gram took her into the house and fed her for several weeks while the wing mended, and then set her free. She flew off but soon returned. In the morning, Gram would step outside and call loudly, "Come, Martha." The bird swooped down from the orchard and, sitting upon Gram's shoulder, ate crumbs from her hand. Sometimes Gram would sit on the glider, and Martha would extract, one by one, her bobby pins. Martha made bird noises, and Gram spoke softly to her. She told me that she might peck me if I touched her, and I never did. I recently came across a photo of Martha perched on her hand, and Gram appearing to speak to it, like St. Francis communing with the birds. Gram was very good with all manners of strays, and also took in a big red dog, part German shepherd, that had been beaten. I can still see the welts. Rusty had always-erect ears and was a formidable watch dog who could leap over the six-foot high chain-link fence into the woods beyond the garden in pursuit of rabbits, deer, and fox. Rusty lived at 44 Bark Street for several years, outliving Grandpa by a year or two.

The four-bedroom house was slightly larger than the others in the neighborhood, but small by today's standards. A porch, or piazza, as it was called, wrapped around two sides and made the house seem grand. The piazza was my coign of vantage for observing movement on the street and in the yard. From there, I waved to cousin Preston Lynn, who pushed his wagon up the hill. "Any raaags, any bones, any bottles," he cried. I also met the mailman, who handed me letters from his leather bag, with a smile.

But when I spied my grandmother's friend, an old crone known as Peggy-with-the-Long-Tooth, walking down the hill, I hid. She squeezed me hard and kissed me whenever she could, and I could feel her tooth against my cheek.

The house had another memorable feature, a standup attic that ran the length and breadth of the house. At either end there was a lunette, a half-moon window which provided the only light—the attic was not wired for electricity. The house faced due south so if I went up in the morning, a few rays of sunlight streamed in on the pine floor boards. Late in the day, the crepuscular light from the north side was softer and slanted differently, transforming the attic into an enchanted chamber, especially in the winter.

To gain entrance, you had to undergo a trial: the Dark Closet. The door to the attic stairs was situated at the back of a long closet on the landing of the second floor. There was a light but the switch, perversely, had been installed at the deep end, hidden behind clothing hanging on a long rack. On days when I was feeling brave, I would take five quick steps into the blackness and then, through the densely packed hanging clothes, and moth-ball odors, furiously grope for the switch. Sometimes I failed, and ran out. But sometimes I'd find the switch, open the door, and slowly climb into the half-light, pausing when my line of sight was just above the attic floor to scan for whatever might be waiting.

The attic floorboards did not go all the way to the wall. There was a gap of a couple of feet, and my grandparents warned me incessantly that if I stepped off the boards I'd drop through the floor. I was tempted, and touched the gray vermiculite insulation with my toe, imagining falling into my grandparents' big double bed. If I stayed too long in the attic, someone, usually my grandfather, would fetch me down.

Before the war, everyone in the house had worked in the spinning mills, and the attic was crammed with crates of complicated tools and hardware for the looms, bolts of fabric and rolls of thread and wooden spools and bobbins of all shapes and sizes. Piled near the chimney were thick display books containing cloth and curtain samples, and boxes of old photographs. Under the south window was a Lionel train set, and nearby a collection of round black cylinders in cardboard boxes with a photo of a white-haired man on each. The wind-up phonograph that played these wax cylinders was also there, and my grandfather sometimes played a song for me, "I Love a Lassie." The singer, I learned much later, was a Scotsman, Harry Lauder, and the man in the photo was the inventor of the phonograph, Thomas Alva Edison.

Over by the stairs stood a chest of 60 small drawers. Forty-eight of them had the name of a state written on the front, and each contained a corked test tube. Six of the tubes—Massachusetts, R.I., Connecticut, New Hampshire, Pennsylvania and New York—contained dirt. My uncle Joe had been a Boy Scout and one of his projects was to collect soil samples from every state. The ambition of this project impressed me deeply, although it was unfinished when he joined the Navy right after graduating from high school. He was on a destroyer in the Pacific. His older brother, Larry, was the crew chief on a Navy flying boat, a PBY, also in the Pacific. The oldest brother, Sandy, was in Gen. MacArthur's army. On the Lennon side, my father was an Army lieutenant in Europe. His youngest brother, Frankie, was in the Merchant Marine, serving on a tanker carrying gasoline to Murmansk. Hughie, his other younger brother, had been in the Marine Corps since 1939, and fought in the battle for Okinawa. Their older sister, Aunt Mollie, was a WAC stationed in a hospital in New Guinea. Our family, like most of those on Bark Street, religiously followed the war news on both fronts.

To this end, my grandfather had repurposed a large, blue-covered book, "The Majestic Line of Brocatelles and Damasks," intended for fabric samples. On its blank pages he pasted in newspaper stories of the naval war around the globe. It contained accounts of numerous disasters, the sinking of the *Arizona* (BB-39) at Pearl

Harbor, the German battleship *Bismarck* in the North Atlantic, and the British aircraft carrier *Ark Royal* in the Mediterranean, as well as photos and stories of the launches of countless destroyers, submarines, and cargo ships. There were several accounts of "Big Mamie," the *Massachusetts* (BB-59), the navy's newest battleship, which took part in the opening and closing battles of the war: Casablanca and Okinawa. Grandpa Mitchell added pertinent dates in pencil. When he gave me the album, I drew crude pictures of battleships, muzzle blasts, and flying shells on the first page, labelled "U.S. WARBOATS." I still have the book, and show it to my grandchildren.

Every Sunday he and I would read the funny papers. "Prince Valiant" was my favorite. He had amazing blue-black hair and his weapon was The Singing Sword, made from the same metal as King Arthur's Excalibur. My grandfather chuckled at "Jiggs and Maggie," about the comic relations of the lace curtain Irish (Maggie) and the shanty Irish (Jiggs), and also Major Hoople in "Our Boarding House." I didn't get the humor. He also explained to me the meaning of the various images in "Ripley's Believe It or Not." This feature appeared in the Hearst tabloid, *The* (Boston) *Daily Record*. "Ripley's" was my first window on the larger world. I could read only a little and when I didn't understand something in "Ripley's," my grandfather explained it to me. The images and stories astounded me. For example, a man in India, missing one arm and with only two fingers on the other one, spent 61 years carving a memorial to his missing arm; Mr. Jerry Elmore of Hall, Indiana, cut his third set of teeth at the age of 75; Queen Muhuma of Kenya lived on milk alone for 105 years; a tribe in the Philippines braided a rope to hold the world together; Jir Kondratik of Trancin, Slovakia, could smell through his ears. One item plucked a string deep inside me: Mrs. Roy Kurz collected 30,000 buttons, all different, and from every state in the Union, an effort akin to, but far outstripping Uncle Joe's dirt collection.

My grandfather got me a large scrapbook and every day we pasted in "Believe It or Not." As it grew, the scrapbook became for me the definitive dictionary of oddities, a compendium of the quizzical, the comical, and the nutty that, collectively, I firmly believed, circumscribed the far reaches of reality, the outer rim of idiosyncratic human achievement. My mother read me poems from Robert Louis Stevenson's *A Child's Garden of Verses*. They were enchanting, but the facts in "Ripley's" had the added advantage of being true, the pure pap of factuality. These bizarre quiddities, I believed, had been verified by Mr. Ripley's team of detectives,* else why would they appear in an esteemed newspaper? I deemed myself fortunate to be the curator of this collection of weird wonders and freakish facts. The scrapbook also had the imprimatur of my grandfather Mitchell, the wisest of wise men.

All my uncles, and Aunt Mollie, made it home safely, although Uncle Larry spent several days on a life raft after being shot down in the Battle of Leyte Gulf. Uncle Joe, who I idolized, was now 19 years old, and would soon be studying at Brown University on the GI Bill. I asked him if his train set still worked and he took me up in the attic to check it out—he knew exactly how to find the light switch in the Dark Closet. I asked him about his dirt collection, but he showed little interest in it, which surprised me. While we were in the attic, he located his Eagle Scout medal and gave it to me. I treasured it for years. One evening after Joe returned, and the family was sitting around the kitchen table, my grandmother announced that we had lost a member of the family: "Martha's gone wild."

Grandpa Mitchell died on his 75th birthday, August 15, 1951 (my mother, reputedly his favorite, had the same birthday and, although not notably superstitious, was somewhat agitated as her 75th loomed. It came and went). The next-to-last time I saw Grandpa, he was lying in the spare bedroom across from the Dark Closet. My mother told me not to go in. When I asked why, she said. "He's turned his face to the wall." I did not know until many years later that my mother got the phrase from a Scottish folk song, "Barbara Allen." Nor did I know that the song borrowed the phrase from the Book of Isiah in the *Old Testament*, where it referred to Hezekiah, a righteous Jewish King.

The last time I saw Grandpa was at his wake. Twice a day for three days, long lines of people, family and neighbors, but also a stream of mill workers, came to say a prayer before his open coffin. At the end of one of the afternoon sessions, I asked Gram if I could touch him. She saw that I was serious, and nodded yes. At a quiet moment I did, putting a finger on the side of his neck. It was very cold and I recoiled. Gram watched me. After the final evening of waking him, Gram, her five children (all then unmarried, save my mother), my father, and I returned to 44 Bark Street. The Tiffany lamp was on and the family gathered at the kitchen table, smoking and drinking coffee. Having been told I was precocious (for reading Lowell Thomas's *With Lawrence of Arabia*), and desiring to impress my uncles, I waited for a quiet moment, and in an assured voice, asked, "Well, are we going to read the will?" This brought laughter, and some nods of approval. I had stepped into the adult world. But there was no will.

For months I made myself cry at night so I could think of how I loved and missed Grandpa, who was alone in his cold grave. I felt very sorry for myself. It was delicious. But I think I cried more when Rusty, our heroic dog, died. My uncles buried him in the Victory Garden.

---

* *From 1924 to 1976, according to* Wikipedia, *Norbert Pearlroth was the chief researcher for "Ripley's," working ten hours a day, six days a week in the New York Public Library to find the oddities depicted in the daily feature.*

Aunt Nellie and the Bigberry Stadium Incident

As my mother and her brothers told it, Uncle Sidney's earlier life followed a seasonal rhythm. He would impregnate Aunt Nellie (my grandmother Mitchell's sister) and then disappear on a Homeric bender before she came to term, returning weeks later haggard and broke to see his new child in the cradle. He looked, my mother said, like the wreck of the Hesperus, a reference to the famous Longfellow poem about "the schooner Hesperus / that sailed the wintry sea." The family, now slightly more impoverished, always took Sidney back, although with less and less enthusiasm as time went by. He held to his pattern through many of Nellie's pregnancies. First the rutting season, then the drinking season, and then rehab.

Uncle Sidney was employed at the municipal water works in Fall River, MA, an impressive granite building built not long after the Civil War, and situated on a large body of spring-fed fresh water, Watuppa Pond. Reputed to have the clearest, cleanest drinking water in New England, the pond and surrounding watershed area was and is fenced off and patrolled to keep out poachers and fishermen. My uncles bragged about climbing the fence on dark nights to swim and fish, and told tales of bass, perch, and tiger muskies so plentiful they would jump in your boat.

When he wasn't off on a toot, Uncle Sidney was the chief breadwinner and made a good paycheck as a hydraulic mechanic. In a loop on his wide leather belt, he always carried a slender, intricate instrument. It was, my uncles explained, a tool for regulating the

(2017)

41

flow from ports and hydrants. When I first knew him, he was already retired, but still proudly wore the leather belt with a loop for the special tool. There was some *sub rosa* chuckling about Sidney's tool among my uncles; I couldn't quite put it together at the time.

Two or three years after Grandpa Mitchell died in 1951, Gram gave up the family home at 44 Bark Street in Fall River, and moved to a cottage next door to my parents in the small town of Somerset across the Taunton River. Now in her late sixties, she was still quite vigorous. Her propinquity was a godsend for my working mother, who needed help with her three small children, and me. I was 12, oblivious to my siblings, and spent my idle hours riding around town on my bike with pals and working obsessively on my stamp collection. Gram held the fort, cooking, doing the laundry, and keeping an eye on seven-year-old Peter, who spent much of his time killing frogs and tormenting our twin sisters, Kathleen and Maureen, who were going on six. When I was in seventh grade, I began sleeping over on a daybed in her bungalow, away from my bothersome siblings. I was an altar boy, and on many mornings she and I walked together to seven o'clock Mass, after which she made me a poached egg and bacon while I watched Dave Garroway and the *Today Show.* We talked a lot. I was curious about her youth in Canada, the wolves that howled, the bears that marauded, the Mohawk Indians, and the clear, bottomless lakes that surrounded the farm. One, she said, was named after her family: Lynn Lake.

Gram was born on a farm in the Laurentian Mountains, about 50 miles north of Montreal, and migrated to Fall River with all her family, save her eldest sister, Aunt Mary, who remained on the farm with her son, Emery Lavois. Her family, like many from Quebec, came south in the early years of the twentieth century to work in the bustling spinning mills of Massachusetts. My grandmother was fluent in French, and used to speak it with my father—which irritated my mother—who spoke it equally well from four years of high school French and his time in the U.S. Army in Europe. Gram

was also fluent in sign language. She explained that her mother
died giving birth to her, and her father married a woman named
Bridget Kelly, who was deaf. At an early age, her step-mother taught
her the sign language created by the American School for the Deaf.

I learned even more about Canada when, every couple of
weeks, I went with Gram to visit Aunt Nellie, her older sister, who
she always described as "the wild one." Nellie ran away from home
when she was 16, and married Sidney Ellis a year or two later. They
and their large family lived on Arizona Street, in Fall River, a few
blocks from Lafayette Park. I'm not sure exactly how many children
Nellie had, either 17 or 18. Gram said she'd lost several as well, and
in a letter to Peter my mother listed the 13 she could remember.
One of them, then in his 40s, was Big Bob, so called, I surmised,
to distinguish him from Nellie's youngest, a high schooler named
Little Bob. At some point, I became curious about two sons named
Bob and asked her why. She told me straightaway, "I always liked the
name." The Ellis home was crammed with Nellie's offspring, and
their offspring, my second cousins. It was a small house, dark and
smoky. All its occupants, save Nellie and Sidney (a pipe smoker),
favored Pall Malls. For many years Nellie prayed a modern picture
window would be installed, and eventually her children chipped in
for one. Unfortunately, it didn't admit much light as it looked out
on the brick wall of the house next door. Years later, in graduate
school, I experienced a thrill of recognition after reading about the
blank wall that Bartleby stared impassively at in Melville's immortal
short story, "Bartleby, the Scrivener." The Ellis family, however, suffered
little from existential angst. They lit up their smokes and pointed with
pride at their impressive addition, a postwar status symbol.

Some of the Ellis children had jobs at the mills, some had
moved away, including two daughters, Marion and Helen, who I
was told performed in vaudeville in Philadelphia. Before World War
II, the family was very poor. So much so, that in the spring when
the dandelions bloomed, the Ellis children came to 44 Bark Street

to pick the dandelion greens for a Depression Salad. In summer, one or another of the clan stopped by every so often and Gram Mitchell filled a basket with vegetables from the Victory Garden. Preston, one of the older sons, lost his mill job, and during the hard years of the Great Depression made his living as a rag-and-bones man, collecting rags to be made into paper, and bones to be made into glue. Preston, ever jolly, was known to everyone in the neighborhoods off Eastern Avenue by his plangent call, "Any raaags, any bones, any bottles," as he trundled his cart about. He often walked down Bark Street, "to my mortification," my mother recalled, although she defended him to her best friend, Bertha, who made a slighting remark about "your cousin the rag man."

During our visits to the Ellis house, Uncle Sidney, now partially paralyzed, sat morosely in his chair smoking his pipe, which he lit by striking a wooden match on the leather patches sewn to the front of his bib overalls. Not infrequently, he'd drop a lit match on his lap. Aunt Nellie, sitting across from him on a large, overstuffed sofa, would croak, "Sidney's on fire," and the nearest person would extinguish his smoldering crotch with the bucket of water next to his chair. Then everyone—save Sidney—would laugh, and Aunt Nellie would smother me in her massive bosoms. My mother was possessed of funds of forbearance, but had nothing but scorn for Sidney. "He was a beaut," she said, "just sitting in that big chair."

Another oft-told story about the Ellis family concerned the infamous Bigberry Stadium incident, which took place when my mother was pregnant with me, on Armistice Day, November 11, 1941, about a month before Pearl Harbor. According to newspaper reports, on a chilly afternoon, cousin Preston, his friend Bill Barlow, and about a dozen of their cronies got together for a drinking party in "The Jungle," a hobo meeting place adjacent to Bigberry Stadium. Long gone now, the Bigberry was where the citizens of Fall River attended stock car races and baseball games for many years. The stadium stood close to where the Quequeshan

River runs into Mount Hope Bay. In the Wampanoag language, Quequeshan means falling river, thus the name of the city.

As the Associated Press wire story explained, one of Preston's pals purchased several jugs of moonshine from two guys peddling them on a street corner near a garage, and then circulated the word to his pals to get together for a party. The celebrants, ranging in age from 30 to 63, were unemployed or worked for the federal Works Progress Administration. One of the group, identified only as "a durable survivor," stated, "We just cracked open the can and mixed the drinks and passed them all around. Big drinks, too. It tasted all right to me." When he woke up, all he could recall was that the booze was "top-notch." He then wandered back to The Jungle and found one of his friends lying dead there. He contacted the police and the search began. "Some were found in alleys, another doubled up in a doorway. One walked alone to the hospital" (probably St. Anne's, where I was born). But before the weekend was over, nine of the drinkers were dead and others were hospitalized. The jugs, it turned out, contained antifreeze, which is made from ethylene glycol. During the early part of the 20th century antifreeze, because of its sweet taste, was often used as a murder weapon.

Ethylene glycol is extremely difficult to detect in the body, which often leads to incorrect diagnoses. The symptoms, including abdominal cramps, cracked lips, diarrhea, and vomiting, can be confused with those of other illnesses. Because of its agreeable taste, and relatively sluggish action in the digestive and renal systems, victims are at first unable to explain what has happened to them. They're too drunk. After several hours, the ethylene glycol begins to crystallize in various parts of the body, including the brain, which turns the drinkers into gibbering idiots. Death, which is often extremely painful, is caused by massive kidney damage after 72 hours.

The culprits who sold the jugs, two gas station employees, claimed that they believed the contents to be moonshine (probably *bagaceira*, made by the local Portuguese from grape skins and stems). They were arrested immediately. This all took place just a few weeks before the U.S. Congress declared war on Japan and national mobilization was underway. The two men pled guilty to manslaughter, and the judge gave them a choice: jail, or the army. They took the latter.

There were at least two Bigberry survivors. One was cousin Preston, whose name, everyone recognized, was damnably congruent with the largest selling antifreeze then and now, Prestone. The other survivor, Bill Barlow, was blinded but otherwise whole. Invincible Preston, however, was completely untouched by the experience, owing perhaps to the aerobic benefits of hauling his rag wagon up and down the stony hills of Fall River. He gained for a time a measure of local fame, but soon, with the war on, it was forgotten, except by my uncles, who marveled at his impervious constitution. Whenever I saw Preston pulling his wagon down Bark Street, I wanted to say something to him, but could never quite come up with the appropriate congratulatory words. We just waved as he chanted, "Any raaags, any bones, any bottles." Bill Barlow, on the other hand, was lauded locally for surviving the Bigberry disaster, even though he was entirely sightless. His enduring fame was enhanced by the adjective used to describe him in the newspaper story. For the rest of his long life, he was known to one and all as Durable Bill.

When I shared the above account with my sisters, who live together, they called me to add something our mother had told them about Nellie and Sidney, something that occurred, we calculated, in the late 1930s, a few years before Bigberry. One day when Gram Mitchell and my mother were visiting, Aunt Nellie announced that she was pregnant once again. Uncle Sidney, who was older than Nellie, must have been in his mid-fifties, but obviously still randy and potent. Gram walked over to his chair, picked up the water bucket and threw its contents in his face. "Keep away from Nellie," she said. He did. It was her last pregnancy, but not her last child. Little Bob, it turned out, was Big Bob's son, taken in by Nellie when the unwed mother deserted.

Altar Boy

My long career as a Roman Catholic altar boy began in fourth grade. Fr. O'Neill, the curate at St. Thomas More, was my instructor. He met me and three or four other boys (girls were not officially allowed to be servers until 1994) one afternoon in the church, a modest wooden building that had been a chapel for many years, and recently upgraded to parish status. We were awed to be inside the communion rail, sitting on the altar steps, as he explained in a sepulchral voice that echoed through the empty building how we would perform our duties during Mass. After this, he took us into the adjoining sacristy and demonstrated us how to tackle the 33 buttons, one for each year of Christ's life, on the front of the long black cassock—you could skip every other one if you were tardy—that servers wore. Worn over the cassock was the surplice, a white pull-over blouse with wide sleeves that our mothers had to wash, starch, and iron. Once dressed, Fr. O'Neill taught us how to walk at the appropriate stately pace with our hands clasped before us like a steeple (right thumb crossed over the left), as we walked before the priest to and from the altar. Proper kneeling was also important—keep the back straight and the hands clasped, no fidgeting.

The following week, Fr. O'Neill took us though a truncated version of the Mass, demonstrating how to ring the bell at key moments, and how to hold the heavy Mass book for the priest to read with his hands free. Trickier was the technique of slowly pouring the holy water from a cruet over the priest's fingers during

(2018)

48

the Lavabo, the handwashing segment of the Latin Mass, while catching the flow in a small bowl and then offering him the towel draped over your wrist.

At our third meeting we began learning how to pronounce the Latin responses during Mass. It was the biggest challenge, and I recall that one of the boys whose powers of verbal articulation were not up to snuff dropped out. The most difficult of the responses was in the Lavabo where the server asks God to accept the sacrifice, or offering, that the priest was about to make. This meant getting my mouth around the concluding words of the prayer: "*ad utilitátem quoque nostram totiúsque Ecclésiae sui sanctae.*" The translation is: "for our good and the good of all His holy Church." I liked the sound of *totiúsque*, the masculine possessive form of "all" in Latin. But I didn't know this at the time; it was sufficient that novice altar boys merely memorize the pronunciations, which we did, and not with too much difficulty, the elastic porousness of a nine-year-old brain being what it is. "*Totiúsque Ecclésiae sui sanctae*" is burned into the tablets of my memory.

Initially, because I was a neophyte, I did not participate in the more complex rituals, and spent most of my time kneeling on the hard wooden steps of the altar. Only after a month or two of serving daily Mass with an older boy would I be allowed to pour water during the Lavabo. An even longer waiting period, and a modicum of poise, was required for holding the communion-plate—a gold-plated disc with a handle—under the chin of those receiving communion. When two of the wafer hosts got stuck together, or the recipient fainted, or the priest fumbled—all of which I witnessed—the altar boy wielded the plate as a sort of holy catcher's mitt. Another pitfall was pressing the edge of the plate too firmly into the throat of a chum or sibling receiving communion, a persistent temptation, and one to which I was prey on occasion. Alertness during the communion service was essential, and woe to the server who allowed the body of Jesus to fall to the floor. Over my eight years as an altar boy, I dropped none and caught a few, for which I received congratulations and, occasionally, a dollar bill from Fr. Welch, the white-haired old pastor.

My father had also been an altar boy, and it seemed to me a wonderful coincidence that he had also served under Fr. Welch—this would have been 20-odd years earlier when Fr. Welch was a curate at the cathedral of St. Mary's in Fall River. Occasionally, he and Dad would exchange memories of old times during the Great Depression. During the years that Fr. Welch was pastor at St. Thomas More, my father often consolidated the offering money from the baskets of the ushers into a large cloth bag, which he gave to Welch after the service. But Dad did not linger after Mass or sit with the family during it. With a crowd of other men, he stood at the rear of the church in the vestibule, within hearing distance of the Mass, but with no clear view of it. This meant, technically, that he'd fulfilled his Sunday duty, but to me it was a dodge, a pro forma fulfillment of the obligation—I was insufferably pious at that age. Dad's explanation that he had claustrophobia, a lingering WWII malady, was unconvincing. When I first watched *The Quiet Man*, John Ford's 1952 movie about Ireland, starring John Wayne and Maureen O'Hara—who had the same red hair and temper as my mother—I noticed that in the Sunday Mass scene most of the men also huddled just outside the church door. "Aha," thought I. The distancing was obviously some kind of Hibernian male bonding practice. Years later, I surmised the custom might be a leftover from the Depression when many parishioners were too poor to pay "seat money" (then a dime, but in the 1950s, a quarter), and consequently stood.

The altar boy schedule at St. Thomas More was rigid and arduous. There were two daily Masses (7 and 7:30 a.m.), and four Sunday Masses (7, 8:15, 9:45, and 11 a.m.). Servers spent a month serving each of the six Masses, and then started all over again, rotating with the same partner through the cycle twice a year. This meant that for four months of the year, altar boys served Mass every day but Sunday, which meant arising at 6 a.m. 100 times a year. This was hard, especially in the winter. My cheerful grandmother Mitchell and I walked the half mile to church for daily Mass, then back home for breakfast and then to school, which was across from the church. If you were lucky, your morning Mass priest was Fr. Medeiros (a loaner from the nearby Portuguese church, later Cardinal Humberto Medeiros of Boston), whose Masses clocked in at 15 minutes or less. The Irish priests were slower.

I was elated when, in my third year of high school, I was promoted to weddings and funerals, and other important liturgical events such as confirmation, when the bishop presided. You could count on getting a $5 tip for a wedding, $2 for a funeral, and a late pass for school if it was a weekday. I was smoking by then, and weddings and funerals allowed me to have a butt before going to classes.

Funeral Masses in the 1950s were often solemn high requiem Masses, lasting an hour. The closed coffin of the deceased was wheeled to the altar gate, which was opened for the ceremony. Before and after the Mass, the priest anointed the coffin with holy water, and also incensed it with a brass vessel on a chain, a thurible, filling the church with the aromatic odors of Frankincense and myrrh. The rising smoke is a symbol of the prayers for the deceased wafting upward to Heaven. The altar boy's job is to spoon the resinous spices onto the burning charcoal wafer.

For the requiem Mass, the priest wears black vestments, circles the coffin, sprinkling it with water and purifying it with incense while chanting, at that time in Latin, now in English. The coffin, always closed, is placed so that the feet of the deceased are closest to the altar (if a priest is in the coffin, this is reversed, an ecclesiastical privilege). There is almost always an organist playing and a singer singing "*Dies Irae*" ("Days of Wrath"), a Gregorian melody from the Middle Ages about God calling all souls to Judgment Day, welcoming the saved and casting the unsaved into eternal flames.

This lugubrious chant, the accompanying organ, coupled with the pungent smoke and the sobbing of the deceased's family, created a moving scene. Catholics know how to put on a show. The end of the ceremony is more upbeat, giving the mourners some relief and hope. The priest recites, in English, the *In paradisum* prayer, just before the body is removed for burial. My mother found this prayer to be uplifting: "May the angels lead you into paradise; may the martyrs receive you at your arrival and lead you to the holy city of Jerusalem."

One funeral Mass is deeply etched. It was for a Greek-American gentleman who had died in mid-life. His large family, headed by his striking, raven-haired widow, wept all though the ceremony. At the end of Mass, as Fr. O'Neill was reading about how Lazarus and the martyrs awaited the deceased, the grief-stricken widow, tears and makeup running down her face, stepped out of the first pew. I was two steps away. She paused for a few seconds—then leapt upon the coffin, full body, and with a long wail of agony scratched its surface with the nails of both hands. The priest stopped praying, everyone froze, and the organ groaned on—a *tableaux vivant*. After a few moments, the two undertakers standing nearby gently prised her off the coffin and passed her to her family. She slumped down and continued to sob. I stared in wonder at the foot-long gouges she'd made in the polished redwood coffin lid. After the mourners had departed, as I unbuttoned and hung up my cassock, Fr. O'Neill, looking grave, handed me an envelope containing two one-dollar bills. Neither of us spoke.

Except for St. Patrick's Day and other holidays when the booze was flowing, my family was generally undemonstrative, and I'd never seen such passion before, and rarely since. The mise-en-scène—the coffin, the organ, the incense, and the cluster of mourners—and the widow's enormous, unfettered anguish reverberated through my school day, but I never said a word about it to anyone.

The Archivist's Apprentice

Becoming an archivist was not my aspiration. I had only a crude idea what one did—sifting through crumbling manuscripts and musty tomes like Sir Walter Scott's tedious antiquarian, Dr. Jonas Dryasdust. My goals in grad school were to saturate myself in American literature, write a doctoral thesis about it, and get a job teaching it. And quickly. My GI Bill benefits were running out, and I was married with three sons in diapers. I was enthralled by the American romantics—Melville, Hawthorne, Dickinson, Poe, and the rest—and my thesis proposal, titled "The Bewitching Difference: Detachment and Ambiguity in Hawthorne," called for an exploration of his dark, symbolic forests and pride-ruined Puritans. Shortly thereafter and before I'd done any writing, I learned that a few years earlier someone had successfully defended a Ph.D. thesis on precisely my topic. Consequently, I'd have to come up with a new proposal.

My first thought was of Norman Mailer, who by the end of the '60s had published a dozen books, and won some major awards. I had a tropism for all he'd written, and a strange sympathy for some of his most disturbing characters, the ones with an enclave of virtue in their pervading ignobility—Sgt. Croft, the sadistic platoon leader in *The Naked and the Dead*; Lannie Madison, the mad Cassandra of a Brooklyn rooming house in *Barbary Shore*; Marion Faye, the Baudelairean pimp who is the conscience of the Hollywood Babylon depicted in *The Deer Park*; and Stephen

Rojack, the parapet-walking professor of existential psychology in *An American Dream* who believes that fear is the root of all neuroses. But I was most taken by his finest creation: a middled-aged, jaded, reluctant Vietnam War protester, who is described in the third person-personal by his writerly self, Norman Mailer, the celebrity author who had "learned to live in the sarcophagus of his image." Seeing himself from another perspective enabled him to distinguish himself from the ways the media depicted him, and to prove and present the pockets and layers of his own mutable self. It was this character in *The Armies of the Night* who moved me from admirer to enthusiast, from enthusiast to votary. Later on, I would become Mailer's bibliographer, editor, flunky, friend, biographer, and eulogist. But first, I was his archivist's apprentice.

When I proposed the idea of a thesis on Mailer, my advisor, a Hawthorne expert, was silent.

"Is there a problem?"

"Mailer's still alive."

"But he's . . . a major figure."

"Not yet, I'm afraid."

Arguing with him was out of the question. My options were to abandon Mailer or get a new advisor. Stunned and baffled, I went to the office of Nancy Potter, whose class on American non-fiction I was then taking. I had recently made a class presentation on Mailer, based largely on a *Life* magazine excerpt taken from his forthcoming book on the Apollo 11 moon shot, *Of a Fire on the Moon*. This heavily illustrated, 26,000-word feature article, the longest nonfiction piece ever published in *Life*, appeared on August 29, 1969. The immediate jewel of the excerpt is a dramatic description of the ignition of the Saturn V rocket and its initially slow ascent, which Mailer likens to the stately movements of Melville's White Whale. His startling simile was more confirmation of my belief that Mailer was a latter-day transcendentalist. As a Harvard undergrad, Mailer had attended the lectures of F.O. Matthiessen, the author of

American Renaissance, and Mailer, I believed then and now, is a literary descendent of Emerson, Whitman, Hawthorne, and Melville, and the other figures of the movement Matthiessen so memorably depicts. The cover of that *Life* issue, featuring a smiling, tousled Mailer in a velour pullover the color of his eyes, hung on my office wall for years.

Dr. Potter, who had encouraged me to present the Mailer report, was a subtle but powerful presence in the U.R.I. English Department. A gay feminist with a shock of black hair, she was a Henry James expert who spoke in paragraphs and had published a collection of chiseled short stories, *We Have Seen the Best of Our Times*. I liked and admired her. Everyone did. She listened to the replay of my conversation with her colleague about Hawthorne and Mailer, and on my unfocused idea of writing about the shift from fiction to nonfiction in Mailer's recent work. I don't think I actually asked her if she would replace the Hawthorne expert. She just announced it. "It's a splendid idea," she said, "Mailer's an important writer, and I'd be happy to direct your dissertation."

At that time, Mailer's reputation among feminists was beginning to tatter—and for good reason—although Nancy never said a word to me about her feminist allegiances. An archetypical WASP, she was unable to conceive of using her position to advance her personal politics. I can only recall one instance when her admiration for Mailer as a writer and her loyalty to the women's liberation movement seemed to be into conflict. In an early draft of my thesis, I quoted Mailer quoting Henry Miller (in Mailer's 1971 memoir-manifesto-literary essay, *The Prisoner of Sex*) to the effect that a vagina was a key symbol for the interconnection of all things, to which Mailer added, that it was the "indispensable step to the beyond." In the margin, she wrote a couple of sentences, but then crossed them out. I could imagine her Kate Millett-feminist side making the rejoinder and her Henry James-forbearance side crossing it out. I never mentioned it to her.

I can further illustrate the fine-hammered steel of Nancy's sensibility. During our interaction on my thesis over the next three years, she learned of my admiration for Henry James and one day told me of her connection with him or his ghost or . . . here's the story as I remember it: She was living in Boston, going to graduate school; this would be a couple of years after the war, 1946-47. James was then all the rage, and nowhere more so than in Boston. A friend of hers called to announce that she had stumbled on a Jamesian artifact in the attic closet of a Beacon Hill building where he'd lived in the 1880s. Nancy rushed over and the discovery, carefully sealed in heavy paper and addressed to James, was brought forth. They paused to savor the moment, almost like the characters in *The Maltese Falcon* before The Fat Man unwraps the black bird. Could it be the conclusion of his final, unfinished novel, *The Ivory Tower*? Perhaps some letters to an unknown lover? Or maybe a preliminary sketch of Whistler's painting of the middle-aged James?

The parcel was opened, and behold: folded neatly were three or four union suits (long underwear) with the monogram HJJR (James was a junior) prominently stitched on the upper torso, over the heart. Nancy and her friend were of course familiar with his 1888 novel, *The Aspern Papers*, which focuses on the intrusive prying of an unnamed biographer in his hunt for the "sacred relics" of a deceased Romantic poet, Jeffrey Aspern, in the possession of his lover, the ancient Miss Bordereau, at her palazzo in Venice. She foils the attempt, and the precious letters are saved from the tawdry desires of the "publishing scoundrel," as she calls him. After they had gently examined the parcel's contents, one of them asked:

"What would James have us do?"

Simultaneously, they blurted out the only answer: "Burn them!" And they did, proudly, solemnly, in an act of literary solidarity with The Master.

Whenever I've told the story of the sacerdotal burning of the Jamesian undergarments, as I have, many times, I couldn't help but reflect that in some unforeseen way the loss perhaps diminished our understanding of James's sensibility. The union suits, while deeply personal, might have been deeply instructive. Perhaps. Time would tell. In fact, the incident enabled me to grasp the prime directive of archival endeavor: Save every artifact, not just manuscripts and journals, letters, and address books, but items whose future significance has yet to be gauged. Wait until the item's utter lack of value is incontrovertible. And then, pause again. This directive explains why, 14 years after Mailer's death, I still retain a small, cheap, broken brass clock he kept on his desk; two oyster shells he brought home from Michael Shay's restaurant because he saw the intaglio faces of Greek warriors on them; and a box containing his complete dental records (obtained from his dentist with the blessing of Norris Church Mailer, his widow), his false teeth, and a partial bridge.

As I worked on my thesis under Potter's benevolent eye, I began to wonder if Mailer might be his own best interpreter. At the time, there was no consensus on Mailer's work—and not much now. The critics were all over the place on its merits and meanings. He was, as James once said of Emerson, "a man without a handle." I'd read the critical estimates of his writings, but found Mailer's unfiltered words in profiles and interviews, which are alternately self-serving and not, to be more valuable. In many of them, the 1964 *Paris Review* interview, for example, he looks carefully over his career, pointing out places where he felt he'd had gone astray, or made an advance. He also talked candidly about growing up in Crown Heights, a profoundly Jewish neighborhood in Brooklyn, the challenges he faced in the Army, and what writers influenced him when he began writing seriously at Harvard—especially James T. Farrell, whose finest work, the *Studs Lonigan* trilogy, is set in an Irish ghetto on Chicago's South Side reminiscent of Mailer's Crown Heights neighborhood in Brooklyn. I found such nuggets to be more valuable than the ongoing, tedious debates among critics of that era about whether Mailer was predominantly a realist, a romantic, or an existentialist.

Consequently, in the early '70s when the literary world was beginning its decades-long affair with deconstructionist theory, I was transforming myself, unwittingly, into an old-fashioned literary archaeologist, assiduously collecting Mailer's public utterances—everything from formal interviews, comments quoted in profiles, letters to the editor, public debates, and symposium contributions to gossip in *People* magazine and Q-and-A sessions at college appearances (the editors of college newspapers usually mailed him accounts of his campus appearances, material otherwise difficult to retrieve). Mailer was often unguarded in these interviews—a journalist's dream—blurting out revealing personal information and outrageous opinions. As Martin Amis once noted of Mailer, "No one in the history of the written word, not even . . . D. H. Lawrence, is so wide open to damaging quotation." I had no clear idea why I was amassing all these clippings and offprints (later I also collected Mailer's blurbs, audio and video cassettes of live events, and campaign buttons from his 1969 run for mayor of New York), no awareness of how valuable the work of seeking, finding, articulating, and cross-referencing this mass of material would be to me, and didn't for several years.

Mailer's original archivist was his mother Fan, who zealously collected his juvenilia (most notably "The Martian Invasion," a 35,000-word sci-fi novel written when he was eight), high school and college papers and grade reports, yearbooks, and every letter he wrote from Harvard and the Philippines during WWII. In the late 60s she gave—not without some pangs and the receipt of repeated assurances—all this material, including thick scrapbooks containing reviews of and ads for his early books (assembled by her meticulous husband, Barney), to a University of Pennsylvania professor, Robert F. Lucid, a close friend of Mailer's.

Lucid, the editor of the three-volume *Journal of Richard Henry Dana, Jr.*, the author of *Two Years Before the Mast*, immediately grasped the value of what Fan had preserved. Over the next few years, and with Mailer's encouragement, he scoured the writing studios, attics, and basements of Mailer's two homes (his brownstone in Brooklyn Heights and a summer home in Provincetown, on Cape Cod), where he found the hand-written and typed drafts, galleys, and page proof of all Mailer's books up to and including *Of a Fire on the Moon*, and a good deal of unpublished material—two unpublished novels written in college, as well a short story, "Love-Buds," a hilarious account of Mailer's disastrous attempt to lose his virginity in a Scranton brothel when he was 17. Lucid later recalled the thrill of finding "the plaster-buried, mouse-nibbled manuscript of *The Deer Park* in a basement tool bench drawer in Brooklyn."

A few years later, my wife, Donna, found the misplaced final print of Mailer's 1968 film *Beyond the Law-Blue*, in a corner of the Brooklyn basement, and Bob and I discovered his still-unpublished 1954-55 marijuana journal, titled "Lipton's" (marijuana was referred to as tea in the '40s and '50s), mixed in with some *Village Voice* material. Typed by Mailer himself, the journal is 104,000 words in length (the ribbon copy is now in the Mailer Archive at the Harry Ransom Center, University of Texas-Austin; Mailer gave me the carbon copy in the early 2000s). In 1970, Fan authorized Lucid to deposit the first trove, now sorted into 36 double archival boxes, in a Manhattan facility on Manhattan's Upper East Side that she had selected. The padlock and key to the storage vault at Day & Meyer, Murray & Young that she gave Lucid now sits on a bookshelf in my study.

I'd exchanged three or four letters with Mailer in early 1972, beginning with my letter of support after his disastrous December 1971 appearance with Gore Vidal and Janet Flanner on the *Dick Cavett Show*. In October 1972, we met in person when he was on a book tour and spent a long evening together in a Macomb, Illinois, bar. My first meeting with Lucid was at Mailer's home in May 1975, the same day I'd successfully defended my thesis. I'd been working on it for three years while teaching full-time at the University of Illinois-Springfield, and now, with "Doctor" before my name and directions to the home of America's most famous writer in my pocket, I was feeling modestly Napoleonic. On the three-hour drive from the University of Rhode Island to Mailer's place in Stockbridge, Massachusetts, I must have smoked a dozen cigarettes. Lucid and Mailer were talking in the library when I arrived, awed, speechless, and over-stimulated from the cigarettes and the celebratory luncheon hosted by Dr. Potter. They were discussing *The Fight*, his new book about the Muhammad Ali-George Foreman championship boxing match in Zaire, The Rumble in the Jungle.

"Okay," Mailer said, "so I've written a minor book," adding, as I walked into the room, that everything he wrote didn't have to challenge Tolstoy.

Lucid, a slight, fair, feisty Irish-American from Washington State, then in his early 40s, conversed easily with Mailer. He'd become his friend and confidante, partly because Mailer was intrigued by his background. One of Lucid's brothers was a major figure in the Communist Party of the U.S., and another was a Jesuit priest who had served as an Army paratrooper chaplain in Vietnam. Bob said he was a cross between them, an alloy of the political and the spiritual. He himself had served in the Air Force and trained to be a pilot in the 1950s. During his time in the service, he did some gambling and in one incredible craps game made a dozen or more consecutive successful passes and won $16,000. The narrator of *The Deer Park*, Sergius O'Shaugnessey, a fighter pilot in Korea, wins a similar amount in a poker game, a coincidence that drew Mailer, always alert to omens and portents, to Lucid right away.

They'd met in 1958 when Mailer spent a week at the University of Chicago, where Lucid was working on his doctorate. Mailer lectured, gave an important interview to Lucid and Richard Stern, "Hip, Hell, and the Navigator," published in 1959, and met students during the day. At night he hit the bars with Lucid and another Irish-American, the poet Paul Carroll. Mailer had many drinking pals with Irish roots, including boxing champ Roger Donoghue, and journalist-novelist Pete Hamill, who wrote about their friendship in *A Drinking Life*. He was also friendly with the legendary Dublin playwright and lush, Brendan Behan, who described himself as "a drinker with writing problems." Lucid, a serious oenophile, once told a morning class that what the world needed was a good breakfast wine. I was another—Irish-American drinker, not oenophile—and relish the memory of evenings sipping single malt whiskey with Mailer at the snug bar in his home overlooking Provincetown harbor. Because I had been a bartender in grad school, I was usually behind the bar pouring, a singular vantage-coign for observing Mailer and his visitors.

After Mailer had introduced me to Lucid on that memorable day in Stockbridge, he returned to demeaning *The Fight*—now generally considered the finest account of a boxing match ever written. Lucid responded by saying that Mailer was now free to get back to his mammoth 1983 Egyptian novel, *Ancient Evenings*, which he had begun researching in the late 1960s. Mailer had shelved this saga-in-progress every time he'd felt impelled to write about the bloody, bizarre events and actors of the time, including his account of the 1967 anti-war March on the Pentagon (for which he won the National Book Award and his first Pulitzer), *The Armies of the Night*, and the seven nonfiction narratives that followed it through *The Fight*. I listened raptly as Lucid and Mailer sorted through the artistic challenges and potential monetary returns of various projects. The Egyptian novel had priority, of course, but the enormous success of Mailer's biography of Marilyn Monroe, *Marilyn*, which sold a half million copies, led him to think about writing a biography of Hemingway, whose death still haunted him. Mailer never forgave Hemingway for not leaving a suicide note. "It was like your own father killing himself," he said. Through the good offices of Hemingway's son, Gregory, Mailer received a large box of material from the Hemingway Archive at the Kennedy Presidential Library in Boston, but he never got beyond the research stage.

Mailer also told Lucid that he was thinking about making another experimental film (he directed three from 1968 to 1971). Listening to the two friends briskly discuss the time and effort required for each project, and the commensurate rewards, as if they were hedge fund risk managers weighing new investments, gave me a mild shock. At the time, I believed, naively, that great books emerged solely from a writer's passion. I had not yet grasped the weight of commercial possibilities in artistic decision-making. Given alimony for numerous ex-wives, college expenses for (at that time) seven children, two mortgages, and a full-time assistant, Norman was "locked in the bowels of cash flow," as he once put it. But, as I learned, his financial needs did not necessarily outweigh prompts from "the navigator," the overseer of his unconscious, when deciding the next project to tackle. It took me years to appreciate the crush of forces jostling Mailer: family obligations (including ongoing relationships with his ex-wives and long-distance relations with a couple of girlfriends), competition with other writers (living and dead), the search for new experience, and the wish, as he once put it, to get his hand "on the rump of history." Standing at the forefront of these considerations was the question of personal exposure or, as he said in 1971, the necessity to consider "in the most ghastly terms possible: how much of yourself should 'go public' like a stock?" For counsel, he consulted Lucid and a few others, but he leaned on his wily but unpredictable navigator.

Lucid left an hour later and Mailer waved me into the kitchen where I gave him an inscribed copy of my thesis, and a bottle of Metaxa, a Greek brandy—he told me later that he poured it down the drain. He produced a bottle of rum and made me one of his favorite drinks, a rum Presbyterian. He only had a couple of small ones, as he was coming off a 20-day fast undertaken to lose weight: too much alcohol or food would shock his system. His ideas on weight loss came from a book, *Fasting Can Save Your Life*, which he liked enough to buy copies for several family members.

As we talked, he began to ask me questions. As an enlisted man in the Army who had been busted from T-5 sergeant to buck private by his commanding officer for insubordination, Mailer was both suspicious and curious about my service as a sea-going naval officer, especially my service on several courts-martial. While we ate cold chicken, he interrogated my Navy experience for novelistic material; it was his inveterate response when someone whose background he found of interest entered his circle. He was intrigued by my account of charting a course across the Atlantic by dead reckoning—this was before satellite navigation (GNSS) was introduced. Given the vagaries of the ocean's currents, and the imprecision of set and drift calculations, exactly where we'd make landfall—Ireland, Land's End in southern England or Cherbourg in France, or some other place on the European coastline—was unknown. I also described taking my ship, the USS *Uvalde* (AKA-88), through the Straits of Gibraltar during a mid-watch, changing course every few minutes to avoid crisscrossing freighters, fishing boats, and Arab lateens.

Finally, we turned to my thesis. I told him about the philosophy professor on the examination committee who found Mailer's philosophical ideas to be confusing, unclassifiable. My response to the professor was that Mailer lived in a no-man's land between rationalism and transcendentalism. A well-read intellectual who could parse Marx, Schopenhauer, and Spengler, Mailer was also as open as William Butler Yeats to the numinous world of spirits, augury, and second sight. When an interviewer asked him how he compared to Gore Vidal, he answered that Vidal was "an atheistic rationalist and I'm a diabolist and a mystic . . . we'd always be on opposite sides in any dispute."

An aside: Years later Mailer told me a long story about how a succubus oppressed him on a muggy summer evening in Provincetown, which he called "a spooky town." In the late '60s

Paul Carroll told Mailer, "I saw the Devil once in an alley in Provincetown. He was beautiful."

Mailer asked, "No shit?"

"No shit," answered Carroll.

Mailer scoffed when I told him that the philosophy professor on my committee was an Aristotelian. He loathed Aristotle's idea of the *aurea mediocritas*, the golden mean, much preferring Nietzsche's adjuration: "Live dangerously!" The only other thing I remember about the end of that evening in Stockbridge was his producing a photograph of the soldiers in his basic training company, and explaining how he had borrowed the lean look of this soldier for Sgt. Croft, and the gait of that one for Red Valsen, and so on, in depicting the characters in *The Naked and the Dead*. He had compiled a list of 161 soldiers that he'd served with in the Army. Elated and adrenalin-drenched by the events of the day, I was unaffected by the booze. I barely slept and got on the road shortly after dawn, leaving a thank you note on the kitchen table next to the unopened bottle of Metaxa and the half-empty one of Bacardi.

In 1971, Lucid published a huge anthology of excerpts from Mailer's work, titled *The Long Patrol*, and the same year edited the first collection of essays on Mailer's work, *Norman Mailer: The Man and His Work*. This collection contained a detailed checklist of Mailer's unpublished and published work (some of it in obscure journals such as *The Poetry Bag, Way Out, East Side Review, Fuck You: A Magazine of the Arts*, and *Big Table*, edited by Paul Carroll), resulting from Bob's collaboration with Fan in organizing her son's papers. Besides the material noted earlier, the Mailer archive he assembled over the years contained numerous foreign editions of his work, extensive research materials for his books, and carbons of his correspondence (approximately 45,000 letters). There were many other items, for example: Mailer's army dog tags, literary award medals and citations, honorary degrees, a letter from Arthur Miller offering corrections to Mailer's *Marilyn*, hundreds of photographs, marked-up copies of Tolstoy's *The Death of Ivan Ilyich* and Priscilla Johnson McMillan's *Marina and Lee*, and, not least, the dog collar of his revered standard poodle, Tibo, who with his equally beloved mate, Zsa-Zsa, produced 34 pups. The dogs are buried in the garden of Mailer's sea-side Provincetown home. Mailer later decided that he also wanted to be buried in this artist colony at the tip of Cape Cod, not far from where the Pilgrims spent six miserable weeks in the fall of 1620 before moving across the bay to Plymouth. The only significant missing item from the archive was the original manuscript of *The Naked and the Dead*, which its fledgling author—gratified to be asked—donated to Yale in 1948, the year it was published.

Lucid's Mailer books and his foundational work in creating the archive cemented their friendship. They also initiated mine with Lucid. I wrote him a fan letter when his essay collection came out, and I asked about some interviews that were missing. He wrote a gracious reply, and our correspondence continued for decades. By the early '80s we were speaking regularly on the telephone, often two or three times a week. I'd call, and Bob would say, "Wait a minute; I'm going to make the biggest drink you can imagine." Then we'd trade stories of Mailer's latest appearances in the media—on Johnny Carson and Dick Cavett, for example—reviews of his books, squibs by and about him in the magazines of the day, radio talk shows in Chicago. By the early '70s Mailer was as close to media ubiquity as Muhammad Ali, and Lucid was the appointed guardian of his mushrooming archive and, to some extent, his reputation.

By the late '70s, I'd become Lucid's apprentice. I had an ugly but roomy white Volare station wagon, and for the next dozen years Lucid and I, and sometimes Donna, filled it up once or twice a year with Mailer's literary remains and transported them from Brooklyn Heights to Day & Meyer, Murray & Young. Since 1928, this secure warehouse storage facility has been the preferred choice for many wealthy New Yorkers, the strongbox where they've stored their valuables—crated paintings and sculpture, furs, silverware,

Robert F. Lucid, Mailer and Lennon, Indochine, New York City, 1989.
Photo by Ron Galella, Ltd. (Getty Images)

furniture, crockery—in twelve-foot-long steel vaults mounted on wheels that roll on steel tracks embedded in the concrete floor of the firm's 10-story building at the time of its construction. The Portovaults, as they are called, are moved about like freight cars on sidings by the company's stevedores and, when necessary, shunted into a freight elevator and locked in place on custom-designed trucks that whisk them to and from summer homes in Newport, Saratoga Springs, the Jersey Shore, and other watering holes of the wealthy.

There was another elevator, rarely used, for customers who needed quick access to their Portovaults. After slipping the stevedores a fiver for an extension cord and light, Lucid and I would take this 3' x 3' x 8' foot elevator cage to where Mailer's papers lay in darkness on the ninth floor. Operated with a wonky speed handle, the elevator often conked out between floors. When this happened, we had to contact the secretary on the first floor—if the cranky intercom instrument worked—to fire it up from below. On more than one occasion, Bob and I waited a good 20 minutes for the secretary to return from lunch. A brilliant lecturer, Lucid used these occasions to school me on Mailer's life and works and on his vision for the authorized biography he was writing—he became Mailer's authorized biographer in 1981, succeeding John W. Aldridge, who gave up after a decade. Bob's elucidations were never straightforward and never hurried. Like Nancy Potter he spoke in fully developed paragraphs, and when we talked during our visits to the archive, I viewed myself as an acolyte addressed by an avatar of Henry James. By all reports, his classes at University of Pennsylvania were just as enthralling. I have never known anyone who enjoyed conjuring the arcs of past and present literary lives more than Bob, and few who practiced it with such easy brilliance. He related the course of Mailer's improbable life to the pulse of a nation undergoing seismic changes, speckling his talk with morsels of gossip about Truman Capote, Jackie Kennedy, and Gore Vidal, and enriching it with sparkling metaphors for the crises and turn points in Mailer's life. What a delicious biography he will write, I thought.

In one way or another, all of Lucid's lectures and essays, as well his plan for his Mailer biography, were part of his ongoing exploration of the American writer as a public figure. One of my sharpest memories of my time with Bob was an impromptu lecture he delivered along these lines at Day & Meyer. He began talking just as the elevator began its ascent. Halfway up the shaft, the lights went off, and the elevator clanked to a halt just as he was launching into a detailed explanation of the abrupt changes in Mailer's life in the early '70s. We tried the intercom, but it was dead. Bob paused for a beat, and then as we stood face to face in the darkness, went on for another 15 minutes delineating Mailer's roiled psychic state when he realized, around the time he was writing his biography of Marilyn Monroe, that the sweeping changes he predicted and desired in American life were not going to happen. Mailer had wanted a shift in American consciousness, a revolution, but the counter-culture coalition that he'd help create—the New Left, Black Panthers, anti-war activists, Timothy Leary and the drug culture—faltered and then collapsed in the heat of middle-class American outrage. In 1972 George McGovern was decisively defeated by Nixon, Abbie Hoffman's Yippies were routed, and Mailer concluded glumly that he was "woefully unsynchronized with the reality of his time," as Lucid put it. Then the lights came on, and we rose to the ninth floor. I see now, at the distance of 30-odd years, that my two dozen visits to Day & Meyer with Lucid, and our many conversations about the organization and future literary uses of Mailer's papers comprised a one-on-one seminar in my education as an archivist.

In 1992, I was appointed Vice President for Academic Affairs at Wilkes University in Wilkes-Barre, Pennsylvania, and two years later I orchestrated the transfer of Mailer's archive from New York to Diversified Records, a storage facility in northeast Pennsylvania.

The Day & Meyer truck struggled through the Poconos carrying a Portovault filled with Mailer's literary remains, 16,000 pounds of paper. Over the next four years, Donna and I slowly revamped the archive, dividing it into five chronologically organized categories: literary works, film, correspondence, personal/family, and business records. The materials were stored in new archival boxes with a detailed contents list in each. With additions made over the next decade, the archive grew to 21,000 pounds.

My state of mind when sorting through the Mailer archive over the years was akin to the way one feels when assembling a jigsaw puzzle, that is, calm and focused, with an occasional jolt when an integral piece is found. Mailer's archive, however, had tens of thousands of pieces, and more kept arriving. Not every page of every manuscript or interview in a college newspaper contained a revelation, of course, but every so often I'd find a piece of paper—an envelope, an invitation to a book party, a matchbook with a name and telephone number, an unmailed letter with a comment about another writer—that would bridge a gap in my understanding of his desires and distastes, fears and ambitions, or his pals and lovers and enemies, his family, beloved authors, favorite restaurants, and the architecture of his psyche. These discoveries produced strong, almost ecstatic surges of pleasure—sometimes my hands would shake. The puzzle was a portrait of him over time, not a historical portrait, but a constantly changing sketch of the man and writer in flux and moving in unforeseen directions. "Lipton's," his wide-ranging, unedited journal written over four months in 1954-55, despite its dull stretches and its repetitions, was one of the key pieces of the puzzle. Finding it was a Eureka moment. Reading and re-reading it slowly, carefully, every day over a stretch of ten days, with the knowledge that only Mailer and possibly Lucid had read the whole thing, was a euphoric experience.

In the fall of 1996, Lucid retired from the University of Pennsylvania and moved with his wife Joanne to the Wilkes-

Barre area—he moved into our house and we went to a University residence—to work on the biography. Two or three times a week, I'd stop to see him for a drink on my way home, and he'd bring me up to date on his work. He worked steadily, and Mailer and Norris, encouraged by his progress, came for a three-day visit. But after two years Lucid returned to Philadelphia when his wife became ill. She died shortly after, and his progress slowed.

In April 2005, the archive was sold to the Harry Ransom Center at the University of Texas-Austin for $2.5 million. Donna and I spent several months that year at the Ransom Center assisting the staff, led by Steve Mielke, in the cataloging of the papers, including the creation of the Mailer Finding Aid. This document helps scholars navigate the archive, which is the largest single author collection at the Ransom Center, approximately 470 cubic feet. Lucid, 76, died suddenly of heart failure in December 2006, and with Mailer's blessing on his longtime understudy, I took over as authorized biographer. Mailer died in November 2007, and was buried in Provincetown.

In his unfinished 180,000-word draft, Lucid took Mailer to 1951, Mailer's 28th year. My prose style is nothing like Bob's, so I did not attempt to continue his draft, and wrote my own. My first draft was over 420,000 words, but was reduced by one-fourth for publication. Lucid's pioneering work on Mailer, which has influenced two generations of scholars and critics, informed my biography in countless ways. *Norman Mailer: A Double Life* was published by Simon and Schuster in October 2013. It is dedicated to Donna, my wife, and Barbara Wasserman, Mailer's sister—and also to "the memory of Robert F. Lucid," my mentor and friend.

Works cited:
Dana, Richard Henry. *Two Years Before the Mast.* 1840. Grand
  Rapids, MI: Sheridan House, 2013. Edited by Rod Scher.

Farrell, James T. *Studs Lonigan: A Trilogy*. 1932-35. NY: Library of America, 2004. Edited by Pete Hamill.

Hamill, Pete. *A Drinking Life*. Boston: Little, Brown, 1994.

Hammett, Dashiell. *The Maltese Falcon*. 1930. NY: Vintage, 1992. Film version, directed by John Huston. Warner Brothers, 1941.

James, Henry. *The Aspern Papers*. London: Macmillan, 1888. London: Penguin, 2015. Edited by Michael Gorra.

___. *The Ivory Tower: An Unfinished Novel*. NY: Scribner's, 1917. NY: NYRB Classics, 2004.

Lennon, J. Michael. *Norman Mailer: A Double Life*. NY: Simon and Schuster, 2013.

Lucid, Robert F. Editor. *The Journal of Richard Henry Dana, Jr.* 3 vols. Cambridge: Harvard University Press, 1968.

___. Editor. *The Long Patrol: 25 years of Writing from the Work of Norman Mailer*. NY: World, 1971.

___. Editor. *Norman Mailer: The Man and his Work*, Boston: Little, Brown, 1971.

___, and Stern, Richard G. "Hip, Hell, and the Navigator: An Interview with Norman Mailer." *Western Review* (winter 1959), 101-03. Reprinted in Mailer's *Advertisements for Myself*. NY: Putnam's, 1959.

Mailer, Norman. *An American Dream*. NY: Dial Press, 1965.

___. *Ancient Evenings*. Boston: Little, Brown, 1983.

___. *The Armies of the Night*. NY: New American Library, 1968.

___. *Barbary Shore*. NY: Rinehart, 1951.

___. *Beyond the Law-Blue*. Directed by Norman Mailer. Supreme Mix/Evergreen, 1968.

___. *The Deer Park*. NY: Putnam's, 1955.

___. *The Fight*. Boston: Little, Brown, 1975.

___. *Of A Fire on the Moon*. Boston: Little, Brown, 1971.

___. "Lipton's Journal." *Project Mailer*, Norman Mailer Society, 2020, https://prmlr.us/liptons. Edited by J. Michael Lennon; Gerald R. Lucas; Susan Mailer.

___. *Marilyn*. NY: Grosset & Dunlap, 1973.

___. *The Naked and the Dead*. NY: Rinehart, 1948.

___. *The Prisoner of Sex*. Boston: Little, Brown, 1971.

___. "Quickly: A Column for Slow Readers." *Village Voice*, January 11 to May 2, 1956.

Matthiessen, F.O. *American Renaissance: Art and Expression in the Age of Emerson and Whitman*. London: Oxford University Press, 1941.

McMillan, Priscilla Johnson. *Marina and Lee*. NY: HarperCollins, 1977.

Potter, Nancy A. *We Have Seen the Best of Our Times*. NY: Knopf, 1968.

Shelton, Herbert M. *Fasting Can Save Your Life*. Tampa: Natural Hygiene Press, 1964.

Tolstoy, Leo. *The Death of Ivan Ilyich*. 1886. NY: Random House, 2009. Translated by Richard Peaver and Larrissa Volokonsky.

Meeting Mailer

I was among many who wrote to Mailer after his appearance on the *Dick Cavett Show* with Gore Vidal and Janet Flanner on December 15, 1971. I had no intention of doing so when I sat down with a yellow legal pad that night to enjoy some predictable verbal sparring between Mailer and Vidal. What I was much more eager to hear, however, was Mailer opening up, expounding about his work. I needed grist for the doctoral thesis I had just begun to write on his insanely ambitious but unrealized plan, announced a decade earlier, "to hit the longest ball ever to go up in the accelerated hurricane air of our American letters." At the time I was going into the final semester of my Ph.D. classes at U.R.I. and living nearby with my wife and children in the oceanside town of Narragansett, R.I. Mailer's appearance on the Cavett program had been widely advertised, and many of my fellow students and professors tuned in to what turned out to be one of most astounding television programs of that era.

After obtaining Mailer's Brooklyn Heights address from his close friend, University of Pennsylvania professor Robert Lucid, I worked over my response to the show for ten days, mailing it off just before Christmas. It was a puddingstone of a letter, reamed with praise for *The Armies of the Night*, comments on Germaine Greer's attack on him in a recent *Esquire* article "My Mailer Problem," a sketchy attempt to link his thinking with that of Jonathan Edwards, an even sketchier effort to link him with Hemingway via St. Thomas

(2020)

Aquinas's notion of "the authority of the senses," all of these tied loosely into my thesis, a Sisyphean boulder I couldn't get rolling.

I opened my letter with my response to his verbal brawl with Vidal, citing Mailer's "basilisk glance" and the "stark terror in Vidal's eye" when Mailer attacked him for betraying their friendship. By inviting the audience to take sides in their argument, by alienating Cavett and Flanner, by head-butting Vidal in the Green Room before the show, Mailer had rewritten the decorous rules of the talk show, rules "as strict and codified as those of a Cistercian monastery," as I put it. He told me later that he received more mail about that Cavett show, ten times more, than for any other of his television appearances—by then he'd appeared on every major talk show in the country. The great majority of the letters he received sympathized with him because it seemed obvious that Vidal deserved what he got for gratuitously linking Mailer and Henry Miller to the notorious murderer, Charles Manson, in a *New York Review of Books* essay, calling the trio the "3M Man." Vidal tried to appear *sans souci* on the Cavett show, but guilt was written on his face, and most of the letters, mine included, noted that when Mailer approached him on the set, Vidal flinched.

In my letter, I also queried Mailer about what he called his "ticklish, dense, incomprehensible and for most readers perverted thicket" of theological views, which I hoped to untangle in my thesis. I made the wild claim that Mailer was "the first writer since Christopher Marlowe to suggest that God could lose [his battle with Satan] even if He was right." Such are the wild and crazy thoughts of graduate students stalled in a dissertation. I ended my letter by proposing that I edit a collection consisting of the best of his many interviews. I had no idea that he would be open to the idea and, looking back, am surprised at my temerity. Ten years later 20 of his interviews, edited by me, appeared in his collection, *Pieces and Pontifications*.

Five weeks after sending off my letter to Mailer, my excited wife called me at the university to announce that a response from Mailer had arrived. I think I told Nancy Potter, my dissertation director, and then rushed home. Donna snapped a photo of me, now misplaced, reading my first letter from my hero. He wrote that he liked my letter enough to do something he rarely did, which was to "answer correspondence which goes toward the root." He was referring to my hypothesis that his recent works of narrative nonfiction (referred to then as "new journalism") represented "a redirection of American prose, new appendages off the novelistic bole." He said that the novel he was then engaged in—*Ancient Evenings* (1983), I learned later—could "do harm to my thesis," but not destroy it because it was "almost impossible to go on with a novel unless one can transcend the domination of actual events, invariably more extraordinary and interesting than fiction." The events he was referring to were the violent upheavals and civil unrest flowing from opposition to the Vietnam War, most notably the savage police riots at the 1968 Democratic convention, which he had chronicled the same year in *Miami and the Siege of Chicago*. With this sentence, Mailer had given me a launch point for my thesis, namely, the conflict between his desire to write long, character-driven, programmatic novels, and his obligation to comment on the bizarre and unpredictable currents and events in the country.

A few months later, in the fall of 1972, I got my first full-time academic job at the University of Illinois-Springfield, a new university in the state capital. During my first semester, while teaching a Mailer graduate seminar, I learned that he was on a speaking tour to promote his forthcoming book about the 1972 presidential campaign, *St. George and the Godfather*. The coincidence startled me; all forces and powers seemed to be conspiring to bring me into contact with Mailer. Sometime in late October, accompanied by several of my students, I drove 100 miles to Western Illinois University in Macomb, where Mailer was speaking. Arriving early, we got front-row seats. At the announced hour, 8:00 p.m. Mailer, dressed in jeans, jacket, and loosened tie, walked on the stage—I was

Lennon at University of Illinois-Springfield, 1972

later surprised to learn that Mailer was precisely punctual for social and professional commitments.

He was carrying a metal pitcher and a glass, and I told the student next to me, "Yes, he's drunk," sure that the pitcher was brimful of Old Grandad—I knew that he liked bourbon. I was wrong; he was cold sober. He almost lost the crowd by opening with clips from his 1968 experimental film set in a police precinct, *Beyond the Law*, in which he plays a police lieutenant, Francis X. Pope. George Plimpton plays the mayor of New York, and several of Mailer's friends are cops or crooks. It was nearly impossible to follow the jerky camera work or understand the soundtrack which, Mailer said, "sounded as if *everybody* is talking through a jockstrap."

In the following Q-and-A session he was much better, handling with ease a range of questions that were by turns informed, personal, ponderous, inflammatory, sweet, sour, and stupid. At least four women asked what he had against the Women's Liberation Movement—his 50,000-word essay analyzing its assumptions, *The Prisoner of Sex*, had been published the previous year. Mailer supported abortion rights unreservedly, but argued that coitus-free conception (sperm banks, artificial insemination, egg harvesting, surrogate mothers) monitored by the state would be the death of heterosexual romance. He also said that the Women's Liberation Movement was in danger of becoming totalitarian by refusing to accept any criticism. His statements, made in his essay and in numerous public forums, created a fierce blowback from the Movement, although *Prisoner* was a finalist for the *National Book Award*.

People wanted to know what he thought of Mayor Richard J. Daley, the Beats, and Percy Bysshe Shelley (Mailer passed on the poet; he knew very little about English poetry), and there was my question about how the war between God and Devil was going. "A draw, so far," he replied. Mailer also read a wonderful selection from *St. George*, the passage where he likens the American bombing of Vietnam and Cambodia to the act of a compulsive suburbanite who defecates on a neighbor's lawn. This righteous shitter unloads a crap every evening, simultaneously feeding his narcissism and adding feculent woe to his neighbor's lot. Mailer went on to note that in the three previous years the U.S. had dropped 7.5 million tons of bombs, double the total dropped in WWII and the Korean War combined. He ended by warning of benign totalitarianism, a soft fascism, coming to the country as a result of our hubris.

After his formal presentation, Mailer, and several dozen admirers, moved to a smaller room where he answered questions for another 90 minutes, after which we moved to a nearby tavern, Tom and Ski's Grin and Beer It. The crowd of students and faculty had diminished, and I was able to ask him a few questions, including one about Hemingway's influence. Papa was a model, he said because "Hemingway, unlike Thomas Wolfe and Fitzgerald, was both able to grow artistically and yet survive." I nodded, but said to myself that Hemingway's art had diminished greatly over time, and unlike the other two, he killed himself.

Then I posed the question I'd been saving: why had he decided to describe himself in the third person in five consecutive books, *St. George and the Godfather*, being the most recent. "It is a tremendous presumption," he replied, "for a novelist to write about what goes on inside of more than one person's head and so after *The Naked and the Dead* I switched to the first person. A novelist needs a completely coherent view of the world to write in the third person and I have not arrived at that position yet. In my journalistic pieces I felt I could gain objectivity and get away from the excesses of using 'I' by describing myself in the third person. But in these pieces, because I am writing about real events, I am able to explore my own consciousness."

Quite a mouthful, I thought, not grasping all the implications. But decades later, my exploration of Mailer's struggles with point of view became a load-bearing wall in my biography. Throughout the middle of his career (1965-79), the period in which he wrote his new journalism narratives, Mailer struggled with how to present himself, how to see himself, how to divide himself into Mailer-then (the participant), and Mailer-now (the observer). Describing himself in the third person in these books was the most important aesthetic decision of his career. This cleaving of self by fiat resulted in his first Pulitzer and a National Book Award for *The Armies of the Night*. As Alfred Kazin noted in his review of *Armies*, "the best American writers of the 19th century wrote about themselves all the time," and in doing so with such bravura, Mailer was following Emerson, Whitman, and Melville in seeing "the self as the prime condition of democracy." An exploration of the optics of Mailer's work became the heart of my thesis, and later my biography of him.

The crowd thinned out more around midnight, and Mailer and I moved to a corner and continued to drink and chat. To my amazement, he was utterly frank, telling me about his expenses and his huge IRS debt. He put it this way in a subsequent letter:

> The simple truth is that I generally wait until the red-hot ire of the IRS is close, bearing on my ass, and then I run out and try to pick up twenty or thirty thousand dollars in a huge, crude overall maneuver that exposes me to the full surrealism of the lecture circuit.

Toward the end of the night, Mailer remarked on my New England accent and asked where I'd grown up. "South of Boston," I said, "not far from Cape Cod." He immediately invited me to visit him the next time I was back East. He had a summer home in Provincetown, the fishing village and artist colony at the tip of the Cape. We closed the bar down after last call.

And so began our 35-year friendship with Mailer. Beginning in 1975, and for most of the summers over that span, Donna and I, and sometimes our three sons, Stephen, Joseph, and James, spent several days with the Mailers either in Provincetown, or Mt. Desert Island in Maine, where he also summered. Our sons connected with Mailer's younger children and were relaxed with Mailer, who talked easily with the boys—Stephen said that he seemed more like a friendly uncle than a famous person.

In 1997, we bought a condo in Provincetown and several years before his death in November 2007, made it our permanent home. From the third floor of our condo you could see Cape Cod Bay on one side of the peninsula, and the Atlantic on the other. Mailer worked there during the winter of 2000-01. He liked the view, and the quiet. At his home, the phone rang all day. He walked over to our place every day, and went to work after a quick hello. He was superstitious about gabbing before he began work, fearing he'd talk something away. Afterwards, back at his waterfront home, we'd have drinks and talk about everything under the sun. Usually, there was a Texas hold 'em poker game after dinner. He didn't reveal that he was writing a novel about Hitler's early years until he was more than halfway through the first draft. Writing in pencil on plain white paper, he completed the first 150 pages of that novel, *A Castle in the Forest*, during that winter. It was published several months before he died on November 10, 2007, and became his 11th bestseller.

Tom Wolfe, Upstart, R.I.P.

Tom Wolfe, the dashing, white-suited, journalist-novelist with a Ph.D. from Yale in American Civilization, and a vocabulary equal to that of William F. Buckley's, satirical skills not dissimilar to those of Kurt Vonnegut, H. L. Mencken and Mark Twain (not to mention Shakespeare's rival, Ben Jonson, the gimlet-eyed satirist), a Southerner whose tradition-battering stories in the *New York Herald Tribune* in the early 1960s made him principally responsible for starting the first new direction in American literature in a half century, the iconoclastic, initially detested-by-the-fourth-estate New Journalism (which really goes back to Daniel Defoe's *Diary of a Plague Year*), has died. Wolfe wrote cantilevered sentences like the foregoing all the time, only much zingier. His passing shunts me back to Springfield, Illinois, 1974. The previous year Wolfe's anthology, *The New Journalism*, was published, although it made no large impression in the state Capitol's sleepy newsroom, where reporters from the Chicago and St. Louis media, as well as most downstate cities, had correspondents. I was an English professor at Sangamon State University (now University of Illinois-Springfield), and Wolfe was one of my heroes.

One day, Paul Simon, outgoing lieutenant governor and later senator and presidential candidate, then a visiting professor of journalism, popped into my office. He was getting ready to run for Congress, but in the meantime decided the university should have a graduate journalism program. He needed someone to design the

Chicago Tribune (May 16, 2018)

courses, and when he found out that I knew Norman Mailer, and was an editor at *Illinois Issues* magazine, he asked me. We launched the public affairs reporting program that year, and Wolfe's anthology was one of the textbooks in the course I team-taught with Simon. The students, mainly bright Midwesterners, were divided, roughly, into two camps: those who read *Congressional Quarterly* and revered *The Making of the President* books by Theodore H. White, and those who thought White was . . . okay. The latter group favored the upstarts: Joan Didion (*Slouching Towards Bethlehem*), Norman Mailer (*Miami and the Siege of Chicago*), the outrageous Hunter S. Thompson (*Fear and Loathing in Las Vegas*), Truman Capote (*In Cold Blood* is the Ur-narrative of the movement), and everyone's favorite, Wolfe and *The Electric Kool-Aid Acid Test*, the story of Ken Kesey and his Merry Pranksters who traveled around the country in a psychedelic bus named *Further*. Simon, a teetotaler from Troy, Illinois, who wore horn-rimmed glasses and snappy bowties, allowed that there was some pretty amazing stuff in Wolfe's writing, but was a Teddy White man. At the time, I had shoulder-length hair, wore bell-bottom pants, smoked weed now and then, and had a mission: bring literature back into journalism. Wolfe, who saw himself to be the inheritor of the techniques of Zola, Dickens, Hemingway, and Orwell—all of whom began as reporters— provided the tools in the introduction to *The New Journalism*.

What particularly stoked Wolfe's ire was conventional journalism's "beige narrator," the bland reporter who spoke with the hushed voice of "a radio announcer at a tennis match." The New Journalists refused to be quiet observers sitting in the grandstand as life's parade passed by, no, they wanted to join the march, tootle the flute, and bang the drum. The writer, Wolfe argued, should be whenever possible in the foreground, taking part in the action so as to see it better. To report on "the whole crazed obscene uproarious Mammon-faced" American scene, Wolfe pointed to four novelistic techniques that could/should be employed: 1) scene-by-scene construction using sensuous description and dramatic flair (loosely linked scenes have been sanctified by nonfiction maven John McPhee, Wolfe's contemporary, in his new book, *Draft No. 4: On the Writing Process*); 2) providing dialogue in full, giving the characters' idiolects, their verbal flavor, and avoiding distorting paraphrasing— Dickens, he points out, "had a way of fixing a character in your mind" using extensive dialogue and only a bit of physical description; 3) using the third person point of view instead of the monotonous first person I-I-I, thus revealing what a character is thinking. This can only be done by reference to letters or diaries, and/or extensive interviewing, something Norman Mailer does successfully in his masterpiece, *The Executioner's Song*; 4) the most demanding and least understood device, Wolfe says, is presenting "the record of everyday gestures, habits, manners, customs, styles of furniture, clothing," in sum, the symbolic status life of the characters. No one does this better than Joan Didion in her report on the "social hemorrhaging" in the Hippie community of Haight-Ashbury in *Slouching Toward Bethlehem*; Capote and Gay Talese, another pioneer of the New Journalism, also excel in this regard.

Wolfe also wrote fiction— his most successful novel, *Bonfire of the Vanities*, was first serialized, à la Dickens, in *Rolling Stone*—but my hunch is that his signal achievement will be seen as pumping new energy into American journalism by moving the writer to the stage of the story. For accomplishing this over a long career, he is now being borne on those historic tides that carry a few authors' boats to the golden isles of posthumous investiture. Salud!

Mailer's Library

Books arrived daily by mail, FedEx, or by hand on the doorstep—a half-dozen was not unusual. At social functions, airports, readings, while walking to dinner along the waterfront of Provincetown, or riding the A Train to Manhattan from Brooklyn, people pressed more into his hands. Not that Norman Mailer was short of books; his library, at four different locations, amounted to more than 7,000 volumes. His last wife, Norris Church, referred to them as Kudzu, the pernicious creeping vine that covers large swaths of the American South. As fast as she gave them away, they reappeared on every flat surface in their two homes. Norman, she said, spent $1,000 a month on books, and received a large number gratis from writers in search of a blurb.

He resisted Norris's efforts to shed them, to the extent that those deemed worthy of further examination were retained on the dining room table in his Provincetown house for a week or two, where he would read the opening pages of more than a few. The scarred dining room table, large enough to seat twelve, was Mailer's cockpit, the place where he conducted all his business, save writing his books. Every morning he sat there for a couple of hours, always facing a wall to avoid the fierce morning light from the harbor coming through the large oriel window. Eating his eggs, he read the *New York Times* and *Boston Globe*, and sorted through the mail. He also did two crosswords to "comb my mind," as he put it, before climbing to his attic study, where he would work two shifts, eleven to

Times Literary Supplement (March 9, 2018)

two, then four to eight. More books were up there, mainly reference works for whatever project was underway, plus a score of dictionaries and thesauruses, some of them nearly clawed to pieces.

On most days during Mailer's final three years, I arrived at his Provincetown home for coffee and talk at around ten. Invariably, the table was piled high with books, several days of mail, printouts of email messages (Norris received the latter; he never touched a computer), bound galleys and manuscripts, and copies of *Vanity Fair, the Nation, Poetry, the American Conservative,* and *Esquire,* among other magazines. When the piles became ridiculous, they were moved to the oriel window shelf, ultimately filling it up and blocking the view. When this occurred, Norris and Norman's assistant Dwayne shunted stuff to recycling, charity, or the basement, where Norman had shelves built a few years before his death in 2007. Three or four times a year, I'd cull items there for his archive.

My wife and I catalogued the books in the three libraries: in Provincetown, about 1,000 volumes; in the Brooklyn Heights apartment overlooking the East River's Buttermilk Channel, approximately 3,400; in his writing studio in DUMBO (Down Under the Manhattan Bridge Overpass), another 1,500. About 1,200 reference books and numerous foreign editions of his forty-odd published books are part of his archive that went to the Harry Ransom Center at the University of Texas in Austin in 2005. A few years after Mailer's death, the rest of his library was donated to Wilkes University in Wilkes-Barre, Pennsylvania, where I teach creative writing.

Mailer couldn't live without books, but was uninterested in them as objects. When he needed some pages for a public reading, he often tore them out of the book rather than carry it. He gave me a first edition of his *Advertisements for Myself* (1959), with four chunks, totaling 106 pages, missing. The inscription, dated May 1995, reads: "For Mike, this working copy of *Advertisements for Myself* with sections removed. God knows what I tore them out for." His copy of

Priscilla Johnson McMillan's *Lee and Marina* (1977), dismembered when he went to Dallas with Larry Schiller to interview Marina Oswald, was later patched together with duct tape. Dostoevsky's *The Idiot* was similarly reconstructed. One of his favorites for public readings was a six-page description of an embalming from the opening chapter of his 1983 novel, *Ancient Evenings*. Norris was furious when he ripped this section from her inscribed copy, and then lost it. Books cringed when they felt his hand. Dust jackets were a hindrance, he said, and were often shucked. He felt similarly about bookmarks. His barbarous method of marking his place was to fold a page twice diagonally so that it stuck out at the top. Limited editions were of limited interest. Unlike John Updike, who published scores of them, Mailer never initiated a single one, but went along cheerfully with about ten proposed by specialty presses—Targ, Lord John, Dolmen, Easton, Caliban, and Franklin Library. Over the course of a week in 1978, he signed 10,180 copies of Franklin's leather-bound thirtieth-anniversary edition of *The Naked and the Dead*, for which he was paid $2 a book.

His disrespect for books as objects provides a clue to the nature of his library: it was assembled over the decades to meet his need for models, reference material, to replenish his toolbox of tropes and techniques, and to keep up with his contemporaries—in short, out of literary need. He didn't collect first editions of his favorite authors, those he listed on seven published surveys. They were: Dos Passos (on all seven), Tolstoy (six), Spengler, Thomas Wolfe and Marx (five), Dostoyevsky, Stendhal, Hemingway and James T. Farrell (four), as well as Malraux and Steinbeck on three occasions. Several other writers are listed twice, including Melville, Jorge Luis Borges, and E. M. Forster, the only English author. There are many cheap used or paperback editions of his favorite authors, none of them worth much apart from the value of some inscribed copies—from Susan Sontag, Colin Wilson, William Manchester *The Last Lion* (1983), his biography of Churchill, and James Jones, who inscribed a copy of *From Here to Eternity* (1951), "To my most feared friend, to my most beloved enemy." Instead of inscribing *The Unmaking of a Mayor*, his 1966 account of his unsuccessful 1965 run for mayor of New York on the half-title page, William F. Buckley went to the index, knowing Mailer would look his name up. When he did, he would see two words: "Hi Norman."

As a matter of principle, Mailer avoided reading his books after they were published. He changed his style for many of his books, sometimes radically—*The Executioner's Song* (1979) is perhaps the best example—and he wanted to avoid being tempted by old narrative modes and gambits. But there were exceptions. For public readings, he had to dip into his books of yesteryear to select cuttings—in later years, *Ancient Evenings* and *Tough Guys Don't Dance* (1984) were the two he most favored—and when I brought him copies of his works belonging to friends of mine to sign, he invariably leafed through some of them, reading a few pages here and there. I remember giving him a copy of *An American Dream*, the 1965 André Deutsch edition with a wonderfully garish jacket illustration, and he read for several minutes from chapter four. When he closed it, he said that it depressed him: "I'll never write that well again." Another time, while signing a copy of *The Executioner's Song*, he remarked that his style was changed by the prose of this narrative. "It was never the same," he said, "flattened out, less lively." I added that his lyricism peaked with *An American Dream*, and he nodded in acquiescence.

Perhaps the first thing one would have noticed about the Brooklyn library is the amount of poetry. Mailer said once that he loved poetry, but added, "I don't approach it critically. To be a great critic of poetry would take a lifetime of work. I read it to replenish myself." In addition to the anthologies of American verse he kept in the loo, perhaps half of the 300 poetry volumes in a floor-to-ceiling bookshelf in the living room of his apartment are by American poets. It was the only one of the twenty-odd bookcases in the apartment devoted to one genre. Some of the volumes came to him from poet friends—James Dickey, Sandra Hochman, and Norman Rosten (the late poet laureate of Brooklyn, who signed his letters to Mailer "Norm II")—but most reflect Mailer's catholic tastes. There are volumes by poets as different as Wallace Stevens, John Berryman, and Amy Lowell, as well as several by her cousin, Robert, whose poem, "For Norman Mailer" appears in his *Notebook 1967-68.* Lowell's inscription, "For Norman, This brief though true return for your kind portrait. Cal," refers to Mailer's depiction of Lowell in *The Armies of the Night* (1968), which Lowell said was "the best, almost the only thing written about me as a living person." There are seven Ezra Pound titles. Mailer visited Pound in Venice in 1970, and gave him a copy of *Deaths for the Ladies (and Other Disasters)*, his 1962 collection of gnomic, Pound-like poems. Asked which of Mailer's poems he liked, "the old eagle," as Mailer described him, said, "All of them!"

There are fewer French poets than British, but a large number of French novelists. Mailer studied French in high school, college, and also at the Sorbonne, which he attended on the GI Bill in 1947-48. His written French was good enough to translate *Souvenirs Intimes*, the memoir of Picasso's first mistress, Fernande Olivier, for use in his 1995 biography, *Portrait of Picasso as a Young Man*, and he spoke it well enough to converse with French friends such as Jean Malaquais (translator of *The Naked and the Dead* into French, published in 1951 with an introduction by André Maurois), and Romain Gary. Malaquais, who Mailer said "had more influence on my mind than anyone I ever knew," introduced him to the work of André Gide, whose 1924 collection of Socratic dialogues, *Corydon*, spurred Mailer to write two long philosophical self-interviews, "The Metaphysics of the Belly," and "The Political Economy of Time," published in *Cannibals and Christians* (1966). His interest in French literature began in his senior year in college when he read André Malraux's *Man's Fate* (1933). Shortly after graduation from Harvard in 1943, he told a friend, "I'd like to be another Malraux."

It could be argued that Mailer became the American equivalent of Malraux, the writer as *engagé* intellectual. Malraux was Minister of Culture under President Charles de Gaulle, and in the early 1960s Mailer hoped to become a key advisor to President Kennedy, a cultural Cardinal Richelieu who would link the White House to the most exciting currents and actors on the American scene. He wanted a seat at the Camelot roundtable, an aspiration which was extinguished in November 1960 after he stabbed his second wife, Adele Morales, with a penknife.

In a 1963 letter to Pierre Brodin, a French critic who asked about his interest in French literature, Mailer said that "the French novel has always been more congenial to me than the English," and goes on to name his favorites. They include not only Proust, Flaubert, and Joris-Karl Huysmans (Mailer adapted his Satanic 1891 novel *Là -Bas* [*Down There*] into a screenplay and published it in *Playboy* in 1976), but Georges Simenon, of whom he said, "He is never a great writer, but he is certainly a marvelous one, so natural, so effortless." Mailer got hooked on Simenon during the war when he read *Faubourg* (*Home Town* in Stuart Gilbert's 1944 translation), and over the years assembled a collection of over 200 of his novels. He numbered them so he could reread them in sequential order, which he continued to do until the end of his life.

Mailer mainly read translations of the French writers, but owned several in the original, including Proust's *Un amour de Swann* and *Le ravissement de Lol V. Stein* by Marguerite Duras (1964). His all-time favorite French novel was Stendhal's *The Red and the Black*. He used the novel's protagonist, Julien Sorel, the ambitious young man from the provinces as a touchstone in several of his essays, most memorably in a 1968 review of Norman Podhoretz's *Making It*, where he compares his erstwhile friend's move from Brooklyn to Manhattan ("one of the longest journeys in the world," wrote Podhoretz) to Sorel's ascension to Paris from Verrières. In 1949, when Mailer and Malaquais were writing screenplays in Hollywood for Samuel Goldwyn, Mailer tried to convince Montgomery Clift to play Sorel in a film version of the novel that he would write. Clift was interested but was called away to another project.

Mailer may have been more influenced by French novelists than English ones, but he nevertheless admired the skills of the British. During a visit to London in the fall of 1961, he told an interviewer, "Sentence for sentence, the good British authors write better than we do. I'm thinking of people like Amis, Waugh, Graham Greene. Some are bad: I've never been able to read Joyce Cary." Mailer may have stumbled when reading the late and largely forgotten novel, *The Fearful Wife* (1947), the only Cary novel he owned. On the other hand, he owned most of Forster's novels. Forster was not "one of the novelists I admire most. But I have learned a lot from him." He was stunned when an important character in *The Longest Journey* (1907), Gerald Dawes, was killed in a football game part way through the novel, causing the other characters to change in unforeseen ways. "It taught me," Mailer wrote, that "character can dissolve in one stricken event and re-form in startling new fashion." In a 1964 *Paris Review* interview Mailer said that "Forster gave my notion of personality a sufficient shock" that after *The Naked and the Dead* he stopped writing in the third person for over a decade. Forster, he said, "had a developed view of the world; I did not."

His best-loved British novelist was Graham Greene; he once said that *The End of the Affair* (1951) was the best anatomy of a love affair he had ever read (the fact that Greene wrote to him to say that he was "moved and excited" by the "magnificent" *Advertisements for Myself* did no harm to their relationship). Besides Greene's great early novels, Mailer owned three later works: *Dr. Fischer of Geneva* (1980), *Monsignor Quixote* (1982), and his nonfiction account of his long relationship with the Panamanian dictator, Omar Torrijos, *Getting to Know the General* (1984). He also owned the three-volume biography of Greene by Norman Sherry. Speaking on the BBC programme, *Omnibus*, in 1971, he praised George Orwell's *Nineteen*

Eighty-Four (1949) for its profoundly prophetic vision of a world filled with "dull, awful, profoundly picayune little wars...that would kill the world slowly." Orwell admired Mailer's work, and said in a 1949 letter that *The Naked and the Dead* was "awfully good, the best war book of the last war yet," a comment that appeared on paperback copies of the novel for decades. Some of the other British books on the shelves are *The Mill on the Floss* (1860), *Women in Love* (1920)—which he discussed at length in *The Prisoner of Sex* (1971)— *The Good Soldier* (1915), Cyril Connolly's *The Missing Diplomats* (1952), a nonfiction examination of the scandal surrounding the Cambridge spies, Guy Burgess and Donald Maclean, which Mailer probably consulted for *Harlot's Ghost*. The earliest book by a British writer is Charlotte Bronte's final novel, *Villette* (1853), a Folio Society edition which shows no dog ears. There is nothing by Austen, Dickens, Trollope, or Hardy.

Mailer's interest in South American writers grew out of the monthlong visits he made to Mexico City almost every year of the 1950s, when he visited his ex-wife Beatrice Silverman, and their daughter Susan. Preparing for a bullfight novel (never written), he took her to the bullfights regularly, and learned Spanish well enough to collaborate with her on a translation of Federico Garcia Lorca's elegy for a bullfighter, "Lament for Sánchez Mejías," published in *Existential Errands* (1972). Besides Lorca, Mailer owned the love poems of Neruda and several of Marquez's novels, but the Latin American book that influenced him most deeply was Borges's 1962 short-story collection *Labyrinths*, and its "magical" explorations of time, which influenced the temporal convolutions Mailer attempted in *Ancient Evenings*. He said in 1980 that Marquez and Borges "are the two most important writers in the world today," adding that Borges's ability with plot enabled him to "do in five pages what Pynchon does in five hundred."

Dostoyevsky's struggle to write *The Idiot* month by month as a serial while suffering from epileptic fits was on Mailer's mind when he was under commensurate pressure during the eight-month span in 1964 when he published his serial novel, *An American Dream* in *Esquire*. *Crime and Punishment* is another obvious influence; Mailer's protagonist, Stephen Rojack, like Raskolnikov, is an intellectual murderer interrogated by the police who goes into spiritual exile, although Dostoyevsky's man goes to Siberia, while Rojack goes to Guatemala and Yucatán. Mailer also had books by Chekhov, Turgenev, Mikhail Bulgakov's *The Master and Margarita* (1966-67), Isaac Babel's *Red Cavalry* (1926), and Henri Troyat's 1965 biography, *Tolstoy* (translated from the French by Nancy Amphoux, 1967). Over the course of a week shortly after his eightieth birthday, Mailer devoured it, and then told me it was the finest biography he had ever read, superior to Richard Ellman's 1959 biography, *James Joyce*.

Many of his large collection of books on Hitler and Nazi Germany are listed in a six-page bibliography appended to his last novel about Hitler's youth, *The Castle in the Forest* (2007). Just as large is his collection of books about the Kennedy assassination, including two sets of the twenty-six-volume *Warren Commission Report*. He also owned several works by Freud, quite a number by Jung, and several books by Wilhelm Reich, including *Character Analysis* (1933), which he said was not a literary influence but valuable for "the idea that a man's physical posture is his character," which he memorably applied to Richard Nixon in *St. George and the Godfather* (1972). He had all the books of psychologist Robert Lindner, including *Rebel Without a Cause* (1944) and *Prescription for Rebellion* (1952). Lindner and Mailer became close friends in the early 1950s, and Lindner, who died suddenly in 1956, gave extensive feedback on Mailer's unpublished 1954-55 marijuana journal, "Lipton's" (tea was then slang for marijuana).

Another essay would be needed to comment on Mailer's collection of Judaica, especially the work of Martin Buber on the Hasidic movement, and another on the large number of philosophical works, from Aristotle to Kierkegaard to the British positivist, A. J. Ayer. One highly influential volume must be named: Walter Kaufmann's 1956 anthology, *Existentialism from Dostoevsky to Sartre*, which Mailer read during the seventeen days he was confined in Bellevue Hospital in New York City while awaiting a determination of his sanity after stabbing and almost killing his second wife, Adele Morales. It is more than likely that he read the Nietzsche chapter, "Live Dangerously," and the passage from which it comes: "For believe me, the secret of the greatest fruitfulness and the greatest enjoyment of existence is: to *live dangerously!* Build your cities under Vesuvius! Send your ships to uncharted seas! Live at war with your peers and yourselves"! One can imagine what resonance this must have had for the lonely reader in the violent ward of Bellevue.

Feathered with Forbearance:
Shirley Hazzard on Graham Greene

A review of *Greene on Capri* (Farrar, Straus and Giroux, 2000), by Shirley Hazzard

Note: I read Hazzard's sketch of Graham Greene after enjoying several of his early novels. Mailer intensified my interest by telling me that Greene's 1951 novel, The End of the Affair, *was the best novel of a love affair he'd ever read, a view he shared with Faulkner. As I noted in "Mailer's Library," Greene called Mailer's* Advertisements for Myself *"magnificent." They met only once, at a 1983 cultural conference in Paris.*

Shirley Hazzard, the novelist (*The Bay of Noon*, 1970, *The Transit of Venus*, 1980), ransacked travel books, histories, and memoirs for nuggets on the lure of Capri to ballast her carefully considered sketch of another novelist, the late Graham Greene. She found that Flaubert visited Capri, as did Henry James, D. H. Lawrence, and Rilke, who spent a night in 1907 looking at "an earth of moonlight, of moon shadow" from the roof of his rented house. Shortly afterwards, the exiled V. I. Lenin arrived there as a guest of Maxim Gorki. Was Lenin jostled by the intense, detached Rilke as they passed each other on the ferry from Naples? Ivan Bunin was also Gorki's house guest. His famous novella, "The Gentleman from San Francisco" is set on Capri. Turgenev made three visits and said his feelings for the island's beauty "will remain with me until I die." Joseph Addison came in 1701; Norman Douglas, the famous classicist and pedophile, lived there for years, and is buried in the non-Catholic cemetery under a green marble slab on which a line from Horace is incised. The earliest pedophile in residence, of course, was the Emperor Tiberius, who had his lover-victims cast from the pinnacle of Mount Solaro, the massif that dominates the island and where the ruins of his palace still crumble. Hazard's memoir rustles with this sort of intertextuality, a term she doubtless despises. Relishing wit, clarity, and the subtleties of literary influence, and quietly loathing Deconstructionism and "the wool of obsessive theory," Hazzard is a senior acolyte in the Henry James Fellowship, perhaps a dean in the now-dwindling college, one in which Greene was prominent. Her memoir is brisk, gem-like, and devoid of languor. It is also an important contribution to our understanding of the necessary contradictions of a major writer, an alternately warm and slightly acerbic feminist arrow, but one feathered with forbearance.

Like Provincetown and Key West, Capri (accent on the first syllable) has long been a haven for lovers, eccentrics, exiles, and writers, those seeking a terminal city, a retreat to make a stand with the sea at their backs. Greene started coming in the late '40s—he owned a house there, *Il Rosaio*, for forty years. Hazzard and her husband Francis Steegmuller, the Flaubert scholar, met Greene and his mistress, Yvonne Cloetta, on the island in the late '60s. The foursome enjoyed dinners and walks and much excellent and old-fashioned literary talk (Hazzard and Greene effortlessly quoting poetry) whenever they were in simultaneous residence. She had countless chances to observe the irascible, charming Greene, a tortured *grande personaggio*, as the Caprese called him, in whom "suffering was the attestable key to imaginative existence," a constant "agitation of the spirit providing some defense against the dreaded accidie," or apathy.

Their first meeting was a Jamesian encounter. Alone with her crossword puzzle and coffee in the Gran Caffe in the *piazzetta* of Capri on a wet December day, Hazzard observed Greene and a friend lope across the square to the café after attending Mass and then sitting near her table. Greene tries and fails to remember the last line of a poem by Robert Browning, "The Lost Mistress," Again and again he repeats it:

> Tomorrow we meet the same then, dearest?
> May I take your hand in mine?
> Mere friends are we—well, friends the merest
> Keep much that I resign.

And then the concluding verse:

> Yet I will but say what mere friends say,
> Or only a thought stronger;
> I will hold your hand but as long as all may,

Here Greene comes up short. Hazzard, taking her time, retrieves her umbrella, pays her bill, and walks by Greene's table, slowing down long enough to say, "The line is: 'Or so very little longer.'"

Greene loved poetry, precision, and certain non-pedantic strains of literary insight, and immediately opened the valves of his attention and regard to those of a similar persuasion. Hazzard is saturated in literature, and that night when she and her husband (no slouch in these matters) arrived at the restaurant, Greene stood up to greet them. "And so began," she said, "our years of seeing Greene on Capri." Their irregular meetings continued until the late '80s (Greene died in 1991), and along the way Hazzard treasured up a dozen or more anecdotes which coalesce in this volume into a portrait of the artist "unhallowed and unmellowed," one who "regularly invited you to step on a rug, which he would then pull out from under." He hated peace and quiet—except when he was writing—and loved singularity and the unexpected. "Agape," she wrote, "was his idea of hell."

The memoir form is tremendously flexible, looser, and baggier in some ways than the novel. It allows Hazzard the freedom to mix and match the history of Capri, anecdotes about its famous visitors (especially writers), natural description, snippets of poetry, asides on the literary life, and a bundle of sweet-sour remembrances of Greene. Unlike biography, the memoir requires no final, summative or (often) forced character analysis. Just slants of insight, casually dressed. What she is really up to is a presentation of the puzzle of Graham Greene, with evidence (but nary a footnote) to push readers to one or more of the cardinal compass points of interpretation.

Take your pick. There is the ascetic Greene, scornful of all possessions, save books; the frugal Greene, leaving dinner early to take the bus and avoid paying a taxi fare; Greene, the generous friend providing support to writers such as R. K. Narayan and Muriel Spark—the latter's checks always accompanied by a few bottles of red wine to "take the edge off cold charity." We also meet the world-weary Greene, seeking diversion and fomenting trouble, "but only on his terms"; Greene, the pilgrim-adventurer, wandering from continent to continent, war zone to war zone, trying to forget the great love of his life, Lady Catherine Walston, who appears as Sarah Miles in one of his three great novels, *The End of the Affair*, 1951 (the other two are *The Power and the Glory*, 1940 and *The Heart of the Matter*, 1948). There is also Greene the professional, producing 350 words a day and always meeting deadlines, and Greene the "Catholic agnostic," who attends Mass but has not gone to Confession in 20 years, and has a complex, Emily Dickinson-like relationship to God, arguing, remonstrating, and negotiating with the Deity. And, finally, there is Greene the sexist, although Hazzard eschews the label. Instead, she says, "In one respect—his attitudes toward women—he remained rooted, as man and writer, in his early decades." His fictional women—Sara Miles is the great exception—are tough, beautiful, devoted to their men, and "sexually disposable." Hazzard returns to Greene's relations with women a few times to skewer him, but gently. She is not one to banish Greene to the outer darkness—as more strident feminists have—for his shortcomings in these relationships. Living the kind of life that he did, and being temperamentally disposed to travel the globe to gather his material, Greene developed an "incomparable relentless freedom in his heart" (to borrow Norman Mailer's line about Henry Miller). So, while Hazzard is not loath to reveal Greene at his most unattractive, to show him lashing out at whomever was handy, even friends, especially friends, ready to hurt before he could be hurt, she usually offers a saving grace on the next page, a compensatory account of hard-won self-knowledge or unheralded generosity. Throughout, she refers to his "blue, extraordinary eyes," the eyes of a demon, as an Italian friend put it. Hazzard wrote:

> In the demon rages, the eyes would glare out, accusatory, engorged with fluid resentment. From under frizzy white brows, the eye sockets appeared then to deepen, the eyeballs to protrude with a playground will to hurt, humiliate, ridicule. At those awful moments, Graham looked for all the world like Thomas Mitchell playing Scarlet's demented father.

As a spindly adolescent, Greene was tormented by a couple of public school contemporaries, clever sadists. It took many adventures and achievements for him to rebuild his self-confidence. World War II and his dangerous intelligence work were factors here, as were his literary successes before and after. But success also made him willful. It is possible that like many a tortured youth, Greene over time re-wired the armature of his personality and developed strident reflexes in reaction to his early humiliations. "More than most people," she wrote, "he did not care to be thwarted." Hazzard's portrait of this "unappeasable, unquiet spirit," will persist in literary memory for more than a "very little longer" than is usual. With this book, she has burnished the memoir form.

Bishop, Pound, and Prospero in Buzzards Bay

Note: The origins of this essay go back to 1983 when my brother Peter wondered aloud how many literary handshakes rearward in time it would take to reach Shakespeare, beginning with a living person. We began planning a book that would trace this handshake chain, beginning with Mailer, whom we both knew, as did my son Joseph, who joined us as third co-author. For months we made numerous lists, trying for a more balanced sequence. Names were added and dropped (including Mailer's), until we had reached consensus on the literary handshakers, each of whom had actually met the individual before and after them in the chain. We also settled on a leadoff figure, Elizabeth Bishop, who knew Ezra Pound who knew Harriet Monroe who knew William Dean Howells who knew Paul Lawrence Dunbar who knew Fredrick Douglass—here we cross the Atlantic—who knew Harriet Martineau who knew William Wordsworth who knew Mary Robinson who knew David Garrick who knew Colley Cibber who knew Anne Bracegirdle who knew Samuel Pepys who knew John Dryden who knew Kenelm Digby who knew Ben Jonson who knew—finally, four hundred-plus years earlier—William Shakespeare. The research, however, proved to be disastrously formidable—it took me nine months to write this, the first essay, and as other commitments surfaced, the project was abandoned. Its assonantic title, "Sixteen Handshakes to Shakespeare" is hereby offered to anyone with the resources to undertake the expedition.

Ocean State Review (2016)

When Elizabeth Bishop visited Robert Lowell in early May of 1948, he took her to see Ezra Pound, who had been incarcerated since late 1945 in St. Elizabeths Hospital, a government psychiatric facility in Washington, D.C. Lowell, then 31, was the most important and ambitious young poet in the country, having won the Pulitzer for poetry in 1946—edging out Bishop's first book, *North & South*—and named the following year as poetry consultant to the Library of Congress (a title later changed to poet laureate). Bishop, 37, unmarried, unstable and still uncertain of her sexuality, had met Lowell a year earlier, and was smitten by this tall, rumpled Yankee who she found to be handsome in "an almost old-fashioned poetic way." He was the first person she had ever met who really spoke with her about how to write poetry—"like exchanging recipes for making a cake," as she put it. For the next thirty years they enjoyed a warm and complex, but not psychically intimate relationship.

As poet laureate, Lowell had an unofficial responsibility to visit Pound in the "bughouse," as the elder poet called it. Both he and Bishop were in awe of the brilliant editor who had acted as midwife to *The Waste Land*, the masterpiece of his friend T. S. Eliot, who dedicated the poem to Pound as *il miglior fabbro* (the better craftsman). Pound had long been an innovative and generous supporter of many writers—William Butler Yeats, James Joyce, Hilda Doolittle, Ernest Hemingway, William Carlos Williams, and Marianne Moore, to name the most prominent—but he was also tendentiously opinionated and surpassingly narcissistic, and perhaps worse, at least in the opinion of a quartet of psychiatrists from St. Elizabeths, led by its superintendent, Dr. Winfred Overholser. They examined him to see if he was sufficiently sane to be tried for making treasonous, anti-Semitic broadcasts, over 300 of them from 1941-45, against the Allies on Italian government radio in Rome. In early 1946 Pound was declared by a federal court to be "a sensitive, eccentric, cynical person" now in "a paranoiac state of psychotic proportions which renders him unfit for trial," and ordered confined to the derelict ward at St. Elizabeths.

He could not be released unless tried and acquitted, but could not be tried unless judged sane, and if found sane he could have been convicted and executed. Two other traitors who made broadcasts for the Axis were hanged in England a few weeks before Pound was judged *non compos mentis*. When Pound's daughter Mary asked about getting her father released, a State Department official commented that "she was lucky he had not ended up in the electric chair." Prudently, Pound went along with the diagnosis, admitting that he was of "unsound mind." At times cogent, he could glissade into incoherence, for example, announcing after his arrest his plan to visit Tiflis where he could learn Georgian in order to discuss his economic theories with Stalin. He remained in St. Elizabeths for over 12 years. Over time, his situation became a cause célèbre with supporters and detractors engaged in a heated public debate. The only thing his friends and foes could agree on was the statement of one supporter, Samuel Hynes: "It is only prudent that we Americans from time to time remind ourselves that one room at St. Elizabeths is a closet which contains a national skeleton."

Bishop likely first encountered Pound in Harriet Monroe's anthology *The New Poetry* (1923 edition), which she received as a gift at age 13. At Vassar, where she majored in English literature and took a number of music courses, she began to read the moderns, including Eliot and W. H. Auden. Later, she recalled that she knew the 1931 edition of Wallace Stevens's collection, *Harmonium*, "almost by heart." She took courses in Shakespeare, admiring the "beautiful, slightly sad lilt" of his sonnets, and the poets of the English renaissance, singling out George Herbert and Ben Jonson as inspirations. For many years, she carried an edition of Herbert's *The Temple* when she traveled, and always listed him, along with Charles Baudelaire, as her favorite poets. Known, because of her aloofness, as "The Bishop," she was named "Class Aesthete." "We all knew with no doubt whatsoever that she was a genius," said her college friend Frani Blough Muser. High praise, considering that Bishop's generation at Vassar included Mary McCarthy, Eleanor Clark, and Muriel Rukeyser.

Her interest in the moderns may have surged at the end of her junior year, when she was chosen to interview Eliot during his campus visit. There is no record of whether they discussed Pound, although she knew of his ties with Eliot. He first appears in her correspondence in 1935, the year after she graduated, when she wrote to Muser about Pound's essays on Arnold Dolmetsch, the French craftsman who helped revive the use of Elizabethan instruments. Following Pound's example, she ordered a new clavichord from Dolmetsch, and then went to Paris to take possession. She took lessons on it, spoke of it "with great tenderness," and transported it with her during the following decades of travel to Brazil and elsewhere. Explaining her purchase, she quoted a line from Pound: "The further poetry departs from music, the more decadent it gets." According to William Carlos Williams, Pound, although tone deaf, had "the most acute ear for metrical sequences, to the point of genius, that we have ever known." Williams added that his college friend was also "the biggest damn fool and faker in the business." Pound had gifts for exasperating his admirers, as Bishop was to learn.

In early 1948, Lowell, along with Williams, Eliot, Léonie Adams and several others had been appointed to a Library of Congress Committee to select the winner of a new annual poetry prize given by the Bollingen Foundation. Pound's *The Pisan Cantos* was the controversial winner, leading Congress to disavow the prize, which went then to Yale University to be administered. These 11 cantos became the sixth book of his masterwork, *The Cantos*. They were begun in pencil on toilet paper in the outdoor "gorilla cage" in Pisa where Pound was jailed for several weeks immediately after the war ended in early May 1945, and completed in the adjacent medical office of the army's Detention Training Center, where he was held until mid-November before being flown back to the U.S. Given her association with Lowell, it is likely that Bishop read *The Pisan Cantos* around the time of her first visit to Pound, and if so was surely impressed with the following lines in which Pound turns an accusatory gaze on himself, often called one of the finest lyrics of the twentieth century:

> Pull down thy vanity,
> Rathe to destroy, niggard in charity, Pull down thy vanity,
> I say pull down.

Superb lines like these are bright spots in the massive, discontinuous tessellation of quips and quotations, Homer to Henry James, that comprise *The Cantos*. Bishop wrote to Lowell two months before their first visit to St. Elizabeths that she was "pretty mystified by most of Pound's message to the world." There is no narrative line to speak of in *The Cantos*, no discernable structure, only a cacophony of voices, some memorable, many muddled. Yeats's comment is instructive: "I have often found there brightly printed kings, queens, knaves, but have never discovered why all the suits could not be dealt out in some different order." Pound told Yeats that Homer's *Odyssey*, Ovid's *Metamorphoses*, and Dante's *Divine Comedy* were his models, but exactly how they were employed is not obvious. Bishop may have appreciated the early *Cantos*, but overall, she found the diffuseness of much of his poetry to be "exhausting," adding that it would "be vastly improved if one could lean on a sense of *system*."

A year passed before she visited St. Elizabeths again, this time as poet laureate (she succeeded Léonie Adams in September 1949). In the interim, she traveled, wrote a little and drank a lot, three activities that took up much of her adult life. As she wrote to a friend, "I've always felt that I've written poetry by *not* writing it, and now this

Library (of Congress) business makes me really feel like the 'poet' by default." Both she and Lowell were regularly treated in hospitals and clinics and rest homes; she for alcoholism, he for manic-depression. Bishop's sympathy for Pound may have been affected to a degree by her knowledge of Lowell's condition, but it was certainly affected by the insanity of her mother, who became unbalanced after the death of her husband seven months after Elizabeth's birth, and was permanently committed to an asylum in 1916 when her daughter was five. An asthmatic shunted between the homes of relatives in Massachusetts and Nova Scotia, Bishop told Lowell that she was "the loneliest person who ever lived." She displayed great empathy for odd, alienated, and disturbed individuals in her life and work. According to one friend, "Elizabeth was absolutely, pathologically terrified that she would go insane," and was always talking about the crazy people in her life, specifically, her mother, Lowell, and Pound. Her poem, "Visits to St. Elizabeths," grew out of her painful but regular calls on him.

Her attitude toward the "maniacal old man," as she described Pound, was anything but simple. She admired his early poems, and his stature as the person most responsible for the modernist revolution in poetry, but when she taught at Harvard, her dismay at understanding *The Cantos* made her feel "terrified" about having to "say anything about Ezra Pound's poetry." Yet their poetics have much in common. The diffuseness of *The Cantos* notwithstanding, Pound valued and wrote much poetry that was spare, secret, and spirited. Bishop wrote: "The three qualities I admire in the poetry I like best are: *Accuracy, Spontaneity and Mystery*." Both also prized clarity and conciseness ("gists and piths," as Pound said), avoided abstractions, despised the forced rhymes, rhetoric, and ornamentation of the late Romantics, and relished unnoticed, telling details. Both wrote largely in conversational tones, and Bishop would have agreed with what Pound told Harriet Monroe about poetic language: "No Tennysonianness of speech—nothing,

nothing, that you couldn't in some circumstance, in some stress of emotion, *actually say*." But while she and Pound are more than a little alike in tactics, they had markedly different ideas of the poet's role. As James Merrill put it, Pound wanted "to write like a God. (Wallace) Stevens and Miss Bishop merely write like angels."

In appearance and social intercourse, Bishop and Pound were separated only by an abyss. Pianist Arthur Gold, who knew Bishop during the 1940s, gave this description of her:

> There was something physically graceful and very elegant about Elizabeth. She had what I call genius hair (vibrant, very alive hair); a delightful smile, when she was familiar with you; and a very warm, rather sad, half-shy and half loving air. She was very, very *soigné*, always going to the hairdresser, always looking terribly neat, extremely well put together, and her clothes were very, very, thought out. Elizabeth loved clothes. They weren't distinguished clothes, but always suggested a tiny bit of British elegance—not American jazzy elegance.

Pound, on the other hand, no longer dressed like the dandy in a velvet jacket (Yeats gave him one) he was during his London years. His biographer Humphrey Carpenter described him during his time in St. Elizabeths:

> "Grampaw" was the persona he invariably adopted in the presence of visitors. He had developed a special costume for the role. The summer version consisted of "floppy sandals, walking shorts several sizes too large gathered at the waist with a belt, his shirt thrown off to take in more sun." Another visitor describes "tan shorts too big for him, tennis shoes and a loose plaid shirt." On less warm days he might be found in "a loose sweatshirt, an old GI overcoat,

baggy trousers, heavy white socks, bedroom slippers, long
underwear showing at his ankles."

Loud, garrulous, utterly unceremonious, and a born meddler,
Pound was full of screwball schemes, and wrote thousands of letters
to supporters, including many racists, while incarcerated. Bishop,
a wicked wit in private, was shy and circumspect in public, which
made some of her trips to St. Elizabeths a subtle form of torture.
She said that she "suffered visiting Pound because he lived in a
room with no doors. He had no privacy whatsoever, so whatever
illness he had was exacerbated by this condition." When the dutiful
Bishop (he called her "Liz Bish") began coming, he gave her a series
of tasks, including the microfilming of various items in the Library
of Congress. Accompanying her on one visit was the poet, Weldon
Kees, who said that visiting Pound was "certainly not an experience
to have missed. He 'receives' at the end of a corridor in the hospital,
which is a pretty gloomy affair, with catatonics and dementia
praecox cases slithering about; but he certainly keeps up a spirit.
Very lively and brisk, and his eyes go through you like knives." Kees
said he didn't think Bishop liked Pound much, "regarding him as a
pretty dangerous character."

Those who wished to see Pound wrote to Dr. Overholser, and
he checked with Pound, admitting anyone he approved. On warm
afternoons, Pound would carry out deck chairs, books, paper and
pencils, string, insecticide, and snacks, including a bag of peanuts he
shared with the squirrels that scampered about. A visitor described
the scene:

> Talking all the while about Henry James or Hemingway, he
> tied the string round the waist of an unshelled peanut, and
> dangled it in sight of a patrolling squirrel. It hopped closer
> and closer with nervous flicks and darts, grabbed the bait,
> and was quickly hauled kicking into the poet's lap ("Come

on, you little devil!"). He briefly caressed the black "oak-cat," untied the peanut, let the squirrel scramble off with it. He then re-baited the string for another squirrel. There had once been an Empress in China, he remembered, who could call down birds from the trees. With his triple-pointed beard he might have been impersonating a Chou dynasty Emperor. The Emperor talking to squirrels.

Numerous poets came to pay homage, including Williams, Eliot, Archibald MacLeish, E. E. Cummings, Marianne Moore, and Charles Olson, who was quite faithful; as did academics and writers—H. L. Mencken, Edith Hamilton (who came in a chauffeured limousine), Katherine Anne Porter, and Marshall McLuhan, driving from Canada. He introduced Pound to the young scholar, Hugh Kenner, who a few years later published his provocative study, *The Poetry of Ezra Pound*. Kenner said, "I suddenly knew I was in the presence of the center of modernism." James Laughlin, Pound's long-time publisher, was a regular, and Alice Longworth Roosevelt, the oldest daughter of President Theodore Roosevelt, also visited. Pound's wife Dorothy Shakespear, who spoke with Bishop on the telephone about her husband, came almost every day.

When Eliot visited his old comrade in the hospital's Chestnut Ward, he tracked in some dirt, and a slippered inmate with a cleanliness fetish followed him about with a sweeper. Eliot, dressed in striped trousers and wearing a gold watch chain, sat with his feet off the floor for half his visit as the inmate worked his obsession. Bishop had an eye like a pair of tweezers, and observed the menagerie around Pound. "During the day," she wrote, "Pound was in an open ward, and so one's visits to him were often interrupted. One boy used to show us his watch, another patted the floor," details that she would use later in her poem about Pound. As her biographer, Brett C. Millier, explained, "Elizabeth did not write her poem about these meetings with Pound until 1956. But it is clear that in 1949-

1950 she had already begun to form the complex sentiment at the heart of 'Visits to St. Elizabeths.'"

During the summer of 1938, Bishop read "Mother Goose," and in a letter to Marianne Moore mentions the venerable nursery rhyme, "The House that Jack Built." Twelve years later, after meeting Pound several times, she adapted the rhyme's aggregating or cumulative technique for "Visits to St. Elizabeths," increasing the length of each stanza until there are twelve, two more than in the Jack poem. Another difference is that she varies the lines—irregularly, noticeably, deftly—to hint at his bizarre history and personality. A friend who accompanied her to St. Elizabeths said that she was not "comfortable in Ezra's presence. I think she looked upon him as a sort of naughty old grandfather whose habits are somewhat questionable, but who, after all, is one's ancestor." Her poem presents the spectrum of her paradoxical feelings about "Grampaw." Following is the final stanza of "Visits to St Elizabeths":

> This is the soldier home from the war.
> These are the years and the walls and the door
> that shut on a boy that pats the floor
> to see if the world is round or flat.
> This is a Jew in a newspaper hat
> that dances carefully down the ward,
> walking the plank of a coffin board
> with the crazy sailor
> that shows his watch
> that tells the time
> of the wretched man
> that lies in the house of Bedlam.

Contending with Shakespeare

Both Bishop and Pound were familiar with and opinionated about Shakespeare's work. Pound called The Bard "the world's greatest dramatist, along with Ibsen and Aeschylus," adding that a reader "can look for real speech in Shakespeare and find it in plenty IF he knows what to look for." But Chaucer, he believed, "had a deeper knowledge of life than Shakespeare." Chaucer "wrote while England was still a part of Europe." By Shakespeare's time, "England is already narrowing." Shakespeare knew and drew on Italian tales and legends, but "they are already an EXOTIC." The reason that Shakespeare was England's great poet, he said, was not merely because of his lyric mastery; it was also because "English opinion has been bamboozled for centuries by a love of the stage, the glamour of the theatre, the love of bombastic rhetoric and of sentimentalizing over actors and actresses."

Writing to Robert Duncan in 1939, Pound said, "Hunks of Shxpr *bore* me; I just can't read 'em. Despite my admiration for other hunks." He had little feeling for the great set pieces in the tragedies, namely, the soliloquies of Hamlet, Shylock, Iago, and Lear made famous by generations of British thespians. Pound preferred the history plays, admiring the gritty eloquence of Falstaff and his crew of cutpurses. He particularly esteemed the histories because they asked the same questions about royal power and the death of young men in unnecessary wars that Pound did in his long, autobiographical poem, "Hugh Selwyn Mauberley," where he excoriated the butchery of World War I:

There died a myriad,
And of the best, among them,
For an old bitch gone in the teeth,
For a botched civilization.

Dante also lamented the slaughter of war, and for this reason, Pound said, he "is the best guide to or illuminator of Shakespeare," although there is no evidence that Shakespeare knew much if anything about the work of the author of *The Divine Comedy*, who

Pound revered. Dante condemned usury in his great poem, and Pound followed his lead unwaveringly. When asked by a visitor to St. Elizabeths why a poet should be so preoccupied with economics and money, Pound replied, "A poet writes what he has to write. All the great poets—Homer, Shakespeare, Dante—all made history a part of their poetry." Usury became his great Satan, an idée fixe walled off from all objections and criticism. Disastrously, it led him to his admiration for Mussolini's fascism, which in turn prompted his anti-American broadcasts, resulting in his long incarceration.

Bishop too admired Shakespeare's history plays, stating that The Bard, like Baudelaire, demonstrated that "poetry is as much a part of the brothel and the slaughterhouse as of the rose garden and the glade." For "North Haven," her memorial poem for Lowell, who died in 1977, she borrowed a line from the song, "When daisies pied and violets blue," in *Love's Labor's Lost*, about how the flowers have "returned to paint the meadows with delight." In her poetry classes at Harvard, she sometimes sang her students the concluding couplets of his sonnets to teach them iambic pentameter, and "the importance and finality of final lines." She also admired his late romance, *Cymbeline*, and enthused in a letter about the splendid funeral song in the play:

Fear no more the heat o' the sun,
Nor the furious winter's rages;
Thou thy worldly task has done,
Home art gone and ta'en thy wages.
Golden girls and lads all must,
As chimney sweepers, come to dust. (IV.ii.258-263)

Unlike Pound, Bishop made no sweeping judgments about Shakespeare, but she cut him no slack on accuracy. She criticized, for example, his description of a deer's death in *As You Like It*, finding the animal's groans and heaving chest, and "the big round tears / (that) cours'd one another down his innocent nose / In piteous chase" (II.i.38-40) to be "full of preconceived notions and over-sentimental." Anne Stevenson, who wrote the first study of her friend's work, said, "Elizabeth saved herself by keeping her eyes on grains of quartz and amethyst while the world pounded around her." Millier notes that although Bishop was "fearlessly observant," she also drank heavily "to escape from the tyranny of that observing consciousness." She groused in letters about what Lowell called her "famous eye." She could also be funny about it. In 1969, when Lowell introduced her as "the famous eye," she stood up and said, "The famous eye will now put on her glasses."

One of Bishop's shrewdest critics, David Kalstone, said this about the keen discernments in her poems: "One finds it all there without any fuss: the most precise psychological connections made between the needs of exact observation and the frail nightmares of the observer, between the strangeness of what is seen and the strangeness of the person seeing it." Epiphanies born of pain and disaster are the stuff of her poems, moments such as the ending of her most famous poem, "The Fish," which comes after she hauls a huge, "battered and venerable," dying Jewfish into her boat, and delineates the five fish hooks firmly seated in his mouth, and the attached lines:

> Like medals with their ribbons
> frayed and wavering,
> a five-haired beard of wisdom
> trailing from his aching jaw.

Cuttyhunk and *The Tempest*

The most curious and compelling instance of Bishop's interest in Shakespeare arose from a visit to Cuttyhunk that she made with her boyfriend Robert Seaver, shortly after her graduation from Vassar. He left after a few days; she remained on the island for eighteen days, and said she never wanted to leave. They continued to see each other, and two years later he proposed to her. When she declined, he killed himself. Three days later a postcard arrived in her mailbox, mailed by Seaver just before he put a gun to his head. It read: "Go to hell, Elizabeth." His death was a heavy blow, but not as tragic or debilitating as the 1967 suicide of her longtime partner, Lota Macedo Soares, with whom she had lived in Brazil for 15 years. Lota took an overdose before Elizabeth's eyes and died several days later. Bishop was devastated, took to drink (bourbon was her favorite), and fell and broke her arm and shoulder, one of many such "accidents" resulting from intemperance.

After graduation from Vassar in 1934, Bishop moved to Manhattan with a vague plan to become a writer. But after setting up an apartment in Greenwich Village, she rendezvoused with Seaver in August for the trip to Cuttyhunk. She probably learned of the small, beautiful island in Buzzards Bay from her college friend Rhoda Wheeler Sheehan, whose family still lives in Westport on the south coast of Massachusetts, about six miles north of the island. Bishop wrote parts of "One Art," one of her finest poems, in a small fishing shack on Sheehan's property. On a clear day you can see Cuttyhunk from its windows. While on the island, Bishop learned that Shakespeare may have used it as the model for Prospero's magical isle in *The Tempest*.

Cuttyhunk is the westernmost of the sixteen Elizabeth Islands, a twenty-mile chain running southwest from the ocean side of Cape Cod. Shaped like a lobster with one claw missing, the island is two-and-a-half miles long and three-quarters of a mile wide. It was claimed for England in 1602 by Bartholomew Gosnold on a voyage financed by Henry Wriothesley, third Earl of Southampton, Shakespeare's patron, and the dedicatee of his early narrative poems, *Venus and Adonis* and *The Rape of Lucrece*. Two of Gosnold's crew, Gabriel Archer and John Brereton, wrote separate accounts of the voyage and their 22 days on the island, where they met the indigenous Wampanoags. Brereton described them as being "of a blacke swart complexion, their eie-browes painted white . . . their women . . . lowe of stature . . . fat, and very well favored, and much delighted in our company." The Wampanoags (literally "people of the dawn") fed Gosnold's men and in return the English "gave them such meats as we had readie dressed, whereof they misliked nothing but our mustard, whereat they made many a sowre face." The colonists ate the plentiful cod, dogfish, mussels, crabs, cockles, oysters, scallops, and wilks (quahogs), but passed on snake, "which the Indians eat for daintie meat, the skinnes whereof they use for girdles." They traded knives and trinkets for the furs of deer, luzernes (lynxes), beavers, otters, and wildcats, and cut down cedar and sassafras trees, the latter's bark then prized in England as a cure for gonorrhea and syphilis.

Gosnold named the island, using a shortened form of the Indian word Poocutohhunkunnof, which may mean "land's end." Gosnold also named Cape Cod, giving it a practical English name reflecting the abundance of this fish, and overwriting the more poetic name—Cap Pallavisino—given in 1524 by the Italian explorer, Giovanni da Verrazano. Bishop visited the island a few times over the years, and loved it the way she did all the places she lived or visited near the ocean, including Nova Scotia, Key West, San Francisco, and Westport. Her last home was on the Boston waterfront. She died there October 6, 1979.

A few scholars have argued that Shakespeare plucked details from the account by Brereton, printed in late 1602, and perhaps Archer's, which was not published until 1625, but may have circulated earlier in manuscript, a common practice in that period. Bishop's belief in Cuttyhunk most probably came, first or secondhand, from Edward Everett Hale (author of "The Man without a Country"), who proposed the island in a 1902 lecture. In 1919 his lecture was published as *Prospero's Island*, with an introduction by historian and U.S. Senator Henry Cabot Lodge.

Lodge mentions three other islands as possible models for Shakespeare: Lampedusa and Pantalaria near Sicily, and Bermuda, 640 miles east of Cape Hatteras. The first two were proposed because they lie near the route King Alonso's shipwrecked wedding party would have taken returning to Naples from Tunis. Prospero, deposed as Duke of Milan by Alonso's brother Antonio, could have landed there after being set adrift in "a rotten carcass of a butt" (II.i.46) with his daughter Miranda. But Lampedusa gets more attention because it was known by mariners as the "Enchanted Island." Bermuda was advanced as the location because the playwright seems to have relied on an eyewitness account of how the *Sea Venture*, flagship of Admiral Sir George Somers, ran aground on Bermuda after a July 1609 storm separated it from the expedition, bound for Virginia. Somers survived, arriving ten months later in Virginia aboard two small pinnaces, amazing the other Virginia Company colonists, in part because Bermuda was known as the Isle of Devils and was avoided by mariners. (Caliban, it will be remembered, was "got by the devil himself" [ii.319-20] upon Sycorax, a blue-eyed witch from Argier, near Tunis, who "did litter" (I.ii.282) him on the island.) The report of the shipwreck by William Strachey, the expedition's secretary-general, was not published until 1625 (in the same volume as Brereton's), but Edmond Malone, the eighteenth-century Shakespeare scholar who first dated the order of plays, believed that Shakespeare read it in manuscript prior to the first known production of the play on November 1, 1611.

Shakespeare, without doubt, heard of the Bermuda shipwreck. News of it reached London in 1610, and was much discussed. His description of the terrible storm that destroyed Somers's flagship is the likely basis for the opening scene of *The Tempest*, and Caliban's refusal to build more fish dams for Prospero (II.ii.180) almost certainly comes from Strachey's description of how the Indians at the Virginia colony destroyed the traps they had previously built for the colonists. The "flam'd amazement" (I.ii.198) created

by Ariel's spooky illumination of the masts and spars of Alonso's
doomed ship does resemble Strachey's comments on St. Elmo's
fire, but a similar description of the phenomenon appears in a
1600 account that Shakespeare knew, Richard Hakluyt's *Principal
Navigations*. Gosnold's *Concord* also ran into gale winds upon arrival
in America, and the weather on Cuttyhunk in early June 1602,
described by Brereton, was just as temperate as Bermuda's in late
July 1609. The companies of both ships, Somers's *Sea Venture* and
Gosnold's *Concord*, felt the same emotions—relief, exhilaration,
and apprehension—after reaching their respective islands: for the
former, Bermuda, an unpopulated, arid, sandy, semi-tropical island
two hundred square miles in extent; and for the latter, the tiny (600
acres), forested Cuttyhunk, which offered a harbor nook, plentiful
food, water from numerous springs, and commerce with the Indian
inhabitants. Bermuda has many palm trees, but no oaks, in one
of which Prospero threatened to imprison Ariel. (Brereton: "This
island is full of high-timbered oaks.") The fresh springs that Caliban
offers to show Stephano are non-existent on Bermuda, where the
only natural source of potable water is rain.

In his introduction to *Prospero's Island*, Senator Lodge points
out what many others have, namely, that while we might not know
the identity of Prospero's island, it was certainly not Bermuda.
For as Ariel explains, "Safely in harbor | Is the king's ship, in the
deep nook, where once | Thou call'dst me up at midnight to fetch
dew | From the still-vexed Bermoothes, there she's hid" (I.ii.227-
29). Lugging dew *from* Bermuda *to* Bermuda, even for Ariel, is too
heavy a lift. Bishop may have known about Lodge's point from her
freshman Shakespeare class with Professor Barbara Swain, who
recalled that Bishop "was an enormously cagey girl who looked
at authorities with a suspicious eye." But it is more likely that it
was the details about Cuttyhunk noted by Edward Everett Hale
in *Prospero's Island*, and how they matched those in the play, that
prompted Bishop to tell Marianne Moore in a 1937 letter that she

was upset about Bermuda being considered the playwright's model, "and not Cuttyhunk, as I dearly believe."

Following Lodge's introduction, Hale lays out his case based on the contemporaneous accounts of Gosnold's voyage. First, the matter of logs. Brereton tells of the strenuous effort needed to cut down the medicinal sassafras and the aromatic cedar: the Wampanoag braves, "some sixe or seven of them, bearing us company every day into the woods, and helped us to cut and carie our Sassafras." Likewise, Miranda's suitor, Ferdinand is put to work by Prospero: "I must remove some thousands of these logs, and pile them up," a "mean" and "odious" task. Ferdinand works happily because his pure, ethereal love of Prospero's daughter "makes my labors pleasures" (III.i.4-10), while Caliban, who loathes lugging logs, lusts for Miranda so he might "people this isle with Calibans" (I.ii.350-51). Hale mentions the springs, coves, and berries of Cuttyhunk, and the "lush and lusty" grass (II.i.53) on both islands, and notes, accurately, that there is not one tropical allusion in the play. He concludes, "I think there can be no doubt that the local coloring of the 'Tempest' is in part derived from the narrative of Gosnold's adventures," which gives him sanction to say "that we have the right to claim Miranda as a Massachusetts girl." It is not difficult to imagine how such an assertion resonated with Bishop, another motherless Massachusetts girl brought up by the sea.

Key Sources: Brett C. Millier's well-wrought and researched biography, *Elizabeth Bishop: Life and the Memory of It* (1986) was my most important source for information on her, and for Pound, Humphry Carpenter's equally thoughtful biography, *A Serious Character: The Life of Ezra Pound* (1988). Regular reference was made to Bishop's letters: *Elizabeth Bishop: One Art* (1994), edited by Robert Giroux. For Pound, I relied on his *ABC of Reading* (1934); *Literary Essays of Ezra Pound* (1954); and *Selected Letters, 1907-1941, of Ezra Pound* (1950), edited by D. D. Paige. For Pound's poems, I used the

1986 New Directions edition, *The Cantos of Ezra Pound*; and for Bishop, the Library of America's *Elizabeth Bishop: Poems, Prose, and Letters* (2008), edited by Robert Giroux and Lloyd Schwartz. For information on the Gosnold expedition, I have relied on *The Gosnold Discoveries...in the Northern Part of Virginia, 1602, Now Cape Cod and the Islands, Massachusetts* (1982), compiled and edited by Lincoln A. Dexter; *The Story of Cuttyhunk* (1953) by Louise T. Haskell; *Prospero's Island* by Edward Everett Hale (1919); and "Cuttyhunk" by Arthur Cleveland Hall, in *Tales of the New England Coast* (1985), edited by Frank Oppel. Special thanks to Eileen Sheehan of Westport, Massachusetts, for information on Bishop's many visits to her parents' home. For *The Tempest*, I used *The Riverside Shakespeare* (1974), edited by G. Blakemore Evans.

The Touchdown Twins:
James Jones and Norman Mailer

Note: Parts of this interview, which was conducted in New York on January 14, 1983, were used in my PBS documentary, James Jones: From Reveille to Taps. *In addition, I quote from it in my biography of Mailer. But the entire interview has never been published. It is probably the most extensive, and revealing, comment by Mailer on Jones, who was his close friend in the 1950s. Their friendship splintered later in that decade, but they never completely broke off relations, and Mailer spoke at a memorial service for him in New York City on February 23, 1978 (Jones died in May 1977). Mailer said more than once that his fiercely competitive friendship with Jones was the strongest male friendship of his life. Jones inscribed Mailer's copy of* From Here to Eternity *as follows: "To Norman—my most feared friend; my dearest rival."*

JML: When did you first meet Jones?

NM: In late 1950 or early 1951, somewhere in there. My editor at Rinehart told me that there was a book that Scribner's was terribly excited about, a war novel by someone named James Jones. His editor, Burroughs Mitchell, wanted me to read it and if I liked it to give it a blurb. They thought that was very important. So I read it, and you know, it knocked me down and half knocked me out. I thought it was an extraordinary book. All the while I was reading it I had a sinking feeling, "Well, you're no longer the most talented writer to come out of World War II. You've been replaced." Extraordinary sensation. I've always felt I understood kings losing their crown ever since. So I gave it a blurb. It was a half-grudging, half-generous blurb, saying that it had marvelous qualities and serious faults, which of course it does, but that it was a terribly important book. Afterwards, I heard the title. I remember writing to Burroughs Mitchell and saying, "Bad title." I thought *From Here to Eternity* was a bad title.

But I didn't meet Jones until maybe a year later, after *Eternity* had come out and had its extraordinary reception. Then one day when I was living down on the lower east side, Vance Bourjaily called up and said, "I'd like to bring Jim Jones over." I said, "Sure." So he came. We met that day.

JML: You became friends pretty quickly?

NM: Yeah. For one thing it was like a joke. I once wrote a one-act play about Eisenhower and Khrushchev called *Buddies* (published in *Advertisements for Myself*, 1959). They were the only equals in all the world so they had to become friends. In a way, Jones and I were the same. We were the only two people who had the same kind of experience, both young, both had written war novels, both had enormous receptions for their books. So in a certain sense we felt like the touchdown twins.

JML: You visited Jones when he was at The Handy Writers Colony in Marshall, Illinois, in 1953. Is that right?

NM: I think it was 1953. I had a blue Studebaker. One of the last ones—marvelous model. I went there with my second wife, Adele, and we stayed there a couple of days and met Lowney Handy (Jones's mentor, who ran The Colony).

JML: What was the situation at The Colony?

NM: Well, you had some very serious writers there and some kids running a scam. They liked the idea of having free meals, a bed, and a roof, and some good athletics. They saw it as an open-air prison, but they could get out. The warden was Lowney Handy and that was pretty easy. There were some who impressed me as being on the edge, kind of scuffling, you know, taking a free ride, and some perfectly serious people. Jones was serious as hell about it, and in a funny way, slightly defensive. I remember he said at one point, "I feel like a goddamn army officer now. Now I know how those army officers feel. If I wrote *Eternity* today, it would be a lot better and a lot different."

JML: What was his relationship to Lowney Handy?

NM: Love-hate. I hate using something so simple but it was the operative definition of it. There was a strong bond between them. They were very much like brother and sister who were fighting all the time, but have incredible family feeling. It never impressed me as a romantic relationship. I found out later to a degree it was. But it didn't seem that way at the time.

JML: Was she as tough and as overbearing as people have described her?

NM: No. Like all legends it was vastly exaggerated. She was terribly opinionated and, like all people from the Midwest, very proud of certain things, but a little uneasy about literary matters—probably because of that old tradition in America that literature started in New England and never went far away from there. So she would protect herself; she would be tentative. She was very gentle with me and handled me with kid gloves. But I found her stimulating and fun. I liked her.

But she was terribly opinionated. I could see if you were under her and she didn't like your work, you could hate her. She had all sorts of interesting ideas, but she was kind of a tyrant about writing. She had these kids copy passages from great books for an hour a day before starting their own writing. A lot of people laughed at that, but I always thought it might be worth trying. If I were giving a writing course I might try it. There are worse ways to demonstrate that writing consists of an awful lot of dreary dull work and paying attention to small details.

JML: I don't think anyone has ever commented on the fact that both Hemingway and Jones were small-town Illinois writers who gained their particular vision by rebelling against overbearing mothers and then going off to war. And that their fathers, both doctors, committed suicide. Obviously, there are some connections there.

NM: Jones thought of Hemingway a great deal. At one point he was talking how Papa had never read his book and he hadn't heard from him, and he was slightly on edge and feisty about it. I think he thought more of Hemingway than anyone else. But I've always assumed that if anyone was ever influenced by Hemingway, it was me. I must confess I've never thought of all those connections. I didn't know, for instance, that Jones's father was a doctor.

JML: He was a dentist.

NM: There's a difference between doctors and dentists. There's also a difference between living in a suburb near Chicago and living in southern Illinois, a huge difference. Southern Illinois is not even Midwest but southern really, northern rim of the South.

JML: Jones was much more interested than you in the implements and the conduct of war, but his ideas about the ideological conduct of war were not really developed like yours. Can you say something about that?

NM: Jones was no intellectual. If he had an Achilles heel, it was that. If you're going to keep living and working as a writer and you've got talents as huge as he had, you simply have to recognize where your shortfall is, and he didn't. So he was always trying to beef up the intellectual side of his writing, which was lamentable because he was not an original thinker. He was a marvelously original novelist and he had wonderful flavor. And he caught the middle of America as maybe no one else did in that whole period. But his thoughts on war were banal.

JML: I assume you're referring to *Some Came Running*.

NM: Well, *From Here to Eternity*, *Some Came Running*, mainly the early Jones, which I know much better than the late.

JML: Jones never really changed his style as a writer. I've just finished reading *Whistle* and it has more polish than *From Here to Eternity* or *Some Came Running*, but his style remained almost the same throughout his books.

NM: I would think so. Unfortunately, I've never read *Go to the Widow-Maker* (1967). I'm still looking forward to it. I have a hunch it's one of his most interesting books. I did start *The Merry Month of May* (1971) and quit it. I was depressed by it. It seemed like the style had burned out. I looked at *Whistle* and it looked pretty good, but my mind was not on that sort of thing at the time so I didn't finish it. But based on the superficial impression that I have of *Whistle*, I think he was going back to his roots, as I believe we all do in one way or another when we feel the end is pretty damn near.

JML: You said that when you visited Jones in 1953 it was in your conversations with him that you first really heard about Karma, or took it seriously. I don't find any references to any kind of mysticism, except on the battlefield, in Jones's writing. Did he hold those beliefs about Karma in a serious way, and did he continue to hold them later in life?

NM: Well, you know we stopped talking to one another for all practical purposes around 1957. So I don't know about his later life. I do know that I had that conversation with him about Karma. And I said, "Surely you don't believe in all that nonsense." And he said, "Of course I do. It's the only thing that makes sense." So I paid attention to it because he was such a tough-minded, practical Midwesterner. When a Midwesterner speaks of something mystical making sense you have to ponder it. I've been pondering Karma the rest of my life. I now have a great belief in Karma. But I'm bewildered by something you said about him being mystical about the battlefield. And I just said his ideas about war were banal. Maybe I missed something.

JML: Well, I'm referring to something you said. You said in one of your comments (in *Cannibals and Christians* [1966]) on *The Thin Red Line* that Jones was able to move back and forth between the mystical nature of combat and practical problems of tactics. You said you admired that quality in him.

NM: Absolutely. I still do. I misunderstood. I wasn't thinking of his sensuous relation to war. I think his ideas about war were relatively ordinary. You know, war is hell. At the same time, war is kind of fun. War is a man's game. No war ever made sense. I think his attitudes about war can be summed up in a series of remarks, some of them half-sententious.

JML: What do you find most valuable in Jones's vision of men at war?

NM: Well, what we were just speaking about: his sense of the sensuousness of combat. I didn't see it again until *Apocalypse Now* (1979). Remember the scene with the helicopters, the attack, and the way these men absolutely enjoyed the combat? Finally, it was more than just theater. It was the Theater of the Gods. It's one of the reasons why so many of us are drawn to war, willy-nilly, and don't know why. It's why there's an absolute opposition to war at all times in all governments. There is something extraordinary about the experience of war. Beyond all the fatigue there's a high in it, and that's why people who are opposed to highs almost always hate the very idea of war. That doesn't mean you go to war because there's a high in it. But you have to recognize this exhilaration before you can deal with war at all.

JML: Can you make anything out of the fact that a great number of Jones's best friends were literary people? Willie Morris, William Styron, James Baldwin, Irwin Shaw, and several others. Jones spent many years in the Army and always wrote from enlisted man's point of view. It's always puzzled me that in his social relations his friends were so consummately literary.

NM: I think it was a symbiotic relation. Writers were enormously drawn to him because he wasn't like other writers. It was like dealing with a redneck who was as gifted as Byron. I'm exaggerating now because Jim was certainly no simple redneck, and he was no Byron. Jones was like so many people whose mentality, finally, was to enjoy driving a car, people who liked the smell of gasoline, people who loved getting drunk and getting in a fight—win or lose the fight, that hardly mattered—but they loved the smell of bar sawdust when your nose is bleeding and stuck behind a cuspidor.

Jones understood all that. We were all agog by it. You know, there's something inextricably effete about the literary world of the East. So writers who lived in the east were drawn to Jones. And he in turn, with that terrible inferiority complex of Midwestern writers, was drawn to Eastern writers. It was symbiotic. But looking back on it, I don't think it did him any good. I say this because I've tended to stay away from writers. The insularity of that world, and the envies that it generates, are consuming. You live your life with blinders, and all you care about is whether so and so's book is selling or not selling. I don't want to get to the point where I live my life hoping that some competitor's book is not doing well.

JML: Someone said in an article on you and Jones that he was a realist and you were a romantic, which is simplistic, of course.

NM: Very. Very. Because you reverse it and it would still be true.

JML: So how would you characterize the fundamental differences between you and Jones?

NM: Jones had his inferiority, I had mine. Mine was ethnic and his was, as I say, coming from the Midwest. But his true inferiority, I think, was that he wasn't a college man, which is always half an asset and half a disaster to a successful novelist who reaches a high level without having gone to college. It means never being quite certain if you're bona fide. It's a little bit like coming from Brooklyn as I did, but very different. Another difference is that he worked from his instincts, while for many years I was working more out of my intelligence and my analytic abilities, such as they were. It was only later that I began to feel that one had to work out of what one felt rather than out of what one could comprehend.

JML: Jones seemed to write best about men at war, and when he wrote about other things, if not in his opinion at least in the opinion of many reviewers and readers, he just wasn't cutting it.

NM: I think he made a terrible mistake leaving America. It was the fundamental error of his life. His roots were here. He wrote about the country. At his best, he wrote about the country better than any of us. He had more claim to be called an indigenous American author than any one of us. And in going to France, I think he dried out his taproot. He got into the literary world in the worse way. He was the literary celebrity of Paris for many years. You didn't account for anything in the literary world if you didn't visit his home when you went there. Jones had great gifts for social life. He was a charming man. You know, he could drink all night and get up in the morning and work. That was part of his doom. If you wake up in the morning and have too large a hangover to work, you recognize that you've got to give up one or the other. He didn't. He was somewhat stronger physically, and in many ways, emotionally, than most people. That was part of what brought him down too early, I think. He had the confidence that he could do it all. And it was false confidence.

JML: Did he always see himself as a Midwesterner, or did he try to distance himself?

NM: He wasn't self-conscious about it. It just came out of him. If you meet someone who's got a strong Southern accent it doesn't matter what they're doing, they're a Southerner. Jim had a southern Illinois accent. It was part of his charm. Here was this man who was so smart and so funny and could say such unexpected things and sounded like a hick. That was terrific. But he didn't know it was terrific.

JML: From everything that I've read and heard about him, he was a generous individual and a gentleman too.

NM: He was a very generous man up to a point, very generous. And warm. You know, if you loved him, you loved him. He did inspire love, I must say.

JML: How would you sum him up as a writer, an American writer?

NM: Well, I'm afraid he falls in the great vein of great American writers—prodigious talent and died too soon.

With the Goddess of the Night:
John Bowers's Memoir

Review of *In the Land of Nyx* (Doubleday, 1984)
by John Bowers

Note: I met Bowers at his Greenwich Village apartment in 1984 when I interviewed him about his friendship with James Jones for a documentary I was making. James Jones: From Reveille to Taps premiered on PBS the following year. We became friends and later colleagues at Wilkes University.

Seal a random sample of people in a windowless building, with all communication cut, and the great majority of them will naturally fall into a 25-hour day. German and French scientists found that after three or four weeks of such isolation about 95 percent of those isolated had lost a full day. Why? No one knows. Nor can it be explained why 5 to 10 percent of humankind prefer to sleep during the day and remain awake during the night.

John Bowers's latest book deals with these nightside questions, especially with people of the night like Larry King, the talk-show host; insomniacs like Jerzy Kosinski, who roams Manhattan gathering material for his bizarre novels; and the late Duke Ellington, who liked to eat cheeseburgers and play his electric piano at 5:00 a.m. Bowers also tracks the nocturnal rounds of those who earn their

(Springfield, IL) *State Journal-Register* (June 25, 1984)

daily bread at night: cabbies, carnies, cops, bartenders, night clerks, cleaning crews and, of course, hookers.

Inspired by memories of his father, a night clerk at a Tennessee railway station, and by James Joyce's Molly Bloom, who free-associates the night away in *Ulysses*, Bowers takes us on a tour of the Land of Nyx (the Greek goddess of night), with a stop in faraway Tromsø, Norway, where the sun disappears for two months at a time, and as nearby as New York City where he accompanies Artie Cappabianca, a policeman, on the graveyard shift. It is a topsy-turvy world populated by eccentrics, loners, and not a few genuine freaks. As Artie says, "From what I've seen, it's as if somebody just turned a rock over and all these strange people come out. You don't see them in daytime. But at night they come out."

Bowers has been writing for more than 30 years; he began in earnest in 1952 at the Handy Writers Colony in Marshall, Illinois, where he lived and worked with James Jones, author of *From Here to Eternity* and *The Thin Red Line*. While there, he met Norman Mailer, then a close friend of Jones's, and later captured their complex friendship in his 1971 memoir, *The Colony*. He also has been a cabbie, night watchman, editor, college professor, State Department bureaucrat, and a dealer at a Nevada gambling casino. Some of the vignettes in the book are based on his job experiences, others on research, His articles have been published in magazines such as *Harper's*, *Saturday Evening Post*, and *Playboy*. Several others derive from pieces he could never quite finish or get published.

But *The Land of Nyx* is by no means a grab-bag of retreads. It is a brilliant meditation on the abnormal and wounded psyches of nighthawks, an exploration of the haunted lunarscape of that "dark night of the soul [where] it is always 3 o'clock in the morning," as F. Scott Fitzgerald put it in *his* book of the night, *The Crack-Up* (1945). The books have a lot in common, but Bowers is free from Fitzgeralds's self-pity, and in places, *Nyx* is as wildly comic as any of Nathanael West's novels.

My hunch is that Bowers had difficulty coming up with a framework on which to hang all his nighttime tales. It is conceivable that he lay awake listening to his refrigerator hum and his children cough while trying to find the right shape for his book. Tossing and turning on the damp sheets and listening to things go bump in the night, he wrestled with the problem until he came up with the solution. Namely, to use his own sleeplessness and troubled ruminations at 3:00 a.m. as the armature for his stories of the con men, jazz musicians, long-distance truck drivers, hustlers, and insomniacs he has known.

It works. All of us, no matter how clean our conscience or how much money we have in the bank, must occasionally count sheep or concentrate on anesthetizing our limbs: "My toes are tired, my toes are asleep, my ankles are sleepy, my ankles are . . . " Bowers begins with a stream-of-consciousness roll of assorted worries, fears, and desires as he lies awake in his Greenwich Village apartment. We learn how much he owes to Mastercard and to the pediatrician, go through his memories of his remarkable parents and an old high-school flame, and are made privy to his desire for literary recognition.

His friend Mario Puzo, author of *The Godfather*, used to be poor, but now pulls "down $2.5 million for a book he hasn't even written yet, for God's sake." He feels no rancor towards his friends, quite the contrary, yet still cannot stop pondering the randomness of literary success: "Bill Smith pulled off *Gorky Park*. Only in Russia three weeks and he pulled off a blockbuster. I remember him working for a hundred a week."

Most of the book's dozen chapters begin with such thoughts, or fantasies about appearing on Johnny Carson's *Tonight Show*, fears of going into heavy debt with ComEd, cold sweats about next month's rent payment, and nostalgic memories of dead friends and family. The passages on his parents are, not surprisingly, the most moving. In what seems to be a single sleepless night, he gives us a lifetime of American dreams.

It is ironic that he uses his own insomnia to hold the book together, since he himself is not much of a raccoon. He has "every characteristic of a night person—a distaste for bosses, a hatred of the unexpected, an obsession with gaining an ultimately nonexistent freedom—every quality except one: I can't stay awake after a while. I fall asleep." No matter. Whether we fall slowly or rapidly into the arms of Morpheus, this splendid moonlight monologue will keep us awake.

Lowney Handy and Her Improbable Writers Colony

Note: I never met Mrs. Handy. But in 1984, in the company of James Jones's son Jamie, and his Colony colleagues John Bowers and Don Sackrider, I visited the grounds of The Handy Colony in Marshall, Illinois, and Jones's hometown, Robinson, about 30 miles south, when working on my documentary, James Jones: From Reveille to Taps. The cliché, a force of nature, fits Handy as snugly as it ever has anyone.

Herman Melville said he needed four things to finish *Moby-Dick*: "time, strength, cash, and patience." Lowney Handy, the president and co-founder (with her husband Harry, and the novelist James Jones) of the Handy Writers Colony in Marshall, Illinois, provided these four necessities to scores of would-be-writers. Because she could not give them the indispensable gift—talent—most of the apprentices she aided, from the late forties to the early sixties, never became even journeymen writers. But the hard, gem-like flame of Lowney's spirit generated the conviction, as she wrote: "Writers are never born, but always made. I believe that I can make a writer out of a mentally ill person (maybe with less waste of energy to myself) than one who is egotistically sure he is God's gift to the writing world." Ambitions like these are bound to be disappointed. Yet Lowney was the midwife to several novels, including Jones's *From Here to Eternity* (1951) and *Some Came Running* (1958), Tom Chamales's *Never So Few* (1957) and

Blue Cross-Blue Shield Life Times of Illinois (September 1989)

Jere Peacock's *Valhalla* (1962). What follows is a sketch of Lowney and the Colony, following Melville's four prerequisites.

TIME: Between five and fifteen writers wrote from 5:30 a.m. until noon every day, seven days a week, no holidays off. No talking was allowed, and Lowney patrolled the compound to make sure the typewriters were clacking. She also insisted that newcomers spend an hour or more of the morning copying the works of the great American realists, word for word, comma for comma. Jones said that he'd copied almost every published word of Hemingway and Fitzgerald. Later, when writers had progressed to Lowney's satisfaction, they were permitted to work full-time on their own manuscripts. In the winter, some Colony members went to Florida or Arizona or California with Lowney and Jones; some went off on their own; a few remained in Marshall, sometimes staying with Lowney's 90-year-old mother-in-law, who was also writing a novel. New writers showed up all the time, usually after corresponding with Lowney. Sometimes she sent them a bus ticket to Marshall, located in the Wabash River Valley of southeastern Illinois. A May 7, 1951, article on the Colony in *Life* by A.B.C. Whipple brought a small flood of new applicants. Once accepted, a writer was almost cut off from the world. No novelistic aspirant (not much poetry was written at the Colony) could give the excuse that a telephone call or a door-to-door salesman had short-circuited a streak of inspiration. Providing long stretches of meditative, grass-growing, productive time was what the Colony did best.

STRENGTH: Meals at the Colony were unmemorable. Instant coffee and raisin toast for breakfast; boiled potatoes, corn on the cob, large curd cottage cheese and a meat dish mixed with pimentos for lunch and dinner. Jell-O for dessert. No milk, butter, eggs, or alcohol (except for Jones, who drank double martinis before lunch every day to unknot his stomach). Lowney was a gourmet cook, but rich food, she believed, was not conducive to creativity. Indeed, she prescribed enemas for writer's block. She chose to invigorate her writers in other ways. John Bowers, author of the marvelously evocative memoir, *The Colony* (1971), said in an interview, "I can count on one hand the pivotal people I've known, people of such awesome personality and will to impress their will that their presence goes into my brain and stays there with a force that's impossible to eradicate. Lowney Handy is one of those people. I will never forget her . . . She changed my life." Like her spiritual mentor, Ralph Waldo Emerson, Lowney gave sustenance to seekers of wisdom and truth. She read daily what every Colony writer wrote and scribbled encouragement in the margins. If negative criticism was called for, she gave that also, especially to manuscripts short on action and dialogue, or that revealed the influence of writers she felt were precious or gay or both: T. S. Eliot, D. H. Lawrence, Marcel Proust, Wallace Stevens, and Franz Kafka. Yet her methods were individualized. "She never handles two guys alike," Jones explained in a 1956 letter. "And yet she infuses them with a confidence and enthusiasm, even when she is riding their ass, in a way that no one else can do. She gives them *belief*. And this belief, which is so hard to come by anywhere else, is why they all come back."

CASH: The largest sums that Lowney doled out to the colonists were for trips to the red-light district of Terre Haute, Indiana, across the Wabash from Marshall. About once a month when the boys got restless, she would give them some cash and off they would go. Ravenous for real food, drink, and sex, the writers quickly exhausted themselves and were back at their typewriters the next morning. Lowney looked on these excursions with disgust, but accepted their necessity. These were the only stipends given out. (Note: Only a few women, including Jones's sister Mary Ann, ever lived at the Colony.) Lowney and her husband Harry supported the Colony generously, however. Harry contributed $400 a month from his salary as superintendent of the Ohio Oil Refinery in nearby Robinson, Illinois. The Colony was built on a five-acre plot that belonged to his family and refinery workers, along with

Lowney's brother, Andy Turner, helped to build the barracks-type buildings where the writers slept and worked. In 1952 Jones gave $65,000 to the Colony from his royalties from *Here to Eternity*, his 1951 blockbuster best-seller, partly to repay the Handys for supporting him after his 1944 discharge from the Army. He supported the Colony generously until he left in 1958. *Eternity* was tangible evidence of what could happen to a Colony writer, and was continually discussed and held up for admiration. There was a loose arrangement calling for Colony writers to give Lowney 10 percent of their royalties, but it was honored more in the breach than the observance. Money was not the golden fleece Lowney held up to her aspiring students. Indeed, she scorned it and told them they would be better off wandering with a yellow begging bowl, like the seers in one of her favorite books, *The Masters of the Far East*, by Baird T. Spalding.

PATIENCE: Two of Lowney's favorite metaphors, according to Bowers, were the story of the Phoenix bird from the Greek myths, and the Biblical story of faith as a mustard seed—Lowney's sources were eclectic; to say the least. In his memoir Bowers records the scene where she tells a faltering writer that all he needs is "the faith of a mustard seed. And you can be a great writer. I don't want any slick, half-ass writers. I only want great ones." And this greatness, paradoxically, would result from the death of the old self. "Kill that ego," she said. "And then rise from your dead ashes like the Phoenix bird. You'll never be a writer until you do. Never, never, never." Jones was proof of all this. From 1944 to 1951 he submitted to her methods, and the result was *Eternity* a masterpiece, which won the National Book Award in 1952. Do the same, she exhorted, copy the works of Hemingway, Faulkner, Raymond Chandler and John Dos Passos, eat bland food, purge yourself of tired old ideas (the enemas were metaphorical as well as actual purgation), avoid women, break from your family and you too will become a great American novelist. Then you can park *your* silver Airstream trailer next to Jones's and drink martinis while the next crop of writers eats their large curd cottage cheese and Jell-O. Such was the force of Lowney's personality, and the power of Jones's example, that a number of writers came back year after year, waiting for the oak of literary greatness to spring up from the seeds of faith dispensed by Lowney.

EPILOGUE: She was an improbable woman, and her copying method was peculiar. Yet Norman Mailer, who visited Jones at the Colony in 1953, said: "There are worse ways to demonstrate that writing consists of an awful lot of dreary dull work and paying attention to small details." Her love affair with Jones seemed unlikely, he being 17 years younger, but it went on for over a decade. She wore her hair in braids and, long before the Women's Liberation came along, eschewed bras; she believed in yoga, meditation, and Emersonian self-reliance. Yet, according to Bowers, she was fiercely maternalistic and controlled life at the Colony like a warden. She disliked intellectuals, rarely found merit in the writing of women, but fourteen published novels and as many short stories came out of the Colony. Her family found her to be exceptional and adored her, but understood why Jones left her in 1958. Her life changed when her star pupil flew away to live in Paris with his bride, Gloria Mosolino, whom he'd met in New York. Jones did bring Gloria back to the Colony for a brief time after marrying her in Haiti, but Lowney could not accept another woman's presence. The Colony came to an end a few years later, and Lowney died in June 1964. It was a quixotic venture from the start, the product of an unlikely alliance between a disgruntled, hugely talented, and tender-hearted writer, James Jones, and an iconoclastic muse of middle America, Lowney Turner Handy.

To Fame from Obscurity:
The Letters of James Jones

A review of *To Reach Eternity: The Letters of James Jones*
(Random House, 1989), edited by George Hendrick

Note: In 1984, when doing research for Reveille to Taps *in
Robinson, Illinois, I met Lowney Handy's sister-in-law, Margaret
Turner, and she generously gave me a tranche of letters, manuscripts,
and photographs that Jones had left in her care before he moved to
Paris in 1958. These materials, which ended up in the archives of
the University of Illinois-Springfield, were drawn upon extensively
for the documentary, and later became a source for Hendrick's
expertly edited edition of Jones's letters, published in 1989.*

From the mid-'40s through the early '60s the word
"experience" had a talismanic quality for American readers.
Dust jackets of many novels, and later the back covers of
paperbacks, bragged about the author's experiences as a short-order
cook, reporter, fisherman, hobo, encyclopedia salesman, migrant
farmworker, and/or veteran of World War II. A college education
wasn't a drawback, but a working knowledge of Stephen Crane, Jack
London, Steinbeck, Hemingway, Dos Passos and—the key figure—
Thomas Wolfe—was much more important. Coming from Boston
or Philadelphia was suspect; Brooklyn or Chicago or Middletown,
U.S.A., was much better.

Chicago Tribune Books (May 14, 1989)

The idea was to rebel against mean-spirited Puritanism, do a hitch in the service and then bum around the country, working here and there, loafing and observing your soul, reading tattered copies of the Viking portable readers, and writing lyrical but realistic prose about the view from boxcars as you rumbled through the great, mysterious American night. Then would come discovery, publication, enormous fame (including critical praise), money, love, Hollywood and a long happily-ever-after. Did anyone ever have such an experience? No, not in such a storybook way, although many tried. But James Jones came closer than anyone. He certainly began obscurely enough.

George Hendrick's edition of Jones's letters begins in 1939, shortly after he graduated from high school in Robinson, Illinois, and enlisted in the Army Air Corps at nearby Chanute Field. The early letters look back on a very unhappy childhood. Like Hemingway, another small-town Illinois boy, Jones had a miserable relationship with his overbearing mother and idolized his father, also a doctor who committed suicide with a revolver after years of depression.

As a boy and in the Army, Jones was a loner. "I've always felt a hunger and unrest that nothing could satisfy," he wrote to his brother Jeff. Reading helped. Jones discovered Wolfe's novels in the post library in Schofield Barracks in Hawaii, where he was stationed, and his simmering literary ambition began to boil. He wrote Jeff that Wolfe was "the greatest writer that has lived, Shakespeare included," and found him to be "an almost exact parallel with myself."

Jones hated the service at first, but as Irwin Shaw, one of Jones's closest friends, once put it, Jones's escape into the Army was "very lucky." He found in the Army's structures, Shaw said, "a sense of authority he admired, a sense of power . . . comradeship with men . . . and the idea of violence close to the surface, which played a big part in all of his books."

Then came Pearl Harbor. Jones was eating breakfast when the attack came, and he rushed outside to see a Japanese fighter "skidding, whammering overhead with his MGs going" and the pilot wearing "a white ribbon around his helmet just above the goggles . . . a *hachimaki*, the headband worn by medieval samurai when going into battle."

Of all the major novelists of World War II–Irwin Shaw, John Horne Burns, Mailer, Joseph Heller, William Styron, Kurt Vonnegut, John Hersey–Jones was the only one on active duty when the war began. He was wounded in the savage fighting at Guadalcanal, and by late 1943 was in a military hospital in Memphis. After going AWOL a few times and spending time in the hospital brig (another crucial experience), Jones was honorably discharged in July 1944. Instrumental in his release was Lowney Handy, an iconoclastic lover of literature from Jones's hometown, and a mother figure to all the outcasts and would-be writers who came her way. With the encouragement of Jones and her husband's support, she founded the Handy Writers Colony. Jones had a rich ballast of experience; he was bursting with talent, anger, and the desire to write. Lowney prescribed Emerson, enemas, and hard work and helped Jones harness his energies.

Although 17 years his senior and married to Harry Handy, superintendent of the local oil refinery, she immediately became Jones's lover. He moved in with the Handys, and they supported him during the six years he spent writing *From Here to Eternity*. The fervor of his letters to her ("we have loved through more than one eternity . . . love overpowering, all embracing, unbeatable") is matched by the intensity of those he wrote to Maxwell Perkins, the legendary Scribner's editor of Hemingway, Fitzgerald, and Wolfe.

Perkins had rejected Jones's first (still unpublished) novel, "They Shall Inherit the Laughter," and was considering a revision of it in early 1946 when Jones wrote to him suggesting several other projects, including "a novel on the peacetime army." The novel would be based on the experiences of army friends, Wedson and Stewart, later known to millions of readers as Sgt. Milton Anthony

Warden and Pvt. Robert E. Lee Prewitt. Jones described Prewitt as a "small man standing on the edge of the ocean shaking his fist"; Warden was "almost a criminal, almost an artist, but not either." Perkins sent him a $500 advance, and Jones started writing what would become *From Here to Eternity.*

Jones was so buoyed by Perkins's support and by the progress he was making on *Eternity* that he wrote his mentor several months later to say it was "a very hard thing to realize that I am in the process of becoming one of the Olympians." Jones was Perkins's last American enthusiasm; he died in 1947 and was succeeded by Burroughs Mitchell, Jones's editor until the mid-'60s. With the support of the Handys and Mitchell, Jones finished *Eternity.* It became a blockbuster success on the order of *Gone with the Wind,* both as a book (1951) and movie (1953). Because he was discovering what he thought as he went along, every line was precious to Jones. Again and again his editors advised compression, but Jones subscribed to a sort of literary manifest destiny and argued against cuts. Yet he did recognize "this tendency I have to try and tell or show everything, to get down exactly every nuance and subtlety so that is easily understood . . . if you keep on you involute yourself right down to nothing."

Jones had his experiences of war, shellshock, bumming around, and finding himself out of step with a society shifting into commercial overdrive. Returning home to Robinson, he wanted more than anything to bear witness. He told one correspondent that "what I have is a very coldblooded merciless dissection and positive knowledge about it (civilization)." To another he predicted his writing would be "a barbed spear up the ass of the world." In letters to his editors, literary critics, and peers (Mailer especially), Jones talked regularly about self-deception, layers of artifice, the difficulties of getting deeper into things. He burned with a desire to get it right, and wrote with the classic novelist's confidence that the world can be understood and explained. If he had not been so apolitical, we could call him the American Zola.

But Jones was not entirely truculent. Even before he broke away from the Handys and the Colony they operated in Marshall, Illinois, Jones had a notable capacity for friendship and enjoyment. Gloria Mosolino, his wife from 1957 to his death in 1977, enriched this capacity, and Jones began to relish his success after the spartan life of The Colony and the tension of life with Lowney. Their marriage was remarkably warm and loving. With their two children, Kaylie and Jamie, Gloria and Jim lived in Paris for 14 years, returning in 1974 when Jones's congestive heart disease began to worsen.

The letters in the last third of the collection reveal a happy family man in full possession of his powers. Rich in friends, he enjoyed entertaining (according to William Styron, in his evocative foreword) "writers and painters and movie stars, starving Algerian poets, drug addicts, Ivy League scholars, junketing United States senators, thieves, jockeys, restaurateurs, big names from the American media...tycoons and paupers."

As is usual with a collection of letters, readers will be curious about the letters of some of Jones's correspondents (some of Perkins's and Mitchell's letters are available elsewhere). An edition of the triangular correspondence of Jones, Mailer, and Styron, certainly three of the best writers of their generation, would be especially fascinating to read.*

Jones's shifting relationship with Mailer is particularly difficult to understand without Mailer's letters. In the early and mid-50s they were close, and Jones said in 1955 that "someday" Mailer will "explode on the world like a nova, with a classic." Their relations later became troubled, although they never lost respect for each other's work. In his introduction and a number of interchapters, Hendrick has provided about as much explanatory material as he could without seriously interrupting Jones's unfolding life as revealed in the letters. He has stayed out of the way, in other words, while doing a skillful job of selecting and editing the letters that reveal the shape of this classic American literary life.

Random House published Styron's letters in 2012, edited by Rose Styron and R. Blakeslee Gilpin, and Mailer's in 2014, edited by J. Michael Lennon.

James Jones's World War II Trilogy

One of the most brilliant intuitions in the long, brilliant editorial career of Maxwell Perkins, the legendary Scribner's editor of Hemingway, Wolfe, and Fitzgerald, was to offer James Jones a $500 advance for an unwritten novel on the pre-war U.S. Army, the pineapple army, set in Hawaii. By this time, February 1945, Jones had already pressed two versions of his first (still unpublished in full) first novel, *They Shall Inherit the Laughter*, on Perkins, who had no intention of publishing it.

It is easy to see why the novel was rejected—and why Perkins was attracted to Jones. "Laughter" is rambling and episodic in structure, self-indulgent and excessively bitter in tone, and patently derivative of Thomas Wolfe, John Dos Passos, John Steinbeck, and even Emerson and the other American Transcendentalists. Toward the end, Jones even borrows Tom Joad's "I'll be there" speech from *The Grapes of Wrath* (1939) and applies it to the returning American soldier. Still, it contains some fine writing and is fascinating as a preview of Jones's later career. It incorporates, moreover, early versions of some of the most memorable scenes from Jones's later work—for example, Lander's speech about "the soldier's responsibilities" to his Indiana hometown Elks Club in *Whistle* (1978); "Mad" Welsh's desperate attempt to help the painfully wounded Tella in *The Thin Red Line* (1962); and several of the major episodes in *Some Came Running* (1958). In fact, "Laughter" is, to a large degree, an early, less successful version of *Some Came Running*. The hero, Johnny Carter, is a prototype for Richard Mast in *The Pistol*

James Jones Journal 17 (Spring 2009)

(1959), Dave Hirsch in *Some Came Running*, Geoffrey Fife in *The Thin Red Line*, and Marion Landers in *Whistle*.

What attracted Perkins to Jones was that he was clearly a writer in the Dreiserian tradition, one who could write novels of saturation about virgin tracts of reality of interest to the large and growing novel readership in the U.S. Jones was not someone who would write small, precious novels of the kind Truman Capote, Jane Bowles, and Carson McCullers were turning out during this time. Jones was an American Balzac but instead of delineating all the levels of French society, Jones wanted to reproduce in prose the pre-war American army. It was only one of the novels that Jones mentioned when replying to Perkins' second, gentle rejection of the "Laughter" manuscript. In the course of outlining the future novelistic work of a lifetime, he described "a real combat novel telling the complete truth" and another, a novel "on the peacetime army, something I don't remember having seen."

This second idea rang a big bell for Perkins. Jones had never seen a novel on the peacetime army, because they didn't exist, not in any realistic form, and Perkins knew it. He also knew: 1) that the "old army" was long gone, swept away by mass enlistments, the draft, and technology; 2) that 20 million GIs had nonetheless heard about the "old army" via the relentless comparisons of their drill sergeants (not a small audience, especially if you add spouses, children, parents, and everyone else touched by World War II); and 3) that Jones was unique in the literary world: intelligent, sensitive, tough, and well-suited to heavy narrative labor and, most importantly; 4) he'd been on active army duty for over two years when the Japanese attacked Pearl Harbor. Jones had actually watched the Japanese strafe Schofield Barracks while he was on guard duty on December 7, 1941. Perkins had a trifecta: the writer, the story, and the demand. He died in June 1947 before his hunch paid off in full, but he did read the first 200 pages of *From Here to Eternity* (1951) and knew it was a winner.

To repeat, *From Here to Eternity* is not a combat novel; it is an army novel, arguably the finest ever written by an American. It is, in fact, dedicated to the U.S. Army, and follows three major characters, Pvt. Prewitt, Mess/Sgt. Stark, and First/Sgt. Warden through the miseries of the caste-ridden, authoritarian peacetime army up to the symbolic moment it undergoes transmogrification, becoming with the Japanese attack a completely different creature. "Authenticity" is the word used over and over in essays and reviews on the novel, a tribute to Jones's massive documentation of the gear, tackle, drills, bugle calls, boredom, KP, masochism, and male camaraderie—in short, all facets of barracks, bivouac, and stockade life in the "old" army. Although it is 860 pages in length, it never flags. Its narrative drive is tremendous. Jones wrote it in the belief that even something as many-faceted as the U.S. army can be detailed and comprehended. Prewitt, who he described to Perkins as "a small man standing on the edge of the ocean shaking his fist," is the novel's tragic hero/scapegoat, and one of the most memorable protagonists in modern American literature.

Exactly when the idea for a trilogy dealing with the before, during, and after of World War II came to Jones is uncertain. His first idea for *Eternity* was to extend it through the New Georgia campaign to the return of the wounded to the U.S. in 1944, and then to the war's aftermath in the late 1940s. But this was impractical for one volume and after *Eternity* was published in 1951 to huge popular and critical acclaim, he turned back to the "Laughter" manuscript and transformed it into *Some Came Running*. It is his longest novel and, he claimed more than once, his best, a judgment that seems less and less personally partisan as time goes by. Set in a Midwestern town similar to Jones's hometown of Robinson, Illinois, it deals with the problems—financial, sexual, spiritual—of returning GIs and (as one critic said), "a continent of towns melting into shopping centers, a world of superhighways and jet flights, where men risk becoming slobs." Not often remembered is that the 1247-page novel begins with a moving depiction of the Battle of the Bulge, and it ends with a tableau of freezing combat in Korea. Jones's prologue and epilogue were clues to his novelistic future.

Jones left the Midwest after completing *Running*, and he went back to the big war, writing first, a novella, *The Pistol*, set in wartime Hawaii. Jones's friend Irwin Shaw claimed that *The Pistol* should be the fourth novel in a quartet, but Jones did not agree. But given its wily insights into the nature of the "new" army, it is fair to call *The Pistol* a pendant to the trilogy. None of the characters in *The Pistol* are carried over from *Eternity*, but there are a few who are congruent with the earlier characters, especially First/Sgt. Wycoff, "a big man in his thirties" who might easily be confused with First/ Sgt. Warden. Jones moved to Paris after he completed *The Pistol* and it was there that he began work on a combat novel set in the Pacific, one he ultimately titled *The Thin Red Line*.

But he now had a problem, one that he finessed in *The Pistol*. He explains it in a preface to the third novel in the trilogy, *Whistle*:

> One of the problems I came up against, with the trilogy as a whole, appeared as soon as I began *The Thin Red Line* in 1959. In the original conception, first as a single novel, and then as a trilogy, the major characters such as 1st/Sgt Warden, Pvt. Prewitt and Mess/Sgt Stark were meant to continue throughout the entire work. Unfortunately, the dramatic structure—I might even say, the spiritual content— of the first book demanded that Prewitt be killed in the end of it... It may seem like a silly problem now. It wasn't then... I could not just resurrect him. And have him there again, in the flesh, wearing the same name... I solved the problem by changing the names... So, in The Thin Red Line, 1st/ Sgt Warden became 1st/Sgt Welsh, Pvt. Prewitt became Pvt. Witt, Mess/Sgt Stark became Mess/Sgt Storm. While

147 r Mailer's Last Days

remaining the same people as before. In *Whistle*, Welsh becomes Mart Winch, Witt becomes Bobby Prell, Storm becomes John Strange.

In the preface Jones also points out that unlike the three novels of John Dos Passos's trilogy, *U.S.A* (1930-36), each of the three novels stand alone as fully realized works. Jones, in effect, had it both ways: he devised a scheme that permitted him to use the same characters, and continue the same master theme, but also permitted him to write three separate narratives, each of which has its own plot, structure, and mood. The careful and systematic depiction of the corrupt and brutal "old" army in *Eternity* is followed by the stark presentation of random and impersonal death in modern technological warfare in *The Thin Red Line*. In this second novel of the trilogy, Jones follows C-for-Charlie Company through an amphibious landing on an anonymous Pacific island that ends, after savage combat, with its capture by U.S. troops. Jones explores three recurring themes in the course of what may be the finest combat novel ever written by an American: the absurdity of anonymous death in combat, the ineffectuality and corruption of the officer class, and the brutalizing effects of warfare on the most decent of men. Of special interest is the episode in chapter three describing Bead's killing of a Japanese soldier in hand-to-hand combat, a scene based closely on an incident in Jones's own experience on Guadalcanal, one that haunted him for the rest of his life.

The unifying idea of the trilogy, the master theme, is "the evolution of the soldier." Jones first fully articulated this theme in his 1975 nonfiction work, *WWII*, which contains Jones's narrative, and a moving collection of World War II graphic art, all by combat artists, and selected by the former art director of *Yank* magazine, Art Weithas. In simplest terms, the evolution consists of green soldiers becoming trained, hardened by combat, and then turned into fearless automatons who know that they will die. A soldier's acceptance of the fact that he is lost, Jones says, changes everything: "Little things become significant. The next meal, the next bottle of booze, the next kiss, the next sunrise, the next full moon. The next bath…It has its excitements and compensations. One of them is that, since you have none yourself, you are relieved of any responsibility for a future. And everything tastes better." If a soldier survives, he must undergo the de-evolution of a soldier; in an ordeal just as painful as the numbing of combat, he begins to feel, begins to hope, and begins to remember even as he tries to forget.

This de-evolution is manifested most powerfully in the final novel of the trilogy, Whistle, which was published posthumously in 1978. Whistle develops Jones's vision of the embittered American soldier returning home from combat overseas only to develop a new kind of alienation in a suddenly affluent and overwhelmingly "new America." The home front had no place for the camaraderie that the returning wounded American soldiers had come to depend on for physical survival. The frenetic mood of the city of Memphis, renamed Luxor, the Peabody Hotel and the army hospital are depicted with ease of deeply imprinted memory—Jones knew these places well. Here the remnants of the old rifle company wait for news of the death or wounding of their comrades while drinking and fighting as much and as often as they can, fighting and drinking to forget and not to forget. The fight with the navy chiefs in the hotel bar is especially evocative of the fierce abandon of these late war years.

A disembodied narrator who speaks for all the members of the old company tells Whistle's first chapter in the first-person plural. Jones's instinct is unerring and the brilliantly evoked "we" perspective proves to be the perfect point of view for capturing the final decline and fall of Prell, Winch, and Strange. In one sense, they are still Prewitt, Warden, and Storm, but markedly different having evolved and de-evolved during the course of over 2600 pages and three novels written over 33 years. It ends with the suicide of

Sgt. Strange who, unable to face more combat, slips over the rail of his troop transport en route to the fighting in western France. Strange's suicide was virtually the last thing Jones dictated on his tape recorder in the hospital before he died in May 1977.

> And then as he's treading water with his woolen GI gloves, he can feel the cold beginning to swell his hands. And from this, in a sort of semi-hallucination, all of him begins to seem to swell and he gets bigger and bigger, until he can see the ship moving away or thinks he can. And then he goes on getting bigger and bigger and swelling and swelling until he's bigger than the ocean, bigger than the planet, bigger than the solar system, bigger than the galaxy out in the universe.

> And as he swells and grows this picture of the fully clothed soldier with his helmet, his boots, and his GI woolen gloves seems to be taking into himself all the pain and anguish and sorrow and misery that is the lot of all soldiers, taking it into himself and into the universe as well.

> And then still in the hallucination he begins to shrink back to normal, and shrinks down through the other stages—the galaxy, the solar system, the planet, the ocean—back to Strange in the water. And then continues shrinking until he seems to be only the size of a seahorse, and then an amoeba, then finally an atom.

> He did not know whether he would drown first or freeze.

At the February 1978 memorial celebration in Manhattan for Jones, Mailer was asked for some words on his friend. He replied, "He was one of the few American writers from whom I learned something: Distance."

Gore Vidal, American Iconoclast

A review of *Empire of Self: A Life of Gore Vidal*
(Doubleday, 2015), by Jay Parini

Gore Vidal often said that his blind grandfather, Senator Thomas Pryor Gore, Democrat from Oklahoma, was the single most influential person in his life. A populist-conservative of the same ilk as Senator Huey Long of Louisiana, Senator Gore was at his best going against the tide. Vidal was raised by his grandparents—his parents were divorced—and in the 1930s became his grandfather's eyes in the Senate, running freely around the floor of the Senate when little thought was given to security. "The blind cowboy," as the press referred to Senator Gore, tutored his precocious grandson in American and Roman history, encouraging him to read Cicero and Suetonius, Gibbon's *Decline and Fall*, and Henry Adams's nine-volume history of the U.S., all of which Vidal later drew on for his historical novels. In 1933, at the age of seven, he watched FDR's inaugural parade with his grandfather, who despised the architect of the New Deal. A strict constitutionalist and pacifist, Senator Gore opposed U.S. entry into both world wars, and most of FDR's programs for the poor and unemployed. He equated the early, virtuous Roman republic with the U.S. in its heroic early years, and deplored the moral laxness of the later empire. Gore Vidal's pessimism, politics, and grasp of history, Jay Parini states in his new biography, *Empire of Self*, "dovetailed in ways that gave pride to Senator Gore."

Times Literary Supplement (October 16, 2015)

Although Vidal wrote in nearly every genre, including poetry, his deepest artistic identity was novelist; he wrote twenty-nine in all, including several murder mysteries under the pseudonym Edgar Box. His screenplays (*Ben-Hur* was a favorite) and plays (*The Best Man*, a 1960 political melodrama) were written during the early 1950s, a period in which, Vidal claimed, he could not get his novels published after being blackballed by the *New York Times* and other publications for having written *The City and the Pillar* (1948), one of the first forthright novels of gay life in the U.S. Parini, suspecting that Vidal was exaggerating, determined that the daily *Times* did ignore Vidal for several years, but not the Sunday *New York Times Book Review*, which consistently reviewed his work. Vidal's several volumes of essays are more important than his dramatic and cinematic efforts, but only the literary essays hold up. When he relishes the virtues of his favorite writers—George Meredith, Oscar Wilde, Henry James, Somerset Maugham, Ford Madox Ford, Dawn Powell, and William Dean Howells— he is vibrant and insightful, and when he is tackling writers he disliked—Henry Miller, John Dos Passos, John O'Hara, and the nouveau roman novelists of the 1950s and 60s—his mandarin tone and mordant barbs are satisfying. He didn't write much about his American contemporaries, many of whom he feuded with, and most of whom he ignored. Vidal preferred being grouped with the meritorious dead than with competitive contemporaries, especially Truman Capote. Most of his later efforts are nasty, shrill, exaggerated screeds. Parini offers a balanced view. "The Political essays," he says,

> seem more improvisational than his solid and acutely sensitive readings of Henry James, William Dean Howells, Dawn Powell, and Paul Bowles: each of them, exemplary, full of sustained reflections that display Gore's wide knowledge of American and European Literature. It was, at times, difficult to take some of his campy and often

malicious essays on politics as seriously as his criticism, but he certainly had a kind of shrill perceptiveness about American politics and many of these ideas needed expression. If, like Noam Chomsky (with whom he was often compared), Gore stood outside the normal range of American discourse, the problem was more with the culture than with Gore and Chomsky.

The most important of his political essays is "Homage to Daniel Shays," a re-examination of one of the earliest American revolts against federal power. Published in 1972, it is a stalking horse for his novel about Aaron Burr, which came out in 1973. *Burr* is the leadoff volume of Vidal's masterwork, seven novels about the defining moments of the American past he called *Narratives of Empire*.

The metamorphosis of the United States from fledgling republic to unprecedented empire is the master theme of his hepatology. Vidal dates the beginning of America's aspiration for power as far back as Jefferson's 1803 Louisiana Purchase (which he claims, unconvincingly, was illegal), and traces its surges and setbacks over 200 years. The novels in the series, like its precursor, James Fenimore Cooper's *Leatherstocking Tales*, were not written in chronological order. Vidal began at the end with *Washington D.C.* (1967), which opens with FDR's failure in 1937 to increase the size of the Supreme Court, and closes in the early 1950s with the Cold War.

The six novels that follow, by order of events depicted, are: *Burr* (1973), *Lincoln* (1984), *1876* (1976), *Empire* (1987), *Hollywood* (1990), and *The Golden Age* (2000). *Burr* displays a premonitory concern about American expansionism—at one point Vidal was going to call the series "Manifest Destiny"—but as he proceeded, he became more and more vituperative. Cooper believed that wresting the continent from Native Americans to be necessary and ineluctable; Vidal makes the case in the novels that American imperialism, especially the savage and racist Philippine-American War of 1899-1902 (presented in *Empire*), was and continues to be conscious policy and a defamation of the principles upon which the republic was founded. To accomplish this, he had to pass over or ignore entirely realities such as mass immigration to the U.S., the conquest of Europe and Asia by the Axis Powers, the liquidation of millions of Jews and other groups, and the not-ignoble motivation of the U.S. to come to the aid of its Allies in two wars, as well as rebuilding Europe and assuaging the suffering of millions of refugees. Despite these and other omissions, America's steady progress to superpower status has never been presented fictionally in such an extended, commanding, and lively fashion.

In this brisk, fluent, and compact biography, Parini has high praise for these novels, especially *Lincoln*, which he says is "the keystone in the arch of Gore's novels about the American past." "The Ancient," as Lincoln's secretaries referred to him, is seen only through his formal utterances, homespun witticisms and the awed or angry impressions of the novel's other characters. as Parini puts it, "Lincoln is a mountain that could only be glimpsed from different sides." The result is a portrait of a partially shrouded figure of iron resolve whose deepest motives are opaque, perhaps even to him. When he does act, it is with acumen and decisive energy, an "American Bismarck coming on like Will Rogers," Vidal said. He believed it would have been wiser to allow the Southern states to secede, a view adopted from his Southern grandparents. The Civil War, or the War Between the States as they called it, was, Vidal believed, a tragic event, "our Trojan War." Lincoln's wily and tenacious efforts to preserve the union were successful, but the centralization of power he initiated undercut republican principles; this is the novel's unstated argument. Implicit in Vidal's masterful reimagining of this critical period in American history is his supposition that Lincoln's assassination destroyed the possibilities of postwar reconciliation and stoked the nation's imperial drive. Parini devotes more pages to *Lincoln* than any of Vidal's other books, and labels it Vidal's "most durable legacy."

Unlike Lincoln's, the mind of the eponymous hero of *Burr* is open for inspection via his fictionalized memoirs and interviews. Vidal claimed to be distantly related to Burr, a New Yorker who was Thomas Jefferson's first vice president and almost won the presidency in 1800. The similarities between Burr and Vidal stand out: both are sardonic revisionists eager to rewrite accepted history. The novel opens with the elderly Burr's unsentimental memories of the Revolutionary War and the founding fathers. For a time, Burr was the most hated man in the country, having killed weak-eyed Alexander Hamilton in a duel, after which he was nearly convicted of treason for attempting to create an empire in Mexico. Like Vidal, Burr has a Dickensian eye for defining details and vanities: Washington's huge hams and famous false teeth (made of hippopotamus ivory); Jefferson's freckles and slave lover, Sally Hemings; Hamilton's short stature and contentious nature.

Burr is a marvelous character, sometimes principled, often opportunistic, a likable swine, but no more ardent for fame and wealth, Vidal contends, than his erstwhile colleagues. In *Burr*, for the first time, Vidal freely mixed fictional and historical characters, anticipating by a few years a similar blending in E. L. Doctorow's *Ragtime*. This technique permitted imaginative invention, while anchoring the key events in history. Having mastered it, he used it in all the novels of the series. Vidal serves up savory descriptions of the rowdy daily life in New York City in the 1830s, and the political battles of the young republic during the boisterous presidency of Andrew Jackson. The novel's narrator, a young journalist, Charles Schermerhorn Schuyler, is revealed at the end to be Burr's son. This is an acceptable twist, but also making Burr the father of President Martin Van Buren is both unsettling and unnecessary. The same is true of the venereal disease with which Vidal falsely afflicts Lincoln.

The only other one of Vidal's novels that belongs on the top shelf is *Julian* (1964), an intriguing depiction of the philosopher-emperor of the fourth century who attempted to reverse the official status awarded to Christianity by his grandfather, Constantine the Great, and restore the pagan gods. Like *Burr* (but not *Lincoln*), *Julian* is a partial self-portrait, and in its deft employment of multiple narrators and perspectives the progenitor of both later novels. Vidal presents the Roman Empire just before its permanent acceptance of Christianity, a woeful transformation in his eyes. The multi-deity pagan world was infinitely preferable to the prescriptive Christianity of St. Paul. Vidal told Parini that *Julian* "was an attack on the church, not on the teachings of Jesus. They're rarely followed, of course. Turning the cheek has never been a popular notion."

Parini met Vidal in Italy in the mid-1980s. He was an admirer of some of Vidal's novels and in agreement with his political protests against the Vietnam War, and the pair hit it off. Parini got along well with Vidal's social circle and, most importantly, his longtime partner, Howard Austen. Vidal referred to Parini as his Boswell and his literary executor, but when Vidal asked him to write his authorized biography, Parini wisely demurred. He recognized that if he took on the task while his prickly subject was still in action, he would be on the receiving end of a barrage of objections about inclusion, emphasis, and interpretation. This is exactly what happened to Fred Kaplan, who got the job on Parini's recommendation, and who published his exemplary *Gore Vidal* in 1999. Vidal directed a series of minatory (one of Vidal's favorite words) legal arrows at Kaplan in an effort to influence the final manuscript and, failing, made a public and preposterous assertion that he had always assumed that it was another distinguished Kaplan—Justin, author of biographies of Whitman and Twain—who Parini had recommended. Vidal was adept at torturing the truth. Parini later stated that he would not write a second biography while Vidal was alive. Vidal agreed to this, but enjoined, "Do notice the potholes. But for God's sake, keep your eyes on the main road!"

The ideal biographical journey, as Vidal saw it, would skirt his social snobbery and namedropping; minimize his alcoholism; rationalize his sexual tourism in Bangkok and cruising for "trade" in Rome; explain away his mean spiritedness towards his mother and other family members; give a wide berth to his ostracizing by the Kennedys—the itinerary is now obvious—while taking a leisurely celebratory ramble through his incontestable literary achievements, accolades, awards, and bestsellers, extolling his Rochefoucauldian wit, Tory-populist grit, and pre-eminence as a sharp-tongued pundit. His Boswell would complete this long, engrossing biography by confidently predicting the maestro's impending arrival at what Mailer called "the golden isles of posthumous investiture." Parini does follow the main road, but he construes Vidal's failings more than his friend would have wished, especially his preference for furtive sex.

Parini relies heavily on Kaplan's massive, thoughtful, and painstaking biography, calling it "immensely helpful" in his acknowledgments. Because Kaplan's study ends in the late 1990s, Parini is the first to cover Vidal's final years—he died in 2012—adding comments culled from Vidal's table talk over thirty years. He also includes a dozen brief inter-chapters of the kind Hemingway used in A Moveable Feast, which provide useful pacing and capture Vidal in emblematic moments speaking candidly with various luminaries—Capote, Rudolph Nureyev, Susan Sontag, Isaiah Berlin, Leonard Bernstein, and Alberto Moravia, among others. Generally, Parini agrees with Vidal's own views on his books, although he has less enthusiasm for his sci-fi and fantasy novels, including the sexual Punch-and-Judy show Myra Breckinridge (1968) and the disastrous Duluth (1983), both prized by Vidal. It could be argued that Vidal is his own supreme fiction, as Harold Bloom remarked of Mailer, Vidal's friend-enemy-friend and an equally accomplished outsider-insider and public intellectual. In sum, Vidal's three finest novels, his achievements as a cultural critic, and his stature as an unforgettable American iconoclast argue for at least a provisional place in Parnassus.

Gore and Norman in Provincetown

In the fall of 2002 Donna and I were living in Provincetown and Gore Vidal was coming to town. I was editing a collection of Mailer's letters and Vidal was a major presence in them. We'd heard a lot of talk at the Mailer dinner table about both the iniquities of Gore, and his acts of generosity, and were eager to meet him. Norris Mailer seemed to have a soft spot for Gore. Norman's relationship with him, which went back to 1952, was potholed. Within minutes of their first meeting, Vidal asked Mailer at what ages his grandparents had died. Mailer told him, and Vidal then proclaimed that he would outlive him, based on the longevity of his own grandparents. Neither of them ever forgot this conversation.

When Mailer was released from the violent ward of Bellevue Psychiatric Hospital in New York City in January 1961 after seriously wounding his second wife, Adele Morales, with a penknife, Vidal was one of the first to contact Mailer. At his invitation, Mailer and Adele, now recovered, spent a weekend at Edgewater, Vidal's historic mansion overlooking the Hudson River about 100 miles north of the city. Mailer, then on parole, was shunned by most of his circle, and was moved by Vidal's generosity. They saw a good deal of each other in the 1960s and remained friends, although they occasionally sniped at each other in interviews and on talk shows—both were major presences on the talk show circuit.

Then things changed. In a *New York Review of Books* piece (July 22, 1971, "In Another Country"), Vidal lumped Mailer and Henry

Mailer Review (2012)

Miller and Charles Manson together as "the 3M Man." Mailer was furious, and six months later butted Vidal's head in the green room before their appearance on the *Dick Cavett Show*. Vidal, however, was the clear winner when they traded insults an hour later on the program. Mailer remained hurt and angry and in 1977, he bounced a booze-filled glass off Vidal's noggin at a New York cocktail party for visiting British publisher, George Weidenfeld, as Jackie Kennedy, Pete Hamill, Barbara Walters, Katharine Graham, Susan Sontag, Gov. Jerry Brown, and 50 others watched. Vidal said later, "Again, words fail Norman Mailer."

They had no further contact until 1985 when Mailer asked for Vidal's help in raising money to underwrite a meeting in New York of PEN, the international writers' organization. Vidal graciously accepted, and shared the stage with Mailer. A few years later when Vidal reprinted the offending essay, he removed the reference to the "3M Man." They were on good, still slightly edgy, terms from that point on.

The 2002 meeting came after Mailer invited Vidal to take part in another benefit, this one for the Provincetown Repertory Theater. At the time, Norris was the theater's artistic director. Gore knew the town, having escorted Jackie Kennedy (with whom he shared a stepfather) there in 1963 so that she could observe the town that Mailer had described to her as "the wild west of the east." Vidal immediately accepted Norman's invitation and flew in from Ravello, Italy, where he shared a seaside villa with his partner of 30 years, Howard Austen. Norris told me that she figured Gore was trying to make up for the "3M" essay.

The benefit at the Provincetown Town Hall was a staged reading of George Bernard Shaw's "Don Juan in Hell." Mailer and Vidal, along with Gay Talese and Susan Sontag, had performed it at Carnegie Hall in 1993. Gore would again play the Devil ("typecasting" was the joke around town), and Mailer, for the first time, would play Don Juan, and also direct. Norris was Dona Ana, Don Juan's former paramour, and I was cast as her father, the

Commodore. The Mailers put Gore up down the street at a guest house, and every morning he came to the Mailer house for Norris's bacon and eggs.

Norris recalled the "wild and wooly week" in her 2010 memoir, *A Ticket to the Circus*: "Rehearsal all day, some kind of lunch and dinner, ending with a late night of drinking and sparring between Norman and Gore in our bar. I didn't for the life of me see how Gore was making it so well. He had more energy than all of us combined. We were all exhausted. There was still a little friction between Norman and Gore, as Norman was the director and didn't hesitate to direct, but for the most part it was civilized." I was there for most of these interactions. One night I dropped Gore off at his guest house late one night, and watched him pour himself a Scotch nightcap, while sitting on his bed. I returned in the morning to find him lying fully dressed on his bed with the glass still in his hand. Seventy-seven-year-old Vidal popped up and went right back to work.

"Don Juan in Hell" is a 90-minute dream sequence in the third act of Shaw's *Man and Superman*. It is often cut from productions of the play, one of Shaw's finest dramas, and performed separately. Mailer trimmed "Don Juan" to 60 minutes, and made further refinements during rehearsals. Vidal knew his part almost by heart, and while he listened politely to Mailer's directorial advice, he played the role his own way. On the night of the performance, Vidal, wearing a jacket with a scarlet lining, told Mailer, "Norman, when I walk out on that stage, you are going to hear a roar of applause the likes of which you have never heard in your life." The applause was indeed thunderous. The Devil stole the show, and the performance raised enough money to keep the theater running. Vidal had a strong, resonant voice and played the role with wicked flair. He was especially memorable when he extolled the superiority of his satanic abode over the dull place upstairs. The four spirits dissect with every weapon of wit and rhetoric the great philosophical questions, culminating in a masterful set of exchanges between Don Juan and the Devil on the merits of the Life Force. It is brilliant exchange, one of Shaw's finest. "If you were scoring the bout, it would go to Vidal," said one reviewer, who called Vidal's portrayal "flawless." Mailer agreed that Vidal was "terrific," just as he had been at Carnegie Hall.

Vidal got another ovation from the 100-plus people at the Mailer home when he arrived after the show. He bowed, and said, "Where's the booze?" He and Mailer posed for pictures, drank from Norman's collection of single malt scotches, and talked into the shank of the night. As the party wound down, Norris recalled, Gore repeated the story of his first meeting with Norman, and pointed out that he, Gore, had demonstrably better family genes, and was going to outlive Norman, which he did. "When that unhappy event occurs," he said, in apparently serious tones, "I will marry you and take care of you." Norris said thanks but no thanks. She didn't want to remarry, she said, if Norman went before her, which he did.

My last memory of Gore is the following morning when he came to the house to say goodbye. He had just undergone a knee replacement a few weeks earlier, and was using a cane. Mailer had bad knees too, and had used one for several years. Standing on the deck behind Mailer's red-brick house overlooking the long curve of Provincetown Harbor, the two old troupers smiled and swung their canes about for Norris's camera just before Gore departed. It was their last meeting.

Norman died on November 10, 2007, at the age of 84 and nine months. Norris died on November 21, 2010, a little more than two months shy of her 62nd birthday. Gore outlived them both and was 86 and 10 months when he passed on July 31, 2012.

R.I.P., Norman, Norris, and Gore.

Triumph at the Biltmore:
John F. Kennedy's Nomination

Introduction to *JFK, Superman Comes to the Supermarket*

Note: Other than Mailer himself, and possibly Muhammad Ali, John F. Kennedy is the most memorably depicted figure in Mailer's historical pantheon, and no national event reverberated more powerfully for him than Kennedy's assassination. Larry Schiller, Mailer's collaborator on several books and films, asked me to write this introduction to a collection he conceived. It contains Mailer's iconic essay on JFK, "Superman Comes to the Supermarket," a second essay on Jacqueline Kennedy, and a huge collection of photographs, many never before published, of Kennedy's dashing, superbly executed campaign in the 1960 Democratic presidential primary.

On November 3, 1960, five days before John F. Kennedy defeated Richard Nixon for the presidency by less than one percent of the popular vote, Norman Mailer wrote to Kennedy's wife Jacqueline. He was replying to her letter thanking him for his extraordinarily favorable report on her husband's campaign, an essay (published in *Esquire* magazine three weeks before the election) titled "Superman Comes to the Supermarket." Mailer had depicted the campaign as the outcome of a dramatic morality play rather than as a realignment of voter preferences

JFK: Superman Comes to the Supermarket by Norman Mailer. Edited by Nina Wiener. Conceived by Lawrence Schiller (Cologne: Taschen, 2014)

based on demographics and party promises. JFK was "a prince in the unstated aristocracy of the American dream," while Nixon was described as "sober, the apotheosis of opportunistic lead." Kennedy would win, Mailer predicted, because the nation was eager for change after eight dull, dispiriting years under President Dwight D. Eisenhower. There was a "subterranean river of untapped, ferocious, lonely and romantic desires" in the American psyche that Kennedy, a war hero with a Hollywood star's glamour, seemed ready to engage. Looking back many years later, Mailer said, "The country began to speed up, the sexual revolution began with Jack Kennedy . . . things began to open up."

Mailer told Mrs. Kennedy that he was troubled by her husband's disapproving, bellicose comments about Fidel Castro, who had just seized power in Cuba, but would nevertheless vote for him because "it is more important than ever that he win." It was the first vote Mailer had cast for a president since 1948 when he campaigned for Progressive Party candidate Henry A. Wallace, who ran a distant third to Harry S. Truman and Thomas E. Dewey. The Kennedy mystique drew Mailer back into mainstream politics, and his essay became one of the earliest exemplars of the "New Journalism" (along with the work of Joan Didion, Gay Talese, and Tom Wolfe, among others), a new kind of writing that moved the observer onto the stage of the story. During the previous decade, Mailer had eschewed any part in conventional politics in favor of a frenetic, controversial role in the New York *demimonde*, where he extolled marijuana, jazz, sexual freedom and celebrated the disenthralled lifestyles of African Americans in magazine essays and columns in the *Village Voice*, a weekly Greenwich Village newspaper that he co-founded and named. Bored and depressed by the kneejerk patriotism and family pieties of the tranquillized Eisenhower era, and oppressed by "the corporations, the FBI, the CIA, and the Mafia . . . working in an overt and covert association," Mailer saw Kennedy's election as "the hairline split in the American totalitarianism of the fifties."

With the 43-year-old president and his elegant, cultured wife in the White House, politics had become exciting. In his speech accepting his party's nomination, Kennedy spoke of America as a "new frontier," a place of "unknown possibilities and perils."

Mailer was present at the Biltmore Hotel in Los Angeles when Kennedy gave the speech, and was dazzled. He saw Kennedy as a hipster president, a bold, canny, ambitious politician who had "the remote and private air of a man who has traversed some lonely terrain of experience, of loss and gain, or nearness to death." For his services in helping get him elected, Mailer felt he was owed— at the very least—a meal, some drinks and the president's ear, but his deeper desire was to become a key advisor, a cultural Cardinal Richelieu who would link the White House to the most exciting currents and actors on the American scene. He wanted a seat at the Camelot roundtable. Some in Kennedy's court called Mailer "an intellectual adventurer," and they had it right.

"Superman Comes to the Supermarket" was the brainchild of one of the top editors at *Esquire*, Clay Felker, who later founded *New York* magazine. He and another editor, the brilliantly irreverent Harold Hayes, as well as the magazine's co-founder and publisher, Arnold Gingrich (a fishing/drinking chum of Hemingway's), were properly impressed by the edgy, self-conscious style Mailer displayed in the prefatory "advertisements" to his 1959 omnium-gatherum, *Advertisements for Myself*. Nevertheless, they believed that their magazine, which was rapidly emerging as the best place for the brightest literary talents of the new decade to publish, was elevating Mailer's name as much as he was lofting the name of the magazine. A contest of egos ensued. Gingrich decided that the last word in the title of Mailer's JFK essay should be "Supermart," not "Supermarket," and made the change before publication. Mailer protested, and was assured by Felker that restoration would be made. But it wasn't, and in an angry letter Mailer resigned from the magazine. "You print nice stuff, but you gotta treat the hot writer right or you lose him like you just lost me. When I'm mayor, I'll pay you a visit and see if you've cleaned the stable." In later years, when admirers asked Mailer to sign a copy of the magazine containing his essay, he invariably crossed out "Supermart" and replaced it with the original word.

Mailer was not joshing about his ambition to become mayor of New York. Bloated by the success of his essay, he decided to run in the September 1961 mayoral primary elections—but not on the Democratic Party ticket. Instead, he planned to run on the ticket of the Existentialist Party, which at that time (and ever after) did not exist. His temper of mind, he wrote later, was "Napoleonic." His friends listened to his plans, but with no enthusiasm. Mailer expected them, and his family, to rally around him the way the Kennedy clan had worked for JFK. Mailer's family thought the idea was crazy, and his wife, Adele, was terrified by the possibility of becoming the first lady of the nation's largest city. He intended to announce his candidacy at a large party at their Manhattan apartment on November 19, 1960, two weeks after Kennedy's victory. Drunk and stoned on marijuana (which he believed unseated unhealthy repressions), a frazzled and belligerent Mailer got into fist fights with several of his guests at the crowded party. The worst was to come. At around 5:00 a.m. on the 20th, he stabbed his wife with a penknife after she delivered a taunt about his manhood. She almost died of the thrust, which nicked the sac surrounding her heart, the pericardium. Mailer received a suspended sentence and was placed on probation after Adele refused to testify against him. They divorced soon afterwards. His literary career was also suspended, and his political career seemed over.

But the influence of the essay was not diminished; indeed, it was enhanced by the notoriety surrounding Mailer at the time. Felker said that it had "an enormous impact," and Pete Hamill, a journalist and novelist who was close to Mailer, said the essay "went through journalism like a wave." Young journalists now recognized

that the venerable inverted pyramid learned in J-school, a form
that front-loaded the most newsworthy information, had become
dull and stodgy, partly because it ignored the array of narrative
techniques developed by novelists over the previous century.
Mailer used them all, including scene-by-scene construction, later
fingered by Tom Wolfe as one of the most important technique
of the "New Journalism." "Superman" is one of the foundation
stones of this movement, one that changed the face of writing
about the news of the day. One difference between Wolfe's writing
and Mailer's is that Mailer, extravagantly confident of the worth of
his explorations, packed everything in: surmises about his subjects,
larger speculations about the amazing changes in American life, and
a filament of continuity extruded from Mailer's own personality. In
his essays and nonfiction narratives of the 1960s and early 1970s, he
consistently included his line of sight on events, coupled with the
nuanced examination of his personal responses to them. His radar
for the mood of events is unerring, and—to extend the metaphor—
his sonar for the depths of his subjects' psyches has rarely been
equaled. Identity and ambition were his touchstones.

In the middle of "Superman Comes to the Supermarket,"
Mailer describes his first meeting with then-Senator Kennedy at
the family compound in Hyannis. The candidate tells the reporter
that he is familiar with his novels, and after a slight but convincing
hesitation says he has read Mailer's most recent and controversial,
The Deer Park, passing over the one monotonously referred to by
everyone else, *The Naked and the Dead* (his 1948 novel of Pacific
combat that spent over a year on the bestseller list). Mailer is
stunned, and ponders whether Kennedy is being truthful, or has
been prepped to name *The Deer Park*, which deals with the lures
and corruptions of contemporary Hollywood. He decides that
it doesn't matter. If JFK's aides had advised him on what to say,
Mailer concluded, it demonstrated the perspicacity of their boss
and his predilection for hiring staff with subtle talents, and perhaps

a sophisticated taste for literature. The encounter is the beginning of Mailer's lifelong admiration for Kennedy—this side of idolatry, as he sharply disagrees with many of his ideas and programs—a fealty which is burnished when Mrs. Kennedy writes to Mailer to say that her husband did indeed read *The Deer Park*, finishing it on a rainy day in Hyannis. Some years later, Mailer spoke of his attraction to Kennedy: "He was a little like (President Franklin D.) Roosevelt: both were enchanting, had personality, and made America more fun to live in. His spell, his wit, the rich and broad life he led conquered us to the point that we would have talked about him for years. I took to him right away. Rather, to be honest, before him I had taken to his wife."

In her letter, Mrs. Kennedy told Mailer that she also enjoyed his novel, and went on to say that before reading "Superman" she had "never dreamed that American politics could be written about that way." She lauded his talent, and encouraged him to use it to write more nonfiction narratives. It was advice he took, writing accounts of subsequent presidential campaigns through 1972, and several novels set in earlier periods, most notably *Harlot's Ghost* (his 1991 novel about the CIA in the 1950s and 1960s), and his 1995 collaboration with Lawrence Schiller, *Oswald's Tale: An American Mystery*, a nonfiction book that explored the life of Kennedy's assassin. JFK's death is a crucial event in both books. Mailer never stopped worrying the bone of the Kennedy assassination (ultimately deciding that Oswald probably acted alone), and continued to ponder what might have been had Kennedy lived.

The slain president remained an inspiration, and in June 1969 Mailer ran in the New York City mayoral primary on the Democratic ticket. The popular newspaper columnist, Jimmy Breslin, ran for City Council president on the same ticket. The key plank in their quixotic platform was making New York City the 51st state; their campaign slogan was "Vote the Rascals In." Mailer came in fourth in a field of five, and Breslin lost as well, and that was the end of

Mailer's direct involvement in politics, although he and Senator Eugene McCarthy seriously discussed running in 1996—McCarthy for president and Mailer for vice president. The idea died aborning. Mailer went on to report on the 1996 election for *George* at the behest of the magazine's chief editor and the martyred president's namesake, John F. Kennedy Jr. Mailer traveled around the country on the press planes of President Bill Clinton and his Republican opponent, Senator Robert J. Dole; and at 73, he was by far the oldest reporter covering the campaign, referred to by the others as "the Dean." The tutelary spirit of his *George* articles was President Kennedy himself, whom Mailer revered until the end of his life as "a real man with a real set of desires to make a good and exciting and interesting change in history."

A Meeting of Giants: Ali and Foreman

Introduction to Norman Mailer's *The Fight*

Note: The first time I met Muhammad Ali was at Mailer's 75th birthday party in May 1998, a huge event at the Rainbow Room in Rockefeller Center. The room was crammed with family and friends and a number of literary luminaries—George Plimpton, Lillian Ross, Rose and William Styron, Kurt Vonnegut, Jay McInerney, and Bret Easton Ellis. When Ali and his wife Lonnie arrived everything stopped, and the waiters crowded around him for autographs. Mailer and Ali traded fake jabs for the photographers and Ali did some magic tricks. When Mailer introduced us, Ali leaned close to my ear, and said, "You're not as dumb as you look."

I t was inevitable that Muhammad Ali and Norman Mailer, two of the most talented, narcissistic, and ferociously ambitious artists America has ever produced, would become friends. Their talents and assets were happily reciprocal. Consummate professionals, the first in boxing, the second in literature, they were amateurs on each other's turf. Mailer, therefore, did not hesitate to call Ali's poems doggerel, and Ali gave faint praise to Mailer's athletic abilities after jogging with him. But it was all superlatives when they spoke of each other's achievements in their chosen fields: Ali called Mailer a "man of wisdom" for his writing; Mailer

Mailer/Bingham/Leifer: The Fight by Norman Mailer. Photographs by Neil Leifer and Howard L. Bingham. Edited by J. Michael Lennon and Nina Wiener. Conceived by Lawrence Schiller (Cologne: Taschen, 2018)

called Ali "the world's greatest athlete." Nineteen years Ali's senior, Mailer's position at the pinnacle of American letters corresponded with Ali's greatest years in the ring, 1964-1979.

"The heavyweight champion of writers" (as Mailer was often called after the death of Ernest Hemingway), and "the professor of boxing" (as Ali sometimes referred to himself) met in July 1963 in Las Vegas, where they attended the rematch of Floyd Patterson and reigning champion Sonny Liston. Liston won, only to lose to Cassius Clay seven months later (February 25, 1964), after which Clay converted to Islam and changed his name to Muhammad Ali. At the time of this fight, Mailer was frantically writing *An American Dream* as a month-by-month serial novel for *Esquire*, but nevertheless took time off to attend the fight in Miami. He was so impressed by Ali's performance that he asked his editor if he could postpone the serial and write about the agile young boxer from Louisville, Kentucky. *Esquire* denied his request, but by then Mailer was permanently absorbed in Ali's career.

In July 1965 Mailer saw Ali fight in an exhibition match in San Juan, Puerto Rico, and was photographed arm wrestling with him at the Hilton Hotel. Baffling reporters, he described himself as Ali's "intellectual precursor" in the accompanying story, his point being that the philosophy of existentialism first articulated in his famous 1957 essay, "The White Negro," anticipated the brand of pugilistic vigilance that Ali essayed in the ring. Ali, in short, was a physical existentialist, ever ready to adapt. From that time on, largely because of the endlessly reprinted photo, he became associated with Ali in the collective mind of the media. He attended several of Ali's subsequent bouts, and wrote about Ali's March 1971 loss to "Smokin' Joe" Frazier—his first career defeat—who became undisputed champion. The essay, titled "King of the Hill," appeared as a *Life* magazine cover story, accompanied by a suite of photographs by Frank Sinatra. Ali's portfolio of punches is expertly analyzed by Mailer, but the essay is more notable for his contention that Ali was not only a superb practitioner of the "sweet science," he was also "the first psychologist of the body," forever pondering the subtle tactics employed by his opponents, as well as his own, to avoid or assimilate incoming blows. He boxed with his head held back, Mailer wrote, and with "his arms low, surveying the fighter in front of him, avoiding punches by the speed of his feet, the reflexes of his waist, the long spoiling deployment of his arms which were always tipping other fighters off-balance."

Further on in the essay, he equated Ali's inner life with those of several literary giants—Joyce, Hemingway, Dostoevsky, Proust, and Conrad—writers with sensibilities so idiosyncratically brilliant they had few peers. Lonely, unorthodox novelists, they were at times nearly deranged, as were heavyweights like Ali:

> The closer a heavyweight comes to the championship, the more natural it is for him to be a little bit insane, secretly insane, for the heavyweight champion of the world is either the toughest man in the world or he is not, but there is a real possibility he is. It is like being the big toe of God. You have nothing to measure yourself by.

Four years later Mailer was back to cover "the Rumble in the Jungle," Ali's majestic, grueling bout with George Foreman in Kinshasa, Zaire, on October 30, 1974. Ali was then perhaps the best-known athlete in the world, and Mailer, who also had an international reputation, had no difficulty obtaining press credentials from *Playboy* to cover the bout. His account of Ali's attempt to win the heavyweight title from the young champion—Foreman was then twenty-five, seven years younger than Ali—appeared first in that magazine in May and June 1975, and was published a month later by Little, Brown, Mailer's publisher. It was generally well-received, but over time its merits became more and more celebrated, and it was often referred to as the finest book ever written about a boxing match. Novelist Larry McMurtry called it "one of Mailer's most perfectly toned books...One could ransack the whole literature of sport and not find a better book than *The Fight*. *Death in the Afternoon* (Hemingway's 1932 study of bullfighting) is a distinguished book, but in this book Mailer simply writes circles around his sometime master, Hemingway."

The Fight is the culmination of a seven-book, eight-year run in which Mailer writes in the third person personal, using himself as a mirror and a lamp to illumine the events and characters of a historical event. It is also one of the masterpieces of the New Journalism, which Mailer, along with Joan Didion, Gay Talese, and Tom Wolfe, were largely responsible for creating in the 1960s. Writing at the peak of his powers, Mailer ransacked his metaphoric armory to depict Ali's complex psyche and his Nijinsky-like ring artistry—the inner and outer modalities of his genius. He compared him to writers, painters, toreros, even chess champions, as well as a number of boxers, some journeymen such as Shotgun Sheldon, and others from the twentieth century's pantheon of great fighters—Sugar Ray Robinson, Rocky Marciano, Sonny Liston, Floyd Patterson, Joe Frazier (defeated by Ali in a January 1974 rematch), and Archie Moore, "The old mongoose," who had fought professionally for almost thirty years. Frazier and Moore were both present for the fight. Also in attendance and portrayed deftly by Mailer are Ali's crafty trainer, the legendary Angelo Dundee, and his assistant, Drew Bundini Brown, Ali's animated doppelganger who loudly echoes Ali's ideas and words. Among the others depicted are Foreman's manager, Dick Sadler, who had spent a lifetime in the boxing game, and his assistant and cousin, Sandy Saddler, a former featherweight champ and one of the greatest punchers of all time. Before the match, Saddler said, "I'm concerned for Ali. I'm afraid he's going to get hurt."

Saddler was not alone. Archie Moore prayed that Foreman wouldn't kill Ali in the ring, and Ali's wife, Belinda, told him, "You better take lessons on how to fall on your ass." A lot of other people were worried, and they had cause. Comparable in height, weight and reach, the two boxers differed in speed, power and styles. Ali had an amazingly fast left jab, and was perhaps the most light-footed heavyweight of all time, but his punches lacked the concussive force of his opponent. Mailer, watching Foreman hit the heavy bag with six hundred punches in less than fifteen minutes, concluded: "They were probably the heaviest cumulative series of punches any boxing writer had seen," enough to crack the ribs or break the spine of an average athlete. Foreman's strategy was brutally simple: wait until Ali weakened after several rounds of dancing, and then "beat on every angle of Ali's cowering and self-protective meat." If Ali desired a victory over the champ, Mailer summed up, "he would have to take more punishment than ever before in his career."

Of the nineteen chapters of Mailer's narrative, abridged here for this volume, only three are devoted to the actual fight. Earlier and later chapters follow Ali around Zaire before and after the match, and paint a grim picture of life under the nation's authoritarian president, Mobutu Sese Seko, the "archetypal African dictator," who changed the name of the country from Democratic Republic of the Congo to Zaire. Mailer admires the "tragic magnetic sense of self" displayed by the people of the country, and the magic of a landscape where everything seems to quiver with meaning. He reads about the Congolese ethos, and finds that one of its underlying precepts is a belief in n'golo, the life force: humans are not merely individuals; they are part of a pattern of forces emanating from nature and history. The championship boxing match, therefore, will be enveloped in the n'golo resonating from Ali and Foreman, their teams, sixty thousand spectators, Mobutu, the weather, the land, as well as "the messages, the curses, and the loyalties of the dead."

Mailer recognizes that he is also a force in this mystical evanescent web, but to what extent is impossible to gauge. He had written about himself and his effect on events before; now, however, the accumulation of these self-renderings weighs on him. "He was no longer so pleased with his presence. His daily reactions bored him." He also has the feeling that his reputation has been "burning low in the literary cathedral these last few years." Despite these uncertainties, Mailer cannot resist insinuating himself into the transcendental aura enveloping the fight. Superstitious to a fault, he measures every one of his actions by how it might help the contender—he is an unambiguous partisan for Ali. One evening, while "good and drunk," he clambers up on a seven-story-ledge in his hotel and squeezes around a partition separating two rooms for the purpose of aiding Ali's cause—don't ask how—although he is angry at himself for being vain enough to believe it will make any difference.

On the big night, Mailer and George Plimpton, who was also covering the fight, are seated in the press row of the outdoor arena. The rainy season has begun, and the sky looks threatening. After a long delay, the fight begins dramatically with Ali hitting Foreman with a series of straight right-hand punches instead of the jabs ordinarily used in opening rounds. Foreman seems surprised, but by the end of the round adjusts and begins to cut off the ring and corner Ali. In the next round, Ali eschews dancing, retreats to the ropes, and lets Foreman pound away. By leaning back on ropes (allegedly loosened just before the match began by Ali's corner man, Dundee), Ali forced Foreman to extend himself while he twisted and bounced on the spring-like ropes. This tactic, which Ali called the "rope-a-dope," went on for several rounds. During all this time, Ali buttoned up as best he could, elbows over belly and gloves in front of his face, occasionally hitting Foreman, as he tired, with a few combinations. Foreman did well in the fifth, but by the seventh was moving as slowly as "a man walking up a hill of pillows." By now he was swinging wildly and Ali was scoring almost at will. As Foreman's strength weakened, Mailer likened him to a sleepwalker in a dance marathon. When Ali hit him several times in succession near the end of the eighth round, Foreman fell "like a six-foot sixty-year-old butler who has just heard tragic news." Until Foreman's powers were greatly diminished, Ali's use of the rope-a-dope, Mailer wrote, was "about as safe as riding a unicycle on a parapet. Still, what is genius but balance on the edge of the impossible?" Like Ulysses, Ali triumphed over brute force with cunning and audacity. He was champion again, and held the title almost until the end of his career.

Coda: Mailer's warm friendship with Ali continued over the decades, and he, along with George Plimpton, added their recollections to the commentary in Leon Gast's extraordinary documentary about the fight, *When We Were Kings*. In 1996 Ali was part of the group receiving the Oscar for the documentary. His Parkinson's disease was now advanced, and when he had trouble climbing the stairs to receive the award, Foreman came to his aid. In 2012 Foreman said that after Ali's 1981 retirement he and Ali became "the best of friends. By 1984 we loved each other. I am not closer to anyone else in this life than I am to Muhammad Ali."

Craftsman of Violence: Muhammad Ali

A review of *Ali: A Life* (Houghton Mifflin Harcourt, 2017), by Jonathan Eig

What clearly distinguishes *Ali: A Life* from the score of biographies preceding it—including even the best of them: Thomas Hauser's *Muhammad Ali: His Life and Times* (1992), David Remnick's *King of the World and the Rise of an American Hero* (1998), and Gerald Early's *Muhammad Ali Reader* (2013)—is the analysis of the number and kind of punches Ali gave and received, round by round, over the long arc of his career. Jonathan Eig enlisted CompuBox Inc. to anatomize Ali's bouts, using film and video recordings. The analysis determined that after his first ten years of boxing, he took almost twice as many punches as he gave. Furthermore, a plurality of Ali's punches were jabs—he probably had the greatest left jab of all time—which while effective at discombobulating opponents, are not as destructive of brain tissue as hooks and uppercuts. The famous rope-a-dope tactic that Ali used to take the championship from Forman may have enabled him to win the fight, but the damage Foreman inflicted was terrible. In his last fight with Joe Frazier, the 1975 "Thriller in Manila," Ali said that the pounding he received from Frazier—"the human equivalent of a war machine"—as Norman Mailer described him, "was like death, closest thing to dyin' that I know of." Eig deploys the CompuBox statistics sparingly, deftly, tellingly to demonstrate that

Times Literary Supplement (November 24, 2017)

a significant part of Ali's unprecedented achievement as a fighter came from his willingness to take much more punishment than he gave out. He defeated Frazier in Manila to retain his title, but urinated blood for weeks. Sitting in his hotel room after the fight, he turned to a reporter, and said, "Why I do this"? Eig's biography comes as close as we are likely to get to the answer.

Eig's is the first biography of Muhammad Ali since his death in June 2016. He quotes James Baldwin to illuminate the teenage boxer's decision to become the greatest fighter of all time. To survive in a racist society, Baldwin wrote, "one needed a handle, a lever, a means of inspiring fear" in the minds of oppressors. "Neither civilized reason nor Christian love would cause any of those people to treat you as they presumably wanted to be treated, only the fear of your power to retaliate" would accomplish that. At the age of thirteen, Cassius Clay adopted a Spartan regimen to become bigger, stronger, faster: no soda pop, alcohol, or cigarettes, lots of milk, raw eggs and garlic water (to lower blood pressure). Run everywhere, train hard every day, go to bed early. His first trainer, Joe Martin, a white policeman in Louisville who worked with young boxers, said he was "easily the hardest worker of any kid I ever taught." His training routine left little time for school work. He could barely read, and was mystified by mathematics. One of his classmates said that he was "dumb as a box of rocks." His hero was Jack Johnson, the first African-American heavyweight champion. "I grew to love the Jack Johnson image," he would say. "I wanted to be rough, tough, arrogant, the nigger white folks didn't like."

Ali: A Life is scrupulously attentive to how deeply and how long Cassius Clay—and after his 1964 conversion to Islam, Muhammad Ali—was despised by both whites and blacks during the early stages of his twenty-one-year professional career. He was celebrated for winning a gold medal at the 1960 Olympics for the U.S., but soon fell out of favor. A combination of braggadocio (the media called him "Gaseous Cassius") and flirtation with the Nation of Islam made him the maligned underdog when he fought Sonny Liston for the championship. Malcolm X (a key figure in Eig's biography) encouraged Clay to see the fight as a battle between Christianity and Islam: "It's the Cross and the Crescent fighting in a prize ring." Ali later became adept at turning prizefights into symbolic encounters that burnished his image, but not in his victory over Liston, who was the fans' favorite. He went on to defeat Liston again, and then agreed to fight the mild-mannered former champion, Floyd Patterson. In the run-up to the match, Ali called Patterson "the Rabbit," and showed up at his training camp with a bag of carrots. Patterson was revered even by those who had no interest in boxing. Ali also called him an Uncle Tom, a name he smeared on many of his opponents.

By the time of the fight, November 1965, Ali had moved into the orbit of Elijah Muhammad, known as "the Messenger," the leader of the Nation of Islam. He prophesized the destruction of "blue-eyed devils" by a hovering "Mother Plane" controlled telepathically by black pilots—the details of the annihilation remain occluded. While the Messenger had a large following, civil rights leaders such as Martin Luther King Jr., as well as a majority of black and white Christians, were scornful of his bizarre separatist dogmas. But as Eig points out, "The Nation had given (Ali) discipline and focus . . . a sense of purpose and community." Gene Kilroy, one of Ali's friends, added, "If it wasn't for the Nation of Islam, he could have been cleaning bus stations in Louisville." The Nation also gave him a premonition of his destiny. Before defeating Patterson, Ali said he felt he'd been born to "fulfill biblical prophecies. I just feel I may be part of something—divine things." It was his custom to thank Elijah Muhammad and Allah after his fights. Even after The Messenger's death in 1975, Ali continued to praise him, though with noticeably less ardor as his own fame grew.

In the fourteen months between his defeat of Patterson and March 1967, Ali defended his title seven times, a punishing series even for a superbly conditioned athlete in his mid-twenties. Eig describes him at the peak of his powers:

Ali...boxed beautifully, changing speed and direction like a kite, cracking jabs, digging hooks to the ribs, sliding away in a shuffle to survey the damage, and then cracking more jabs, moving in and out with no steady rhythm, no pattern. He was a revolutionary, like Charlie Parker, with an innate style and virtuosity no one would ever reproduce. He turned violence into craft like no heavyweight before or since.

Ali was now "the most widely recognized athlete on earth," Eig states, and also probably the wealthiest. A few months later, however, after refusing to be inducted into the U.S. Army, he became the most hated. Stripped of his crown, he did not fight again for three-and-a-half years. With the encouragement of Martin Luther King, he became involved in the anti-Vietnam War movement, which he, like King, saw as inseparable from the civil rights movement. In one interview he said, "I don't have no personal quarrel with those Viet Congs." Another statement—dubiously but permanently attributed to him—became one of the mantras of the movement: "No Viet Cong ever called me nigger." Staunch in his refusal to compromise with the government, Ali was broke, scorned, unemployed, and convicted of draft evasion.

His situation began to improve after the October 1967 protest march on the Pentagon, and the January 1968 Tet Offensive launched by North Vietnamese and Viet Cong forces. Anti-war marches grew in number, and protest grew into resistance. Ali's actions and words were rallying cries. After a long legal struggle, his reputation was restored in January 1971 when the U.S. Supreme Court unanimously reversed his conviction. By then, however, he was now in his thirtieth year, out of shape, and just one of a dozen boxers who had championship ambitions. It took seventeen fights over nearly four years for him to earn the right to challenge and defeat George Foreman, who had been champion for almost three years. Their epic 1974 match in Zaire, the "Rumble in the Jungle," is arguably the best-known boxing match in history, in no small part because of the 1996 documentary, *When We Were Kings*, and Norman Mailer's unsurpassed 1975 account, *The Fight*. Eig makes no comment on the film, the only significant omission in this deeply researched, comprehensive biography. His prose is fast-paced, uncluttered, and rich in personal insights from the 600-plus interviews he conducted in the years just before and after Ali's death. Eig managed to get the recollections of most of Ali's entourage, including his doctor, Ferdie Pacheco, and the impresario and hustler, Don King ("Cash is King and King is cash"), many of his opponents, his brother Rudy, and his four wives. The assistance of the last, Lonnie, who was married to Ali for twenty years, was extensive. He also received assistance from others who had written about Ali. Eig had both the advantage and the obligation to tell the story of Ali's slow retreat into silence, a result of Parkinson's disease.

She Is Her Own Most Memorable Character: Joan Didion

A review of *Joan Didion: The 1960s and 70s*
(Library of America, 2017), edited by David L. Ulin

Note: Mailer first heard of Didion in 1965 when she gave a warm review to An American Dream, *calling it "the only serious New York novel since* The Great Gatsby." *She was even more laudatory in her 1979* New York Times *review of* The Executioner's Song, *the finest and most influential appreciations of his Pulitzer-Prize winning "true life novel," which she called "an absolutely astonishing book." Mailer later returned the compliment, saying, "If one wants an example of superb dialogue where the bar is set about as high as it can go, then read Joan Didion." She and Mailer were not close friends, but met several times over the years. Didion spoke at Mailer's Carnegie Hall Memorial in 2008, reading from her* Times *review. I spoke with her before the event, my only meeting with a writer I'd esteemed and taught for over thirty years. I was nervous and mumbled something about how she and Mailer defined the arc of achievement in postwar American nonfiction prose. She listened graciously and thanked me.*

Joan Didion's late husband, John Gregory Dunne, once pointed out that "Joan never writes about a place that isn't hot." During the late '60s and '70s, Didion lived in and wrote about climes

Washington Post (November 7, 2019)

of shimmering heat where apathy, violence and paranoia jostle, and snakes glide through the swimming pools.

Draw a line from Hawaii that runs the length of California, jogs across the desert to Las Vegas, moves east-southeast to New Orleans and Miami, then due south to the countries near the Equator and you will find the settings for Didion's novels: *Run River*, *Play It As It Lays*, and *The Book of Common Prayer* as well as the majority of the essays in *Slouching Toward Bethlehem* and *The White Album*. All of these works are gathered in *Joan Didion: The 1960s & 70s*, the first of several planned volumes of her work from the Library of America. (The only significant departure from these balmy settings is New York City, which Didion has written about occasionally, most notably in an evocative valedictory essay "Goodbye to All That.")

As in the work of Tennessee Williams, whose affection for sultry weather and nostalgia for a mythical past are mirrored in Didion's work, sexual activity in these three novels is roughly congruent with the temperature of the locale, although less so in her emotionally persuasive first novel, *Run River*. The book, which takes place mainly in the '50s in the Sacramento River Valley, is the portrait of an always-failing, never-dissolving adulterous marriage between the scions of two of the richest landowning families, Lily Knight and Everett McClellan. Despite mistakes and betrayals, Knight never relinquishes her desire to return to a stable past, "to that country in time where no one made a mistake," the Edenic California celebrated by her (and Didion's) parents.

The Old West of legend, now somewhat tarnished, is also present in Didion's next novel, *Play It As It Lays*. The central character is Maria Wyeth, a minor film actress who grew up in and around Reno, Nevada. She is raised by a gambler father who teaches her that the lessons of life are akin to the action at the craps table, and a mother whose corpse is eaten by coyotes after a desert car wreck. Drenched in dread, Wyeth's story is told mainly by an anonymous narrator via 84 flashback scenes reamed with abrupt, enigmatic silences. Didion and Dunne, who worked on a number of films, wrote the script for the 1972 film of the novel. The frame for the novel's action depicts Wyeth confined in a psychiatric hospital watching a hummingbird outside her window, and recalling the debilitating events of her recent life—bad lovers, a semi-pornographic film, an abortion, her parents' deaths, her director-husband's desertion, and a daughter born with a neurological illness. Perhaps the most dazzling of these chapters is an early one which describes Wyeth taking daylong daily drives on the California Freeway, an activity which is both an escape and a desperate attempt to exercise some control over a life in shambles.

Her third novel, *The Book of Common Prayer*, is the most complex and to my mind the least realized. In *The White Album*, Didion describes a time in the late 60s when she was deeply distressed by the shocking events of that period—the assassinations, protests, riots, the Manson murders, and the rest. Her life at that time had lost its narrative line. "All I knew is what I saw," she wrote, "flash pictures in variable sequence, images with no 'meaning' beyond their temporary arrangement, not a movie but a cutting-room experience." This vision captures precisely the jagged, baffling flow of *The Book of Common Prayer*. The narrator, Didion's version of Conrad's Marlow in *Lord Jim*, is Grace Strasser-Mendana, an American who has married into the country's ruling family. Sick with terminal cancer, she observes and tries to understand the purposes of another American, the psychologically damaged Charlotte Douglas, a 40-year-old woman from San Francisco, who is murdered in one of the small-bore revolutions that periodically roll through this fictional equatorial nation.

In *The White Album* Didion said that her highest admiration is for fictional characters who believe that "salvation lay in extreme and doomed commitments, promises made and somehow kept," but Charlotte Douglas's are a dark mystery. Her listlessness reinforced my conclusion that Didion will be best remembered for her autobiographical nonfiction where she crisply parses and delineates her feelings and observations. As she remarked in a 1979 interview, "If you want to write about yourself, you have to give them something." The two essay collections in this volume and her 2005 memoir, *The Year of Magical Thinking* (not included in this collection), are where Didion gives the most, putting herself, firmly but gracefully, on the stage of the story and delivering her finest character.

Motion Slowed into Choreography:
Didion Drives South

A review of *South and West: From a Notebook*
(Knopf, 2017)

J oan Didion's latest work seems, at first glance, to fall into that category of books rushed into print after the death of a famous writer—an unfinished narrative, a journal, or fugitive prose yoked into rough order—while there is still sufficient name recognition for monetization. But Didion, although quite frail at 82, is very much alive, has published this book with a very clear-cut if unspoken purpose that has nothing to do with royalties. *South and West: From a Notebook* is comprised of two fragments written over 40 years ago. The first and longest, "Notes on the South," is the first draft of a piece based on notes she took during a monthlong driving trip through Alabama, Mississippi, and Louisiana with her late husband, John Gregory Dunne, in the summer of 1970. The second piece, "California Notes," was written in preparation for a report, later abandoned, on Patty Hearst's 1976 trial. It runs to around 2000 words; the first piece is ten times that length. It's a tiny book, bulked up only a bit by Nathaniel Rich's valuable introduction, which provides some hints on why it is coming out at this particular time, seven weeks into the administration of President Donald Trump.

Rich notes that Didion planned to write about the South in 1970 because at the time she felt it was a way to understand the

Times Literary Supplement (February 24, 2017)

West. Many California settlers had arrived from the Gulf Coast, a place in her mind that seemed to represent what California had long been for Americans, a place of "earnest, eternal optimism," a place to start over. "The future always looks good in the golden land," she wrote in "Some Dreamers of the Golden Dream," the opening essay of her 1967 breakthrough collection, *Slouching Toward Bethlehem*. But her hunch proved wrong, and she never published the piece, although the visit gave her a sense of the tropics. She saw the Gulf Coast as a "gateway to the Caribbean," and her 1977 novel, *A Book of Common Prayer*, is set there in the fictional country of Boca Grande, a setting as foreboding as the symbolic tropical landscape in Conrad's narrative romance, *Victory*, Didion's favorite novel.

"The idea was to start in New Orleans and from there we had no plan." The narrative begins with this explanation and then presents a series of evocations of the city in all its overripe decay, and a weird kind of light in which

> random objects glow with a morbid luminescence. The crypts above ground dominate certain vistas. In the hypnotic liquidity of the atmosphere all motion slows into choreography, all people on the street move as if suspended in a precarious emulsion, and there seems only a technical distinction between the quick and the dead.

The city's endemic fatalism leads its citizens to countenance the bad weather, fevers, tarantulas, rotting bananas on the quays, graft in highway building, sexual jealousy and knife fights—bouillabaisse New Orleans style. Her premonitions about the city are further confirmed when she reads that Tennessee Williams wrote, "Here surely is the place that I was *made* for on this funny old world."

She and Dunne have connections and spend an evening with a patrician family who are interested in the restoration of New

Orleans Greek Revival houses. Willie Morris, the Mississippi journalist, and later editor of *Harper's*, was supposed to join them, but cancelled to meet with the director of an educational program for poor children, which the male host, Ben C., finds inexcusable. "I only hope he doesn't get too mixed up with the Negroes," his wife says. They agree that this is what happened to another writer, George Washington Cable, who "ended up having to go *north*" for writing essays opposing Jim Crow laws and promoting racial equality. This was in 1885. Morris's fate was the same, although he returned to Mississippi at the end of his life. Didion and Dunne drink bourbon and get restaurant recommendations from their affable hosts, but leave with a vivid sense that the southern ethos, with "its dense obsessiveness, its vertiginous preoccupation with race, class, heritage, style, and the absence of style," has changed little since G. W. Cable fled to Massachusetts.

From New Orleans they drive to Mississippi stopping along the way to watch baseball games and visit a reptile farm. In Biloxi they attend a Southern Broadcasters' convention at a coastal hotel. At the luncheon the state's lieutenant governor complains about "unruly, unwashed, uninformed and sometimes un-American" demonstrators, referring to the civil right activists, the "freedom riders" who have been challenging segregation in the south for a decade. They stop at other Gulf coast towns, eating red beans and rice at restaurants and overhearing conversations. She notes the ubiquitous freight trains running through all the towns, describes the many churches, beauty shops and gumbo restaurants. People smile and say "Howdy," but most are not forthcoming. When she tries to set up an interview with the director of the Academy of Cosmetology in Townsend, Mississippi, she is rebuffed. She has an appointment with the head of the Mid-South Business College, but the doors are locked when she arrives. Residents complain of getting "a lot of bad publicity down here," and the disapproval of strangers engenders an unusual solidarity.

It seemed to have reached a point where all Mississippians were bonded together in a way simply not true of the residents of any other state. They could be comfortable only with each other. Any differences they might have, class or economic or even in a real way racial, seem outweighed by what they shared.

Much of the book is a tessellation of images: the sluggish brown water in the rivers and "a sense of water moccasins," a trailer-sales lot with signs that say REPOSSESSIONS, and the cashier at a truck stop, a sullen "blonde girl with a pellagra face." Atlanta (which they do not visit) is booming, but "a somnolence so dense it seems to inhibit breathing" hangs over the rusty, dusty, economically struggling small towns. Didion includes a long conversation she had with the white manager of a large gospel and soul music radio station that caters to the black community, one of the few locals who opens up to her. He tells her that the state is in a "transitional stage." The Klu Klux Klan is almost completely gone, public schools are all integrated, and some blacks attend Ole Miss, the University of Mississippi in Oxford. He notes defensively that George Wallace got a lot of votes in Indiana. "I'm not saying I'm going to have a colored minister home to dinner tonight," he concludes, "'cause I'm not." What is most apparent, Didion concludes, is "the isolation of these people from the currents of American life in 1970," which she finds bewildering. "All of their information was fifth-hand, and mythicized in the handing down." Oxford is also Faulkner's hometown, and Didion is distraught by the hostility towards him among his fellow citizens, which he ignored. She goes to the graveyard where he is buried, but is unable to locate his grave among the many Faulkners (and Falkners) there.

Things are much the same in Alabama. Twice she is told that outside of the big cities like Birmingham, what you see is "the last of the feudal system," with blacks working the land and as house servants in the wealthier homes. In the hill country, which is "more reactionary" than the Delta, it is hard to buy a meal after 7:30 or 8 p.m. When Didion goes for a swim in a motel pool, the people in the bar are surprised: "Hey, look, there's somebody with a bikini." Eventually, she gives up trying to connect and spends days hanging around in drugstores. "I was underwater in some real sense," she writes, "the whole month."

The short concluding notebook entry, "California Notes," was apparently added for two reasons. First, it provides readers with a portrait of the Sacramento girl who grew up to be the woman touring the South with a bikini and a notebook, the slightly remote, slightly pampered Joan Didion, whose high school classmates predicted would be the first woman president. We also see her as an adult in San Francisco looking out the windows of the Mark Hopkins Hotel on Nob Hill into the apartment owned by the Hearst family where Patty listened over and over to a recording of *Carousel*. Toward the end she underlines the very different sense of destiny felt in the South and West: "In the South they are convinced that they have bloodied their place with history. In the West we do not believe that anything we can do can bloody the land, or change it, or touch it."

Rich ends his introduction by noting that the defiant way southerners in 1970 resisted "with mockery, then rage, the collapse of the old identity categories...resisted the premise that white skin should not be given special consideration," far from disintegrating under the weight of Enlightenment values, technology and globalism, has actually moved north into the Rust Belt and the rural Midwest. This attitude "has taken root among people—or at least registered voters—nostalgic for a more orderly past in which the men concentrated on hunting and fishing" and the women on running a home, a past where corruption, injustice and segregation were the order of the day. "The force of this resistance has been strong enough to elect a president."

Crafted Confession: Re-reading Mary McCarthy's
Memories of a Catholic Girlhood
(Harcourt, Brace, 1957)

Note: Mailer and McCarthy were not close friends, but from the 50s through the early 80s moved in the same Partisan Review/ New York Review of Books *literary circles. They first met at the Cultural and Scientific Conference for World Peace held at the Waldorf Hotel in March 1949. McCarthy, Dwight Macdonald, and Robert Lowell attended to challenge speakers whom they saw as being soft on Soviet Communism, including Mailer, but eventually all of them became friendly with him. McCarthy disliked Mailer's novels but admired his political nonfiction, especially* The Armies of the Night, *and he liked some of her early novels. She said she preferred Mailer's "perceptive but unfavorable review" of her best-known novel,* The Group *(1963), to the "bitchiness" of most of the others.*

Mary McCarthy planned to write a three-volume autobiography late in her life, but only finished the first, *How I Grew* (1987), before she died at the age of seventy-seven in 1989. It was politely received, as due the "First Lady of American Letters...our Joan of Arc," as Norman Mailer referred to her, but the praise was generally tepid, largely because it was a twice-told tale. McCarthy had covered roughly the same years of her life in an earlier book, *Memories of a Catholic Girlhood*. Published in 1957,

Times Literary Supplement (July 10, 2020)

it is considered by some to be the best of her two dozen books, including eight novels and several volumes of essays, reportage, and criticism. Its superiority derives not only from the passionate sense of justice that imbues the depiction of her ghastly Cinderella childhood, but also the singular circumstances of its composition.

Between 1944 and 1957, McCarthy wrote and published the memoir's eight chapters separately in magazines, during which time she also published six other books. Each chapter was built around a character or cluster of incidents from her childhood. At first, she had no plans to shape them into a continuous whole, and as a result, the usual anticipations and retrospections are missing. When she did gather them into a roughly chronological narrative of her life up to the moment of entering Vassar College at the age of seventeen, she added cohesive foreshadowing and backward glances. More importantly, she also added an italic reconsideration after each chapter, except the last, a portrait of her Jewish grandmother, Augusta Morganstern Preston. These afterwords further knitted the chapters, but they also raised questions about McCarthy's veracity and motives.

Rereading McCarthy's memoir as the Coronavirus is sweeping the planet is a portentous experience. McCarthy does not cite mortality figures or the massive economic dislocations caused by the 1918 influenza pandemic. The immediate jewel of *Memories of a Catholic Girlhood* is its moving depiction of the gaping holes in family life and memory wrought by cataclysmic plagues, wars, and other disasters. Her memoir is a valiant attempt to repair the breaches.

When she was six, her young parents died in the 1918 influenza pandemic. She and her three younger brothers, and all four grandparents survived (one of the hallmarks of the 1918 pandemic, unlike the current one, is that a disproportionate percentage of its victims were young adults). She lived beneath the overhang of their early, sudden deaths for the rest of her life, more so than Kevin,

Preston, and Sheridan, who were four, two, and one, respectively, at the time. Roy McCarthy and his wife Tess (née Preston) died shortly after arriving in Minneapolis, where the McCarthy clan lived, after a train journey from Seattle in October 1918, the height of the pandemic. In the prologue to *Memories of a Catholic Girlhood*, McCarthy writes that her father drew a revolver when the conductor tried to put the family, all sick with the flu, off the train in North Dakota.

Unlike her brothers, she had sharp memories of her fun-loving, indulgent parents and missed them desperately. The separation was made immeasurably worse by the relatives that her McCarthy grandparents assigned to raise the orphans. As the oldest, she suffered more under these keepers, the fiendish Uncle Myers and his wife Aunt Margaret (grandmother McCarthy's sister), a sour martinet who prescribed castor oil, stewed prunes, root vegetables, and long after-breakfast sessions on "the throne." But in another way, McCarthy wrote, "I was less affected because I had another standard. I remember my parents. My uncle couldn't get to me mentally; I feared him physically." She had a permanent footprint in the past, the lost Eden. Recollections of happy days in Seattle with her doting parents contrasted with her existence under the thumb of Myers, a figure right out of *Oliver Twist* (Dickens was one of McCarthy's favorite authors).

The first two chapters detail the five years that the children spent living with Myers and Margaret, who was thirteen years older than her husband. There were no books, no movies, no friends, and only a few battered toys. The children recalled "sitting for hours in their cold, dark cellar, pungent with the odor of stored potatoes, peeling the raw peanuts Myers used for his candy," but none of them remember being given a single piece. They were beaten regularly, often for no apparent reason. A hairbrush was used for venial sins and a razor strop for "special occasions." When Mary was ten, she won the $25 first-place prize in a statewide contest for her essay,

"The Irish in American History." Her aunt was in the audience for the presentation and looked "for once, proud and happy."

> But when we came to our ugly house, my uncle silently rose from his chair, led me into the dark downstairs lavatory, which always smelled of shaving cream, and furiously beat me with the razor strop—to teach me a lesson, he said, lest I become stuck-up. Aunt Margaret did not intervene. After her first look of discomfiture, her face settled into folds of approval; she had been too soft. This was the usual tribute she paid Myers' greater discernment—she was afraid of losing his love by weakness. The money taken was "to keep for me." And that, of course, was the end of it. Such was the fate of anything considered "much too good for her," a category rivaled only by its pendant, "plenty good enough."

The whippings had little effect on her and her siblings, as Myers provided no inducements to behave. Like Kevin, Mary ran away several times, once hiding all day in the confessional of a Catholic Church, and another behind a statue in the Art Institute. It is no coincidence, that the Church and art would be her twin passions over the next decade. The children's goal was to escape *to* a nearby orphanage, on the assumption that things couldn't be worse there. The random enforcement of Myers' regimen, the docility he sought, and his sadistic punishments led, McCarthy said, to her adopting "a policy of lying and concealment." Recalling her mistreatment in 1978, she said: "It took me a long time to realize I wasn't going to be punished for something I had or had not done."

Finally, the many escape attempts led her maternal grandfather to intervene. Mary returned to Seattle with him, and the boys were sent to military school. At the Sacred Heart Convent School, she earned a reputation for fervent religiosity, academic brilliance, and dramatic flair verging on exhibitionism. A problem liar starved for attention, McCarthy renounced her faith to the Mother Superior, the prelude to her plan to dramatically regain it. The staged renunciation led to an examination by a priest who presented her the five Catholic proofs for the existence of God, the flimsiness of which she immediately recognized. Consequently, just as she was announcing she had miraculously recovered her faith and was returning penitent to the fold, she was shocked to realize that she had actually, permanently, lost it. She became a lifelong atheist at the age of fourteen. When she acted rebellious in class one day, Madame Barclay, the prefect of studies, told her: "You're just like Lord Byron, brilliant but unsound." McCarthy, "simulating meekness," did not look up, but "never felt so flattered in my life." Her classmates gave her glances of wonder and congratulation, "as though I'd been suddenly struck by a remarkable disease, or been canonized, or transfigured." Her time with the sophisticated, French-speaking, Voltaire-and-Byron-reading Sacred Heart nuns gave McCarthy the poise and assurance to select, over time, the lineaments of a new personality, not, as she later explained, "a Yeatsian mask," but a deliberately chosen self.

The penultimate chapter in the memoir describes a hilarious summer trip to Montana she made with a high school friend, and the last is a brilliant, unflinching portrait of her raven-haired Seattle grandmother, reputed when younger to be the most beautiful woman in Seattle. Grandmother Preston sequestered herself in her own rooms most of the day, pampering herself with creams and ointments, and the rest of it shopping or in her flower garden. Although she could be a wonderful *raconteuse*, she was on the whole a slightly remote guardian whose beauty and mystery had the effect of "indescribable daring" on her granddaughter. She and her husband, a distinguished social justice lawyer who drafted one of the first worker compensation plans in the country, treated Mary generously, but most of her time at their house overlooking Lake Washington was spent alone. The commonest sounds in the elegant home were of the maid vacuuming, and the sound of the mail coming through the front door.

McCarthy writes in her prologue that "the chain of recollection, the collective memory of a family," had been broken, and necessarily the first drafts of her chapters were written from memory, her only other resources being some photo albums (there are twenty-seven photographs of the family) and newspaper clippings about the pandemic. But in the first edition of *Memories of a Catholic Girlhood*, more than a fifth of the total number of pages contain her later commentary on the now-revised eight chapters. Some of these reconsiderations are based on conversations and correspondence with her eldest brother, Kevin, a smaller number from Sheridan, her youngest brother, and some from Uncle Harry McCarthy, her father's brother, who defended the way the clan handled the four orphans. These pages constitute an extraordinary layer of punctilious emendation that bolsters some interpretations, and undercuts or qualifies others, similar to the way the prefatory "advertisements" in Norman Mailer's collection, *Advertisements for Myself* (1959) serve as corrective or qualifying commentary to most of the major selections.

McCarthy opens her prologue by admitting that in writing it "the temptation to invent has been very strong, particularly where recollection is hazy and I remember the substance of an event but not the dates—the color of a dress, the pattern of a carpet, the placing of a picture. Sometimes I have yielded, as in the case of conversations." She goes further, admitting that in some instances she "arranged actual events so as to make 'a good story' out of them. It is hard to overcome this temptation if you are in the habit of writing fiction: one does it almost automatically." Perhaps the best instance of the mixture of fact and fiction concerns the train trip where McCarthy remembers seeing her father pull a revolver on the conductor as they approached "a small wooden platform in the middle of the North Dakota prairie." She says in her prologue that it was her grandmother Preston —"no special partisan of my father"—who told her this story.

> But my Uncle Harry, who was on the train, tells me that this never happened. My father, he says, was far too sick to draw a gun on anybody, and who would have told my grandmother except my Uncle Harry himself, since he and his wife were the only adult survivors of our party? Or did my grandmother hear it from some other passenger, on his way east during the great flu epidemic?

McCarthy continues to worry the bone of the incident in another of the afterwords, saying that, if Harry was right, then she didn't "see" the revolver, but rather—when she heard the story from her grandmother—"I had the feeling that I almost remembered it. That is, my mind supplied me with a picture of it." To further complicate the matter, she concludes, "Actually, I do dimly recall some dispute with the conductor, who wanted to put us off the train." Who are we to believe? Mary, the grandmother, the uncle, or the suppositional "other passenger"? McCarthy's method of revealing the past via a layered cross-hatch of memory, speculation, fictionalizing, reliable and unreliable testimony from multiple sources is the impressionistic way we know much of the past.

In a long essay on McCarthy's memoir written in 1965, John W. Aldridge concluded that her afterwords are a reflection of her erstwhile Catholicism. He compared her to another apostate, James Joyce. Both writers demonstrate "the truth that when Catholicism ceases to be a matter of faith, it tends to linger on like radioactivity in the bones as a secret infection of the moral life." The morality of the confessional, Aldridge says, taught McCarthy that "if you want to lie, do so, but remember always to confess you have lied." Her hidden plan, he says, was to have it both ways: she wanted the advantage of first presenting a partially false but presumably more dramatic account of her experience and getting all the literary mileage she could out of that; but she also wanted to square herself with her conscience or God or whomever by adding her palliating and expiating corrections. Not to put too delicate a point on it, she wanted simply to lie about her experience, then make things all right by confessing the lie, while at the same time capitalizing on the fact that the reader would come upon the lie first, accept it as the truth, and be impressed by it before he would come upon the notes informing him that he had been duped.

All very neat, but the way Aldridge hammers this nail for the length of his thirty-seven-page attempt to demolish McCarthy's reputation is too much of a muchness for me. Also, he neatly suppresses the fact that she had no plan to consolidate the free-standing pieces when she first published them in the mid-1940s and early '50s. Calculation of the kind he avers was inimical to McCarthy as an adult.

Mary McCarthy was addicted to the truth, however painful. Towards the end of her life, when asked what kind of self-portrait she would provide in her two planned (but never written) volumes of autobiography, she said, "Not too favorable. But then it'd be awful if one formed too favorable a self-assessment of oneself."

James Baldwin: Preacher vs. Writer

Review of *Talking at the Gates: A Life of James Baldwin*
(University of California Press, 2021) by James Campbell

ol Stein, who went to DeWitt Clinton High in the Bronx with
James Baldwin, and edited one of his best books, his first essay
collection, *Notes of a Native Son* (1955), told Campbell, "As
time went on (Baldwin) allowed the preacher in him to overtake the
writer." This is one of the two fundamental conflicts in Baldwin's
life. The other one, which Campbell says "dominated" his life to
the very end—he died in France in 1987 at the age of 63—was the
struggle between his life as a writer and his life as a lover. Campbell
explores these two related struggles in his fair-minded, revealing,
and evocative biography, which was first published in 1991, and
re-issued in 2002. This latest edition has a new introduction that
comments on the explosion of interest in Baldwin's life and works
that came in the wake of the Black Lives Matter Movement, and
Raoul Peck's 2016 documentary on Baldwin, *I Am Not Your Negro*.
It also includes a chronological list of Baldwin's books and essays
(including op-ed pieces), and a fascinating, previously unpublished
1988 interview with Norman Mailer.

Campbell met Mailer a few times, and reviewed some of his
books for the British periodical *Times Literary Supplement*, where
he was an editor for decades, but he knew Baldwin much better
and saw him many times over a ten-year period, beginning in 1978.

(*Mailer Review*, 2021)

He also met and interviewed many of Baldwin's relatives, friends, editors, and rivals, and uses his interviews with them to great effect, although he conducted fewer than David Leeming, who knew Baldwin for 25 years, and was his assistant for four. Leeming wrote Baldwin's authorized biography in 1994, and discusses fully his romantic life, something about which Campbell has much less to say.

Where Campbell's biography is most accomplished is in its careful expositions and evaluations of Baldwin's work, and how it grew out of his life on the streets of Harlem and his stint as an electrifying teenage preacher at the Fireside Pentecostal Assembly. He is insightful on Baldwin's work in the *Nation, New Leader, Commentary,* and *Partisan Review* where he earned his chops with a series of elegant review-essays. Baldwin never attended college, but he was as well-read in classic literature as anyone of his generation. "Baldwin had read *everything*," according to Mary McCarthy, who met him when he was 20, adding that "he had what is called taste—quick, Olympian recognitions that were free of prejudice." This included French literature, a language in which Baldwin became fluent. Campbell reports that Baldwin imbibed Flaubert, Camus, Gide, and Balzac's *Comédie humaine*, which "taught him about the place of French institutions from the universality of bureaucracy to the role of the concierge." His extensive reading—Hemingway and Henry Miller on Paris life were also devoured—attracted him to France and helped him settle in Paris where he lived off and on for years.

Campbell, himself a Francophile, has written two other books with French connections. *Exiled in Paris: Richard Wright, James Baldwin, Samuel Beckett, and Others on the Left Bank* (1995) examines the English-speaking literary scene in postwar Paris, and was "shaped from a rib" taken from his biography, and it, in turn, provided material for *This Is the Beat Generation* (1999). Baldwin figures in all three, which can loosely be called Campbell's trilogy. He also was chiefly responsible for gaining the release of Baldwin's FBI record, a huge, decades-long legal effort that demonstrated without a doubt that J. Edgar Hoover unfairly singled out Baldwin for extensive surveillance not only because he was Black, and had been briefly involved in the early 1960s with the pro-Castro "Fair Play for Cuba Committee" (as was Mailer), but because he was gay. The FBI was not alone in mistreating Baldwin because of his sexual preferences, quite a few Black writers also demeaned him. He was called an "arty upstart," and "the colored darling of avante garde (sic) magazines." Worse, he was given the nickname "Martin Luther Queen." If Baldwin had been unfairly vilified by a white adversary, Campbell states, he "would probably have responded with a volley of superarticulate fury; confronted by black opposition, he was just as likely to break down in tears." This abuse was one of the key factors that prompted Baldwin to go abroad for long periods.

Campbell is at his best when describing the conflicting pressures on Baldwin in the 1960s and '70s, when he was, on the one hand, a leading spokesperson for the Black civil rights cause and, on the other, a major novelist in the American social realist tradition. He could lay fair claim to both. But during the mid-60s,

> whenever a way of escape opened, he went down it. And when he found time to take a deep breath, he privately renewed his purpose: not to sacrifice all his energy to the movement, but to contain some in his art. The book of stories (*Going to Meet the Man*, 1965) had been published, there was a new novel, a long one, in the typewriter (*Tell Me How Long the Train's Been Gone*, 1968). But with the mood outside his study so tempestuous, when he wanted to work he found it necessary to leave the country. Paris, London, Helsinki, Rome, and Istanbul were among the places where he turned up between the summers of 1964 and 1965.

Baldwin's writing gained and lost from the push-pull of his stature in the movement. He was immensely proud of speaking out and protesting against the Jim Crow laws of that time: "I will always consider myself among the greatly privileged," he declared many years after his first trip to the American South in support of Black protesters "because, however inadequately, I was there." But as Campbell learned firsthand, this role rasped against his equally strong literary ambitions. In 1979, Baldwin spoke at Edinburgh University at Campbell's invitation, and subsequently Baldwin invited him to pay a visit in St-Paul de Vence, about ten miles from Nice, where Baldwin had a home. While there, a close friend of Baldwin's told Campbell, "Jimmy was touched that you called him an American writer in your magazine, not a black writer. That meant something to him." In point of fact, he had referred to him as "one of the greatest American writers." Campbell was entranced by Baldwin's writing voice. "It was," he wrote in his introduction, "a unique tone among many in the cacophony of discordant timbres and inventive scales that comprise the great modernist symphony of twentieth-century American prose and poetry."

Baldwin wrote six novels. Campbell finds all but his first two, *Go Tell It on the Mountain* (1953) and *Giovanni's Room* (1956) to be badly flawed. *Another Country* (1962), notable for its bold presentation of interracial love affairs and bisexuality, and its depiction of the gritty streets of Harlem and Greenwich Village, reminds Campbell of Balzac's novels, but he points to its "startlingly clumsy" prose, sentimentalized characters, and "poor control of form." *Tell Me How Long the Train's Been Gone* (1968), a retrospective narrative, looks back on the conflict between Leo Proudhammer, a New York City actor who dies of a heart attack on stage, and his older brother, Caleb. Campbell says that "almost everything that can go wrong with a novel has gone wrong here," including lack of a firm structure, and uninventive language. His fifth novel, *If Beale Street Could Talk* (1974), is told by a nineteen-year-old Black woman, Tish, who works in a New York City perfume shop, a choice Campbell calls a "bold step." The problem is that she sounds as sophisticated as Baldwin, which deprives her of her own identity. Campbell asks rhetorically, "Was Baldwin so bent on reminding white people that they had no idea how blacks thought and felt that he had lost sight of it himself?" Missing is what Baldwin could have delivered: "the intelligence of Harlem street talk...its ironic wit, its poetic double-edge, its full-speed ahead rhetorical 'rapping.'"

Campbell succinctly lays out the problems of his final novel, *Just Above My Head* (1979): "too many bloodless characters, too neatly divided into goodies and baddies; too strong a dependence on color as an indicator of virtue." The novel's rambling plot—generally a weakness for Baldwin—and the book's length, 600 pages, are also problematic. Yet, Campbell finds residual merit in the novel because it looks at the related issues of American history and "the variable treachery of individual memory." In this last major work, Baldwin wrestles somewhat successfully with the question that all autobiographical writers ponder: "If one's memory is not to be trusted—and apparently his was not—then how does one prepare to face one's own experience, and how, in the end, is it to be recorded?"

I agree with Campbell on the considerable merits of his first novel, the semi-autobiographical *Go Tell It on the Mountain*, specifically, its "compact jeweled prose" and the Jamesian aplomb with which Baldwin ranges over seventy years of family history. The deftness with which he explores and links spiritual and sexual themes also adds to its luster. It is regularly included on lists of the best novels of the twentieth century. *Giovanni's Room* is not as accomplished, as Campbell notes, and suffers from too many and too perfumed (to use Mailer's adjective for Baldwin's prose) poetic flights, but its early bold examination of gay themes demonstrates his courage.

Campbell is much more admiring of Baldwin's nonfiction, especially his first three collections: *Notes of a Native Son* (1955); *Nobody Knows My Name* (1961); and *The Fire Next Time* (1963). Perhaps the most important set of remarks Campbell makes in the biography concerns the relative merits of Baldwin's fiction and his essays. Baldwin's interest in literary form, as revealed in his letters to friends and editors, was focused entirely on the novel, short stories and plays. He considered many of his essays to be "magazine work," undertaken largely for money, and the esthetic problems surrounding them were, to his mind, non-existent. As Campbell points out, "it is the essay and not the novel—especially not the social realist type of novel that Baldwin was writing—that provides the space for the play of intellect, and the intellect, not the imagination, was Baldwin's strong suit . . . (his) quicksilver intelligence was the quality about him that most impressed his friends in Paris," just as it impressed Mary McCarthy when she met him in 1944. "The essay form," Campbell continues, "enabled Baldwin to write as he spoke, to unfold his experience by discursive methods, until he came upon the meaning at the core." His skill at recalling moments of his past and ruminating on them, and his willingness to address difficult questions of race, memory, and the experience of Black Americans was revealed in the three books named above, which are the core of his artistic achievement.

The Fire Next Time, a long essay, built around Baldwin's meeting with the leader of the Nation of Islam, Elijah Muhammad, was first published in the New Yorker in 1962. Campbell notes that it is "probably his masterpiece." Re-reading it two decades later for his biography, Campbell, always admirably frank in revealing his reservations, finds it somewhat soft on the leader, and says it gives a "foretaste of the sentimentality that flowed from Baldwin's pen whenever he wrote about other blacks." Nevertheless, it made Baldwin an international figure and was no doubt instrumental in the decision of Time to put him on the cover on May 17, 1963. Besides his account of his meeting with Elijah Muhammad, Baldwin in 20,000 words, ranges over his childhood in the ghetto, his pulpit eloquence, his Oedipal struggle with his father, and his defection from fundamentalism to humanism.

"The essay," Campbell says in summation, "comes closest to representing his ideas *in toto*"—

not in a schematic way, but in the form of a mature and exemplary worldview. Baldwin's essay reads like the conversation of a genius; his critique of American society ranges over the poor state of American bread as a reflection of the national soul, the importance in life of the acceptance of death, the illusion of the "Russian menace," the reality of the Negro's past—"rope, fire, torture"—and the healing power of love and reconciliation.

I'll leave off here with one final quote from Campbell's astute, engrossing, critical, deeply felt and indispensable biography, one that gives hints of the richness of his portrait of that complex, indispensable American writer, James Baldwin:

He was magnetic, compulsively sociable, elaborately extroverted, darkly introverted, depressive, magnificently generous, self-absorbed, incorrigibly self-dramatizing, funny, furious, bubbling with good intentions, seldom hesitating over a breach of promise—and capable of demonstrating all those traits between lunch and dinner, and again between dinner and the final Johnny Walker Black Label at 4 a.m.

Drenched in Dread: Don DeLillo's *Moribundi*

A review of *Zero K* (Scribner, 2016)

Note: DeLillo and Mailer got to know each other in the mid-80s when Mailer invited DeLillo to readings at Actors Studio in New York. Later, DeLillo joined The Dynamite Club, an informal group assembled by Mailer, Dick Russell, and Edward Jay Epstein to discuss various theories about Kennedy's assassination—G. Gordon Liddy attended one meeting and Mailer engaged him in a head-butting contest. Mailer had high praise for DeLillo's 1988 novel about Lee Harvey Oswald, Libra, and told me that DeLillo was his most important successor. In confirmation, DeLillo said that it was Mailer's "ambition, risk, broad vision, wide range— aspects of the American tradition that put me on the path I've been following all these years." I became friendly with DeLillo in 2010 after he gave me a generous interview for my biography.

The reticence of Don DeLillo, regularly remarked on, is a canard. For decades he has threaded a course between over and underexposure. Although he has never taught, dislikes being photographed, and only rarely gives readings, he has been interviewed dozens of times, delivering well-considered if sometimes flinty answers to questions about the leanings and aversions of his art. For example, he has often noted his propensity to describe place, both interiors ("I sometimes feel I'm painting

Times Literary Supplement (May 6, 2016)

a character in a room, and the most important thing I can do is set him up in relation to objects, shadows, angles"), and exteriors ("I'm interested in what real places look like and what names they have . . . with memory and roots and pigment and rough surfaces"). He has pointed to the Ouroboros shape of his plots ("a looping action from the end of the book to the beginning"), and noted his admiration for novels like Malcolm Lowry's *Under the Volcano* (1947) and Joyce's *Finnegans Wake* (1939) that employ this action.

DeLillo has also explained that his novels attempt to give "a sense of something extraordinary hovering just beyond our touch and just beyond our vision." These intimations, he says, are "somehow related to the extraordinary dread, to the death ear we try to keep beneath the surface of our perceptions." It would be difficult to name a contemporary writer whose work is more thoroughly saturated in manifestations of *memento mori*. His first novel, *Americana* (1971), ends in Dealey Plaza in Dallas, where President Kennedy was assassinated. His subsequent novels, especially those following *The Names* (1982), which concerns a cult of assassins intoxicated by linguistic coincidence, link death with something else. Each relationship is different, and to delineate the multifarious ways that DeLillo relates death as an idea, a reality, a memory, a desire, a constricting and an ennobling force and so on to these phenomena would take considerable space, a long essay. A partial list: sex (*Running Dog*, 1978), ecological catastrophe (*White Noise*, 1985), conspiracy (*Libra*, 1988), nuclear weapons (*Underworld*, 1997), grieving and ghosts (*The Body Artist*, 2001), financial speculation (*Cosmopolis*, 2003), celebrity (*Mao II*, 1991), terrorism (*Falling Man*, 2007), time (*Point Omega*, 2010), and religion (*The Angel Esmeralda*, 2011). Death is also considered in tandem with commodification and waste, and with paranoia, in several of his books—he was once called, with some exaggeration, "the chief shaman of the paranoid school of American fiction."

Zero K, DeLillo's sixteenth novel, is a probing examination of the ethics and techniques of cryonics, that is, the freezing of dead people. In the rugged Tian Shan mountains of Uzbekistan, under many feet of pre-Cambrian rock, lies the Convergence, a structure for the cryogenically preserved that could have been designed by Piranesi. The Convergence was built by the Stenmarks, twin brothers who might be described as two-fifths genius, three-fifths fraud, lured by immortality and hedge-funded. Within layers of blast walls that provide isolation worthy of a pharaoh, a certain number of enormously wealthy multi-nationals wait for the day when radically new technologies will reanimate their freeze-dried bodies (Zero K refers to absolute zero, minus 273.15 degrees Celsius). The Convergence has its own durable energy sources, redundant cyber-security systems, and roving armed guards. In a manner eerily similar to how serial murderers are executed by lethal injection, the *moribundi* who come to the Convergence die chemically prompted deaths.

In the opening chapter, Jeffrey, the son of the billionaire Ross Lockhart, recalls going as a boy to a Catholic church in New York City on Ash Wednesday to receive a mark of ash on his forehead as the priest intoned, "Dust thou art, and to dust thou shall return." This ritual stands in stark opposition to the purposes of the Convergence. Jeffrey, the deeply skeptical narrator, agrees to accompany his father to say farewell to Artis Martineau, his brilliant, beautiful stepmother who is close to death in this hi-tech catacomb. He describes her upcoming experience as "a highly precise medical procedure guided by mass delusion, by superstition and arrogance and self-deception." The brunt of the novel consists of brisk delineations of the routines and meetings of the Convergence, and detailed descriptions of its physical locus. Both are punctuated by painful conversations between Jeffrey and his grief-stricken father, and those between Jeffrey and the staff, discussions about the merits of the cryonic enterprise which are by turns clinical, profound and humorous—DeLillo's comic gifts have been insufficiently recognized. The presentations of some of the hucksters who run the Convergence bring to mind late-night television spiels by pop psychologists and Santoku knife salesmen. Jeffrey weighs his doubt as he undergoes an indoctrination during his two visits to the grim premises. He attends meetings where groups of benefactors, technologists, economists, philosophers, and a few nutters attempt to convince him and each other that the Convergence is "a radical technology that simply renews and extends those swarming traditions of everlasting life."

The novel is drenched in last things: headless sculptures, a mausoleum of fine-grained marble, insulated receptacles reminiscent of the canopic jars used by ancient Egyptians that are used to store the excavated organs of some of the departed residents, a stone auditorium filled with adepts chanting before a giant, jewel-encrusted skull and, at every corner of the endless corridors, video screens replaying images of war, torture, assassination, self-immolation, ecological catastrophe, and many scenes of fearful, raging crowds (including clamoring, distraught immigrants). DeLillo's pictures of massed humanity are the immediate jewel of the novel, and call to mind Elias Canetti's important study, *Crowds and Power* (1960). Jeffrey studies the videos, attempting to determine if they are documentary in nature, or the product of computer wizardry.

Narrative tension is provided at the outset by Ross's impending decision: go into cryogenic preservation with his wife, who is dying of an MS-type illness, or return to the upper world and suck on the marrow of his guilt. Artis, an archeologist, with a deep respect for preserving the past, assumes that Ross will accompany her. In her final hours, as she awaits her transmutation in an antiseptic hospice room, she whispers a dare to Jeffrey: "Come with us." DeLillo's remarkable ability for setting is displayed in such *mise-en-scène* within the vaults of the Convergence—macabre dumb shows, camp meetings of McNugget philosophy and bizarre gatherings resembling timeshare sales presentations.

Jeffrey accidentally encounters a Serbian monk several times at the Convergence who gives succor to less-wealthy *moribundi*, who seem to be charity cases. The monk is of the old persuasion and believes death to be the precious upshot of life—the novel's underlying theme. Over a meal of "medicated sustenance" with the monk, Jeffrey hears his account of how he circumambulated the high rim of Mount Everest, prostrating himself and praying after every step. "The thinness of contemporary life," he tells the younger man, "I can poke my finger through it." Jeffrey manages to cull only a few fractured insights from the mystical monk, but their deftly rendered meetings are among the finest moments in the novel.

There is another remarkable scene in a faux English garden within the Convergence where plastic greenery and fake roses flutter in a mechanical breeze. Here, Jeffrey speaks to Ben-Ezra, an ancient gentleman in a silver skullcap who, in his hushed manner, brings to mind the High Lama of Shangri-La welcoming visitors to the mountain-top lamasery in James Hilton's novel, *Lost Horizon* (1933). Both the Convergence and the remote Tibetan lamasery have the same purpose of extending life, but Shangri-La is a place of enlightenment and art; the Convergence is the abode of shills and their prey, as well as a number of personages whose motives and beliefs are uncertain. Ben-Ezra is one of these. Like the High Lama, he eschews hortatory rhetoric, but he quietly espouses the mission of the Stenmark twins, while painting a detailed and horrific picture of the planetary woe without. Like the lamasery, the Convergence has "fallen out of history." Ben-Ezra gains Jeffrey's attention by his understated recitation of pandemics above and attempted life-extension below: "He spoke in a subdued tone that carried an eloquence . . . about food systems, weather systems, the massive die-offs of birds and ocean life, the levels of carbon dioxide, the lack of drinking water, the waves of virus that envelop broad geographies." Jeffrey seems pleased when Ben-Ezra denigrates "all the voice commands and hyper-connections" of wearable "puppet technology" that permit one to "become disembodied."

Near the end of the novel, a Convergence official makes a presentation to rich clients who choose "to enter the portal prematurely," telling them:

> It will not be total darkness and utter silence. You know this. You've been instructed. First you will undergo the biomedical redaction, only a few hours from now. The brain-edit. In time you will re-encounter yourself. Memory, identity, self, on another level. This is the main thrust of our nanotechnology. Are you legally dead? You will have a phantom life within the braincase. Floating thought. A passive sort of mental grasp. Ping. Like a newborn machine.

In another chapter, we enter this phantom life as experienced by Artis: "Where is my body? Do I know what this is? . . . . Am I someone or is it just the words themselves that make me think I am someone? I only know the word and I know it out of nowhere . . . But all I am is what I am saying and this is nearly nothing." Safe in her plastic chamber after her quasi-death, Artis faces an existential question: "Am I someone without others?" Her disturbing catechetical monologue recalls both the voice in Samuel Beckett's *The Unnamable* living his half-life in a barrel, and also the plight of the Cumaean Sibyl, who, granted long life by the gods, failed to ask them for a youthful body, and shrivels to a leathery wisp, a voice asking for death from her home in a bell jar. The proprietors of the Convergence sidestep, parry and reject ontological questions like those from Artis, and offer instead a new definition of death: "a cultural artifact, not a strict determination of what is humanely inevitable." *Zero K* is DeLillo's answer to this sophistry.

DeLillo's novels, like the plays of Chekhov, attenuate plot and characterization to heighten the presentation of environments and the historical events and philosophical issues they embody. His characters are not presented in the round as major or iconic protagonists, rather, they are the interlocutory servants of his investigations, and are revealed in dramatic flashes. *Zero K*, the summa of DeLillo's engrossment in cultural morbidity and human mortality, is another milestone in his long, relentless, and prescient examination of life in these parlous times.

Dread Persists: DeLillo's Digital Disaster

A review of *The Silence* (Scribner, 2020)

Don DeLillo's latest fiction takes place on Super Bowl Sunday 2022. Three people, a retired physics professor, Diane, her husband Max, a retired building inspector, and Martin, a visiting former student, now a high school teacher, await the start of the game and the arrival of two friends, Tessa and Jim, who are flying in that evening from a vacation in France. Except for two early chapters, one on the plane (which crash lands), and another in a clinic where Jim gets his head wound bandaged, the *mise-en-scéne* is the small ninth-floor apartment of Diane and Max on the Upper East Side of Manhattan.

The flight from Paris, as described by Jim, an insurance adjuster, is a long, boring "immersion in a single sustained overtone," which he attempts to counter with a mulishly persistent reading aloud of the information on the overhead monitor—air speed, ETA, external temperature in Celsius, etc. Tessa, a poet who works as an editor for an online service that provides answers to questions about things like hearing loss and dementia, takes notes on their visit to Notre Dame ("crippled but living") so she can remember them 20 years later, "if I'm still alive"—an ominous foreshadowing. Then the plane begins bouncing violently, there is a massive knocking below, and the overhead screen goes blank. The next scene in the apartment is the equivalent of a cinematic match cut. It opens with

Times Literary Supplement (October 23, 2020)

Max listening to the football commentators babbling away as they await the kickoff. As Martin, who is only "fitfully present," states his preference for the ancient traditions undergirding World Cup football, the image on the superscreen TV begin to shake, dissolve into geometrical shapes, and then goes blank.

From this point on, the entire novella—really a long short story of approximately 15,000 words—is devoted almost entirely to three lines of discourse. The first is a range of suppositions from the five characters about the possible causes of the massive power disruption, including internet and cell phone service. Some are plausible: a power station overload (similar to the blackout in New York, New England, and parts of Canada on November 9, 1965); the flyover of military jets at the game; "a selective internet apocalypse" initiated by the Chinese. Others are more bizarre, but most are congruent with the disasters and plagues of other DeLillo novels, most notably *White Noise* (1985), *Cosmopolis* (2003), *Falling Man* (2007), and *Zero K* (2016). They include: mass surveillance software overruling itself; phantom waves from an unknown source; an internet arms race, "hack and counterhack"; satellites that "can see the socks we're wearing"; autonomous drones, cryptocurrency manipulation, surging microplastics, germ warfare, and a takeover by hidden networks "changing by the minute, the microsecond, in ways beyond our imagining." DeLillo's mastery of the fragmented nature of spoken language is displayed in these paranoiac blurts, which every year seem less crazy.

The second set of responses are felicitous memories, visions, and yearnings, uttered as a counter-narrative to the hidden force that "has crushed our technology . . . our secure devices, our encryption capacities, our tweets, trolls and bots." Most of these seem to be protective emanations from the subconscious, talismanic prayers. Diane recalls visiting museums in Rome:

> The paintings, the furniture, the statues in the long galleries. Arched ceilings with stunning murals. Totally,

massively incredible. . . In one gallery tourists with headsets, motionless, lives suspended, looking up at the painted figure on the ceiling, angels, saints, Jesus in his garments, his raiment . . . Voices in how many languages. I think of them even now before I go to sleep, the still figures in the long galleries.

Max's contribution is two-fold, first to recall, in "a kind of plainsong, monophonic, ritualistic voice," the language of the play-by-play announcers at football games: "During this one blistering stretch the offense has been pounding, pounding, pounding." Secondly, he recalls with fondness his work as an inspector, climbing to rooftops and descending into basements, "looking and finding violations of the building code. I love the violations. It justifies all my feelings about just about anything." Jim and Tessa also contribute anti-dread memories. He recalls reaching for Tessa's hand as the plane plummets, and Tessa talks about the snippets of poetry she writes obsessively in tiny 3" x 4" notebooks. She wonders if the entire disaster is "a kind of virtual reality," which is an echo of Martin's question about whether people have some kind of controlling communication device implanted subcutaneously, something Morpheus and Neo might discuss in one of the *Matrix* films.

The third line of discourse in *The Silence* is Einstein's *1912 Manuscript on the Special Theory of Relativity*, fragments of which Martin quotes regularly through the evening. Einstein's vision of the universe in this work, which includes a facsimile of his hand-written pages, is Martin's way of contextualizing or subduing the events of the day by pointing to a circumambient scientific structure that might explain and resolve the spate of contradictory explanations for the massive cyber and electrical calamity that is the novella's narrative premise. In quoting from it, Martin even lapses into a version of Einstein, a native German speaker, speaking English, an

215 of Mailer's Last Days

amazing bit of ventriloquism on DeLillo's part. Martin's Einstein gambit is a sacerdotal anti-angst measure; it is calming, but far from being fully or permanently successful. Dread persists. And for most readers, Einstein's theories are as inexplicable as Joyce's *Finnegans Wake*, which is quoted from by Diane, in passing.

DeLillo's tale brings to mind three other dystopian works: Cormac McCarthy's post-apocalyptic novel, *The Road* (2006), the Wachowski sisters' sci-film, *The Matrix* (1999), and Poe's 1842 short story, "The Masque of the Red Death." All three have truncated plots, but none of the three are as severely abbreviated as DeLillo's, which covers a six-hour period immediately before and after the inexplicable silence in which the five Manhattan pilgrims find themselves ensconced. In writing this brilliant, pointillist tale, DeLillo, it seems, was listening to the shrewd advice Chekhov gave to Ivan Bunin about how to write a short story: "It seems to me that when you write a short story, you have to cut off both the beginning and the end. We writers do most of our lying in those spaces. You must write shorter, to make it as short as possible."

A Mistake 10,000 Miles Long: Robert Stone

A review of *Robert Stone: Dog Soldiers, A Flag for Sunrise, Outerbridge Reach* (Library of America, 2020), edited by Madison Smartt Bell

Note: Stone gave a warm review to Oswald's Tale (1995) in the New York Review of Books, calling Mailer "the American master of dark and swirling purpose" for his moving depiction of Oswald's tangled motivations as an assassin. Stone's biographer, Madison Smartt Bell, thinks that Mailer and Stone must have met in passing, adding that Stone, like Mailer and Vidal, was a public intellectual. He also resembled them in being a vociferous critic of the Vietnam War.

In interviews two decades apart (1985 and 2006) Robert Stone recalled what happened after finishing a difficult section at the end of his second novel, *Dog Soldiers* (1974), while working in the basement of a university library. He staggered out of his carrel, crying and talking to himself, and "ran right into the security guard. He almost went for his gun because it's the middle of the night, and I looked completely demented. You can get very, very affected." He equated his passionate immersion in the lives of his characters with that of Charles Dickens, who he described as a *haluciné* whose evocation of the private world of his characters is so powerful that "you cannot refuse his reality."

Times Literary Supplement (March 12, 2021)

The section that triggered Stone's emotional upheaval is a magnificent passage describing the last hours of Ray Hicks, a Nietzsche-reading ex-Marine who acts out a samurai fantasy in the California desert just south of Death Valley. Three years earlier during the Tet Offensive—the novel is set in 1971—Hicks lost six of his comrades in Hue City and now, back in the States, sees himself as a species of enlightened desperado. Bleeding steadily, and burdened with an M60 machine gun and a backpack of pure Vietnamese heroin, Hicks sings Marine cadence calls as he marches, observes hawks gliding in the wind, mentally chants lines from the Buddhist Heart of Wisdom Sutra ("Form is not different from nothingness. They are the same"), and remembers his mother washing pots in a Chicago Salvation Army shelter. At the base of his skull he erects a psychic triangle of dark blue, encases within it a circle of bright red, and then impounds his pain inside the two perimeters. When the pain throbs too much, he titivates the triangle, hones the edges. This extended, wrenching depiction of Hicks' ebbing consciousness is rendered flawlessly.

Hicks's spiritual guru, an-ex Jesuit named Dieter, describes him as "a natural man of Zen . . . there was absolutely no difference between thought and action for him."

> In the end there were not many things worth wanting—for the serious man, the samurai. But there were some. In the end, if the serious man is still bound to illusion, he selects the worthiest illusion and takes a stand. The illusion might be of waiting for one woman to come under his hands. Of being with her and shivering in the same moment. If I walk away from this, he thought, I'll be an old man—all ghosts, and hangovers and mellow recollections. Fuck it, he thought, follow the blood. This is the one. This is the one to follow till it crashes.

The Dog Soldiers of the title refers to the Cheyenne warrior bands who were the point of the spear in the battle against white encroachment before and after the Civil War. Dog Soldiers were expected to fight as if already dead: in compensation they were deemed holy warriors. Although the central action of the novel follows the violent struggle over the smuggled heroin, it is the intense inner life of its major figures, including the horrid crew of miscreants who pursue Hicks, that is of paramount interest. In addition to Hicks, the novel's roster includes Dieter, the drunken *rōshi*; John Converse, Hicks' feckless Marine buddy; Converse's plucky wife, Marge, who flees with Hicks and the drugs; and a rogue federal drug official and his two sadistic sidekicks, who torture Converse to extract information on the whereabouts of Hicks and Marge. All are complicit in placing themselves in situations not unlike those of the Dog Soldiers; all are on a pilgrim's journey. Stone put it best in his description of the characters in his next novel, *A Flag for Sunrise* (1981): "They're always getting little glints of what may or may not be God. All of them are pursuing something beyond themselves . . . everybody's after a new morning."

Outerbridge Reach (1992), the story of a solo, round-the-world sailing race, is the third novel in the Library of America volume edited by Stone's biographer, Madison Smartt Bell. Like the other two, it calls to mind the novels of Graham Greene set in Africa, Mexico, Cuba, and Vietnam. Stone dismissed claims of influence, however, and was negative about Greene in several interviews, claiming that their concerns were quite different, but his comments probably should be chalked up to what Freud called "the narcissism of small differences." In their creation of memorable characters receptive to the numinous, susceptible to God glints, their novels are damnably congruent. Both explore the same kind of existential sinkholes in deftly plotted, character-driven action narratives set in a mixture of cosmopolitan and remote settings. Both suffered the same kind of bullying as adolescents, and both were congenial with the tenets of Catholic eschatology on the importance of the moments before death. Stone claimed that one of the key characters in *A Flag for Sunrise*, the drunken Father Egan, did not derive from the unnamed whiskey priest in Greene's 1940 novel, *The Power and the Glory*, which is set in Mexico, but readers might remain unconvinced.

What distinguishes Stone's work from Greene's is his belief that America politics, at its best, has been a means of carrying out the moral ideals of the Enlightenment enshrined in the Constitution. This idealism, of course, was severely damaged by the nation's Vietnam involvement, which he called "a mistake ten thousand miles long," referring to the military supply chain that also returned 50,000 American corpses, some of them sharing a coffin with smuggled drugs. But the peace party ultimately triumphed and the soldiers came home, partially justifying Stone's belief. Greene's indictment of America's blind arrogance in Vietnam, as displayed in his 1955 novel *The Quiet American*, was more unforgiving. He didn't see anything exceptional about American politics or morality, far from it. Stone, who spent a couple of months in Vietnam in 1971 as the Americans were handing over the fighting to the ARVN, had a more complex view. On the one hand, he decided that the North Koreans and Viet Cong were not as virtuous as he had previously supposed, but on the other concluded that "America is a state of mind that you can't export."

The central character of *Outerbridge Reach* is Owen Browne, a fortyish salesman of fancy sailboats. After valorous service in Vietnam, he feels spiritually empty. When his tycoon boss disappears in a financial scandal, Browne embraces the chance to replace him in a globe-girdling race, sailing south from New York via Outerbridge Reach to the South Atlantic on an untried 45-foot sloop built by his company. Another Vietnam veteran, a documentary filmmaker, is recording Browne's voyage. Stone admitted that his novel was based in part on Donald Crowhurst's fraudulent, fatal, single-handed circumnavigation attempt in 1968-69. Browne, however, is a more complex figure who recalls both Lord Jim and Billy Budd in his psychic dimensions. T. S. Eliot's line about risk-taking sums up Browne's psychological stance on the eve of his departure: "Only those who will risk going too far can possibly find out how far one can go."

The long novel moves sluggishly until its final 100 pages, but after Browne gets underway on the *Nona*, the novel begins to amass force in its adroit intercutting between the filmmaker's venality and the disintegration of Browne's mind as he moves through forty-foot waves in the Roaring Forties. After cutting off contact with his handlers in the U.S., his only human contact is Mad Max, a blind ham radio operator who sends him riddles in Morse code. Intermittently, his dilemma begins to cohere: continuing the race will lead to insanity, but discontinuing it and returning ignominiously to New York will lead to rack and ruin. And so, like Crowhurst, he begins creating a detailed false log of his positions, with appropriate wind and weather notations, as if he is sailing east toward the Cape of Good Hope, rather than moving in circles beneath the Southern Cross off the coast of Argentina.

All three novels unfold in the long shadow of the Vietnam War—most of the major characters spent time there, and were alternately beguiled and scarred by their experiences. A number of debts from the disasters of the war began to come due in the 1970s. The drug epidemic and a loss of faith in government lead the list. Despite Vietnam, the American appetite for intervening in under-developed countries continued. Frank Holliwell, a leading character in *A Flag for Sunrise*, gets enmeshed in a failed revolution after a former CIA colleague in Vietnam inveigles him into investigating a medical mission in central America. The mission is run by the sodden Father Egan and a nun-nurse, Justin Feeney, both of whom are sympathetic to leftist revolutionaries. Holliwell's blundering implicates Feeney and leads to her capture by the reactionary government supported by the U.S. Stone has been praised for his portraits of women, and the portrayal of Feeney may be the finest. None of the Americans' efforts succeed and the government, with the a few nudges from the CIA, brutally quells the revolt. Towards the end, the novel's half-cynical, half-hopeful observer, Holliwell, reflects on heroism:

> Apparently it was his fate to witness popular wars; Vietnam had been a popular war among his radical friends. As a witness to that popular war he had seen people on both sides act bravely and have their moments. Popular wars, as thrilling as they might be to radicals, were quite as shitty as everything else but like certain thrilling, unperfected operas—like everything else in fact—they had their moments. People's moments did not last that long.

In a career spanning half a century, Stone wrote eight novels and two collections of short stories, a memoir and a collection of nonfiction essays, as well as several screenplays, including the one for the 1977 film starring Nick Nolte as Ray Hicks, *Who'll Stop the Rain*. The novels collected here are advertised as his "three greatest," and it's a fair claim. The editor has wisely skipped over Stone's first, immature effort, the hallucinatory *Hall of Mirrors* (1966), which deals with the counterculture in New Orleans, and also his least successful novel, *Children of Light* (1986), a Hollywood story of drugs and schizophrenia. Stone taught creative writing for decades at Yale and several other schools and drew on his experience in two novels with academic settings, *Bay of Souls* (2003), which was not well-received, and *Death of the Black-Haired Girl* (2013). The latter, published a year before his death in 2014, the story of an adulterous, deadly love affair between an unsteady, brilliant professor at a small college and his extraordinary and beautiful student, is propelled by paranoia and fear, like all Stone's best efforts. More than one critic has pointed out that *Black-Haired Girl* explores the same web of lust, religion, and guilt to be found in *The Scarlet Letter*.

The only novel excluded from this collection that ranks with the "three greatest" is Stone's longest and most ambitious, *Damascus Gate* (1998), a reflection of his long-standing interest in the existentialist tradition of an absconded God. This passion led him to make a serious study not only of the Old and New Testaments, but also the Koran, the Kabbalah, and the Nag Hammadi Gnostic Gospels. All come into play in a novel that links Stone's absorption in the religious traditions and texts of the three Abrahamic religions with his abiding interest in international intrigue and violent revolutionary schemes.

The range of Stone's accomplishments notwithstanding, it is likely that his reputation will endure as one of finest American writers of the Vietnam War. In his punctilious depictions of the conflict and its aftermath (Stone once referred to himself as "a slothful perfectionist"), he stands in the company of Tim O'Brien (*The Things They Carried*, 1990), Larry Heinemann (*Paco's Story*, 1987), Philip Caputo (*A Rumor of War*, 1977), and Michael Herr (*Dispatches*, 1977). What Herr wrote of himself, applies equally well to Stone: "I went to cover the war, and the war covered me."

A Magnificent Keening: Philip Brady

A review of *Phantom Signs: The Muse in Universe City*
(University of Tennessee Press, 2019)

Note: The essay collection by Philip Brady reviewed here gave me sanction to assemble this one. A friend and colleague for nearly two decades, Brady and his partner at Etruscan Press, Bob Mooney (my editor for this collection), met Mailer when he spoke at Wilkes University in 2004, a memorable evening.

A blurb on the back cover of professor-publisher-poet Philip Brady's new book, *Phantom Signs: The Muse in Universe City* describes it as "high-spirited flash memoir." This phrase could lead innocent readers to anticipate juicy tales of the author's life as an American variety of Kingsley Amis's Lucky Jim, a farouche academic who will take us on a frisky ride through the postmodern cultural landscape where we'll encounter eccentric editors and nasty provosts (Brady's particular bogeymen), attend poetry readings, ponder manuscripts and blurbs, get tutored in small press publication, pedagogical conundrums, and literary politics, all of this reamed with apercus about the miseries of social media and technology, remembrances of youthful erotic escapades, and punctuated by mildly astringent appraisals of poets past and present—Homer, Yeats, and H. L. Hix are the book's tutelary

Hippocampus (April 1, 2019)

spirits—as well as comical portraits of fellow litterateurs and beloved family members, the whole shebang battened together by droll wit and admirable forbearance. Brady's dazzling new memoir (he wrote an earlier, more conventional one, *To Prove My Blood*, 2004), is all of these things, but it is the dream-like manner that he employs for the majority of the volume's essays that transforms the volume into something rich and strange.

Here I must make some disclosures: Brady is a friend and colleague, and I make a cameo appearance in the book, although under a different name. At the beginning of the book, I am also included in a four-page list of individuals, some living: Joan Baez, Sheriff Joe Arpaio, LeBron James, to name a few; some dead: Sir Roger Casement, Robert Keeshan (Captain Kangaroo), Virginia Woolf; some ancient: Sappho, Genghis Khan, Gestas (the Bad Thief); and some fictional-mythological: Molly Bloom, Batman, and Osiris King of the Dead, all of whom express their "collective outrage at the usage of our names, monikers, aliases, titles, and appurtenances without notice or permission." The letter serves as a kind of dramatis personae for the volume, in that every one of the 365 named personages have their moment to strut upon the page. It also includes the candid admission that the book "is rife with dubious claims, fake news, jaundiced insinuation, and factual error." Forewarned, the reader buckles up.

But before Brady assumes a new name (Thersites, a disgruntled Greek soldier in the *Iliad*, who tells Commander-in-Chief Agamemnon he wants to go home), and glissades to oneiric realms, he provides an introductory chapter explaining that *Phantom Signs* replaces a conventional memoir of his youth abandoned out of a growing distaste for dealing directly with the "nightmare landscape of terror and humiliation" of a youth so skinny that "the fingers of one hand could encircle a thigh." He was also weary of the earlier book's discursive prose, of sentences that "can't breathe for long away from print," sentences "devoid of mystery." In 2010 after by-pass heart surgery, he finds a new modality for his story while recuperating in a rocking chair. He rocks and thinks, rocks and remembers, rocks and conjures blank verse lines in the manner employed by bards of yore. He also notes his dissatisfaction with another kind of poetry in some of the manuscripts he's read as poetry editor at Etruscan, a small press he co-founded with his friend, novelist Robert Mooney. His characterization of these poems coincides with my own grim recollections of certain poetry readings I prayed would end long before they did. The poems submitted, he says, "were good, but not that good, or all good in the same way":

> a setting and observation about the setting developing into three or four related observations strung together in a short time span; usually walking was involved, sometimes driving. All were rectangular and they began to look like clumsy interpolations translated from the Etruscan and it was mile after loose-stepped mile of chopped prose. Did I say all? Not so. Some were served straight from academic Delphi, where the oracle was deconstructed into semiotic salads (read: language poetry) only a tower-dweller could digest.

Now-heart-healthy Brady explains in the opening chapter of *Phantom Signs* how after surgery he recast his prose memoir into a long narrative poem, *To Banquet with the Ethiopians*, where his painful seventh-grade experiences at a Long Island Police Athletic League Boys' camp are re-imagined as events in the *Odyssey*. Brady's humiliations are akin to those endured by Leopold Bloom in Chapter 15 of James Joyce's *Ulysses*, another memorable re-imagining of the *Odyssey* (the Circe episode), and Bloom is another of Brady's avatars. In one of the most hallucinatory and hilarious chapters of *Banquet*, Homer and Joyce, along with Dante, Pope, and T. S. Eliot drink pints and argue poetry in Nobuddy's Bar below the El in Queens, N.Y., where Brady grew up. Homer, a Yankee cap

hooding his marble eyes, arrives via subway; Ezra Pound pounds
the table and calls for gists and piths. On the wall hangs a signed
glossy of Boss Steinbrenner hugging Agamemnon. You get the idea.
In some chapters, Brady is an adolescent at summer camp, in others
he's grumbling Thersites, and occasionally he's Homer—identities
elide with ease in this phantom poem. His fellow campers (friends
and fiends) are recast as Agamemnon, Achilles, Ulysses, and the
rest. *To Banquet with the Ethiopians* is an astounding, genre-busting,
18-chapter seriocomic marvel that unfolds at the intersection of
myth, memoir, and history, unfurling in time and not, as Brady is
fond of saying. Engraved on the tablets of his capacious memory,
several of the book's chapters are spoken from the stage at the
semi-annual residencies of the Wilkes University MFA Program in
which he teaches, and in other literary venues. It was published
by Broadstone Books in 2015. The book reviewed here, *Phantom
Signs*, is both a gloss of the earlier volume, and a web of tributaries
flowing from it.

Some of the new volumes most successful chapters—there are
18, the same number as in *Banquet* and Joyce's *Ulysses*—are impressionistic portraits of Brady's professors, including Galway Kinnell,
W. D. Snodgrass, and James F. Carens (with whom he edited *Critical Essays on James Joyce's Portrait of the Artist as a Young Man*), and
those of several of his friends: sturdy Mooney (and his ghostly double), poets H. L. Hix and William Heyen, memoirist Carol Moldaw,
and Steve Reese, the acoustic guitarist and leader of Brady's Leap,
a new-Celtic band, in which Brady plays the bodhrán, a small hand
drum known as the heartbeat of traditional Irish music. As for the
band's title, it's the name of a rest stop somewhere on I-80 at which
Brady's mother, "Pet," was once forgotten by her family . . . and
remembered after 20 miles. To this day, Brady stops there in re-
membrance of her.

H. L. Hix, a prolific poet and finalist for the National Book
Award, is Brady's closest poet friend. A dozen of his books have

been published by Etruscan, so many that some believe that Hix is more than merely another of Brady's avatars. No photograph of them together has surfaced, and doubts persist in some quarters of Hix's corporality. I am happy to report that I was privileged to sit for an hour between the two poets in a seminar room beneath a bust of Tennyson, although I must admit that because one was fore and one aft I could not see them together in the prism of my parallax. Hix may not be Brady, but he is at the very least a muse for Brady, who reports various borrowings from Hix's treasury of poetic wisdom. The slogan or epigraph for Etruscan Press, "Nothing attested, everything sung," comes from Hix's 2009 collection, *Incident Light*, published by Etruscan in 2009. The line is the occasion for one of *Phantom Signs'* liveliest chapters, a forensic battle among Hix, Brady, and the shades of two novelists, Norman Mailer and John Gardner. The debate centers on whether attestation, or factual accuracy, on the one hand, "signifies a failure to mix, a hardening of boundaries" or, on the other, is the evidentiary roof tree of story-telling. Aristotle is one of the signatories in the letter at the start of the book, but Brady apparently skipped metaphysics class the day Aristotle's "Principle of Non-contradiction" was discussed. It states: "A thing cannot both be and not be at the same time and the same respect." No matter. Double identities, temporal interleaving, and the morphing of quiddities are the three tent poles of Brady's literary endeavors.

Brady is large, contains multitudes and, like Whitman, worries nought about contradiction. Indeed, the numerous felicities of his book flow from the way many of his 365 characters flout every boundary. Line judge Aristotle may fulminate, but he is over-ruled by Proteus, a higher magistrate. Transmogrification, we could say with justice, is the operative principle of the volume. This is most apparent in the long final chapter, "Nine Phantom Signs," which is both a non-chronological autobiography of the making of a poet, and a lament for the lost time when poets, in the absence of writing instruments and written language, muttered and uttered their songs. Brady and Hix insistently point to the fact that "the alphabet is a technology—the first to which we are exposed, at so young an age that we see it not as a tool but as a source of identity." This technology, first created in the 8th century BCE by the Greeks, gave civilization a new way of recording history, but at the loss of the oral bardic culture that had for millennia conserved the past. The bards were all but wiped out by tablets, papyrus, scrolls, the codex, and the paperback. The Internet, mere pixels, continues the effacement. Much was gained with the alphabet, much lost. *Phantom Signs*, Brady's beguiling multi-generic collection of poems, tales, jokes, gibes, eulogies, rants, pontifications, and memories, explores this contention from nine perspectives in the concluding cumulative chapter. Like the early Irish myths and sagas, his utterances comprise two worlds: one real, tangible, and testamentary; the other (an idealized simulacrum of the first) densely metaphoric, oneiric, and mythic. Again and again in the volume, he summons up the memory of sitting in his rocking chair after surgery composing the poem which became *To Banquet with the Ethiopians*, and then linking it to moments forty years earlier in his parents' row house where his younger self "rocked back and forth in front of the cabinet hi-fi, listening to Father's Clancy Brothers records babble from another world." *Phantom Signs* is a magnificent keening for a time before written history "when lines were conceived and spoken in one breath" and gods walked the earth. In this magical time of pre-history, Brady says, poets composed "right at the vortex of forgetting." Then and now, he concludes, "poetry isn't written; it is the impression left after everything not a poem has dissolved."

Well, it has to be said . . . or uttered: Brady rocks.

Murder, Sex, and the Writing Life: An Interview with Mailer's Biographer by Ronald K. Fried

Note: I met Ron Fried when he was a Mailer Fellow in Provincetown a few years after Mailer died. I was giving a tour of Mailer's house to the Fellows and we hit it off. A novelist and literary journalist, he knows Mailer's work, especially the boxing narratives, as well as anyone I know. He is also the author of a play, The Two Mailers, *based on* The Big Empty *(2009), a collection of conversations between Mailer and his son, John Buffalo.*

It took J. Michael Lennon seven years to write *Norman Mailer: A Double Life*, the 947-page authorized biography of Lennon's longtime friend. But when you think about it, that's pretty fast. Mailer's very public life was as rich in incident as a 19th-century novel, fueled by what his longtime rival and friend Gore Vidal called "an extremely radical imagination." Besides the familiar litany of Mailer's triumphs and humiliations, Lennon read Mailer's almost 50,000 letters and the more than 700 interviews that Mailer gave in his lifetime. And, of course, there's Mailer's 40 books, ranging from the brilliant (*The Naked and the Dead, Armies of the Night,* and *The Executioner's Song*) to the unfortunate (*Death for the Ladies, Marilyn,* and *The Faith of Graffiti*).

Any definitive biography must also treat what Lennon calls the three great crises of Mailer's life: his near-fatal stabbing of his second

The Daily Beast (November 19, 2013)

wife, Adele Morales; his championing of the convict criminal Jack Abbott, who killed an innocent man shortly after Mailer helped Abbott get out of prison; and the near-break-up of Mailer's sixth—and most enduring—marriage when Mailer's ongoing infidelities were revealed. Throw in the four feature films Mailer directed, his six wives and nine children, plus innumerable feuds, friendships, and mistresses, and it's clear that any attempt at writing a definitive life of Mailer is a prodigious—maybe impossible—undertaking.

But Lennon, an emeritus professor of English at Wilkes University in Pennsylvania and president of the Norman Mailer Society, has spent almost a lifetime preparing for the job. He wrote his 1975 doctoral thesis on Mailer, and went on to edit several collections of Mailer's work, as well as a book of interviews with Mailer, *Conversations with Norman Mailer*. Lennon interviewed Mailer at great length, was granted exclusive access to the letters and diaries, and had the cooperation of Mailer's family. The result is a sympathetic but impressively objective narrative which treats Mailer's actions and scandals, his ideas, and literary accomplishments with equal seriousness.

RKF: Do you think that Mailer's celebrity has colored his literary reputation and how your book will be perceived.

JML: I've met dozens, scores, hundreds of people in my life, young and old, who have a received opinion of Mailer based on an article that they read in the *New York Post* or on seeing him on television, when he was not usually at his best. As far as the book is concerned, I am sure there will be reviews that are based on a conclusion about Mailer that was reached a long time ago. My hope is that my book will be able to get beyond that, that people will be able to re-configure, re-perceive Mailer based on the evidence I am bringing up.

RKF: What would you like your book to make people see about Mailer that they don't usually?

JML: I guess his generosity of spirit, his compassion, his interest in people who were not famous. He was interested in people who were famous, absolutely, and he had ideas and opinions and theories about fame and identity and ambition and so forth. But he was also terrifically interested in his neighbors in Provincetown, people he met in bars in Brooklyn, people who just knocked on his door. It was Gay Talese who said that Norman Mailer may be the most accessible famous American writer in the 20th century, because he was never too busy or too high and mighty to talk.

Literary Reputation
RKF: Do you think Mailer's literary legacy suffers because he never wrote a short book that can be assigned to college students?

JML: I think it's a big problem for understanding Mailer. Colleges do not like to teach thousand-page novels. I mean, every sophomore who goes to college in this country reads *The Great Gatsby*, or they'll read *The Scarlet Letter*. Mailer is taught more in journalism, history, American studies, and sociology courses, than he is in English classes.

RKF: How would you assess Mailer's strengths and weaknesses as a novelist?

JML: He's got a great sense of character. Character is his strength. Plot is his weakness. His dialogue is a little soupy sometimes. But his settings are fantastic. His sensitivity to the resonances of nature and place, cityscapes and landscapes, is terrific. His characters are people you remember. His plots are a disaster. He could never figure out how to do them. He always wanted the story to rise out of the character and the plot would take care of itself. Well, it doesn't. It doesn't take care of itself.

RKF: Later in his career, he turned to history with novels about ancient Egypt, the CIA, and Hitler. Do you think that was a way to compensate for the fact that he wasn't that great with plot?

JML: Yes, I do. He wrote a letter to me that said it is impossible to escape and transcend the power of historical events, which are invariably more interesting than fictional ones. But I think he felt very at home with the historical novel, very at home with biography, too.

Omens, Portents, and a Succubus

RKF: In *The Spooky Art*, a wonderful book that you edited in 2003, Mailer said that whatever else it does, a novel reveals the character of the novelist. So what do Norman Mailer's novels reveal about his character?

JML: Well, they reveal that he lived in a numinous world where there were forces all around him. Let's say that not everyone shares that belief today. But he would walk in the room, and the way the furniture was set up would give him a shiver, and he would say, "Something bad is going to happen." He was very open to all sorts of omens, portents, and forces. He was sometimes afraid to go out of the house on the full moon. So he lived in what you almost might say was a medieval world. He had a medieval world view in which there were demons and forces all around him all the time. You know he told me once that he had been oppressed by a succubus. I didn't put it in the book because I didn't have enough to thread it out. It was just a kind of passing remark. He told me that it happened in Provincetown. He pointed to the house. But I could never get him to talk about it in any detail. He said it was a very unpleasant experience. So he lived in that world, and yet he was raised and educated as a rational, thinking Jewish intellectual, Marx and Freud, and Spengler and so forth.

And so he had that rational side to him, and then he had the transcendental side. I think his books reveal that everything about

Mailer is doubled. There are dueling personalities, there are dueling points of view jostling within of all his books and certainly within his own character. He could be the most rational, thoughtful person you ever met, and then he could also sound like you were dealing with a medium sometimes.

RKF: In his books, he's always talking about all these portents and signs, and I can never tell if they're intended metaphorically or literally.

JML: Mailer, if he were here, would say, "Well that's the interesting thing about life, isn't it?"

Mailer and Women
RKF: How do you explain Mailer's astonishing number of mistresses?

JML: Attractive male celebrities are usually followed by a hoard of women. He loved women. He was so terrifically attracted to them. He felt that he needed to learn about himself by being in intimate relations with women. So here's an opportunity to learn about yourself and another person, another way of being. Part of it was just selfish, sensual, sex. The normal drives.

RKF: But wasn't part of it being dishonest to the person he loved most, his sixth wife, Norris Church?

JML: Yes, yes, and of course that was a great lesson for him because when push came to shove he wanted his marriage to Norris to survive more than he wanted to have more affairs with women. The door was shut. He might have fallen off the monogamy wagon a couple of times after that, but I have to tell you, not very much.

RKF: I remember a prominent New York literary woman years ago saying to me, "Norman Mailer is not a father, he is a procreator."

JML: I wouldn't agree with that at all. He was a very good father. He cared deeply about all his kids. They will all tell you that when they had a personal situation, he was there. He was understanding, he was helpful, he listened to them, and he encouraged them mightily in all their pursuits.

RKF: Do you think that Mailer's beef with feminism has had an enduring negative impact on how he is seen?

JML: I think it had a strong impact on how he was seen in the '70s. He said some remarkably stupid things that, you know, were intended to be incendiary and to get a debate going and start an argument. I don't think he was a misogynist. He made some terrible tactical errors in dealing with women. But a lot of what he was saying—and there is a long discussion of it in the book— was because he was worried that everything was going to become unisex. That procreation would become an automated assembly line. Heterosexual romance would die. That's what he was afraid of more than anything. But in the short run, all the things that women wanted, Equal Rights Amendment, equal pay, etc.—he supported all of these. So in a way he got a bum deal, but he certainly pushed himself into that position with the stupid things he said.

Mailer and Violence
RKF: Let's talk about violence. Why did he write so much about murderers? If you sit down and read a dozen of his books in a row, you are spending a lot of time with murderers: Gary Gilmore, Lee Harvey Oswald, Hitler.

JML: Yeah, sure. And *Tough Guys Don't Dance* is all about a murder and it's based on an actual murder case.

RKF: And there's a murder in *An American Dream*.

JML: He was trying to write about the enclaves of goodness and virtue that you will find even in the most horrible people. He went to a women's prison in the early '50s with a psychologist friend, Robert Lindner, and he watched interviews with 15 inmate women. Most of them were in there for violent crimes, stabbing their husbands and things like that, and Mailer was stunned by the beauty of these women's lives. How candid they were. And how, as he said, "crime is just another arrow in their quiver. It's a very natural thing." He said, "I realized then and there that you should never write a person off just because they have committed a crime, even a violent crime. You should try to understand and contextualize. Look to understand the motivation. Look for the hidden virtues even in people like that."

RKF: But I think that there's a perception that he somehow enjoyed violence.

JML: I don't think he enjoyed violence at all. I don't think he liked violence at all.

RKF: We have to talk about Jack Abbott, the convicted murderer Mailer helped get out of jail.

JML: He did not lead the charge to get Abbott out of prison. He was asked to write a letter attesting to Abbott's literary ability. That's all he did. The reason that Abbott got out of jail, was that Abbott snitched on fellow prisoners. That's a fact. The pardon board said, "We examined him and he's passed a psychological test for letting him out." So Mailer was a very small part of it. But people wanted so much for Mailer to have led the effort. They desired it devoutly. But it's not true. Did he help? Yes. Did he then do a lot for Abbott when he got out? Yes. More than anybody? Yes. Did he bring him home for dinner several times? Yes. Norris was helping at every turn. Norris spent more time with Abbott than Mailer did. And Mailer accused himself. He said, "I didn't spend enough time with the guy. I could have done more. I should have seen this. I should have anticipated this. I'm supposed to be good at these things. I should have seen that this guy was falling apart." And he never stopped blaming himself for it. He said, "I am not trying to get out of this. I am responsible. I have blood on my hands."

RKF: Norris's comment, which was in her memoir, was: "You wrote that book about Gary Gilmore, and you didn't learn anything?" Do you think that's fair?

JML: Absolutely. It's a brilliant remark. She understood Norman as well as anybody who ever lived. And she was absolutely right. He didn't heed the lesson of his own book.

Mailer's Legacy
RKF: Do you think his literary style is underappreciated? To me that's what makes him great—his prose style.

JML: I think his prose is the most remarkable thing about him. It's so characteristic of him. I say somewhere in the book that he had two compositional modalities, fast and slow. *The Armies of the Night*, *Miami and the Siege of Chicago*, *Advertisements for Myself*, were written in a white heat, and they're probing, they're self-reflective.

RKF: Ironic.

JML: Ironic, sardonic, and yet he has those beautiful, long Melvillian sentences that roll out, those beautiful long periodic sentences. He had a great ear. He sounded out every sentence. When dictating his letters, he would say everything twice. He would mutter it, then he would utter it. We have all the dictation tapes. Even in his letters he didn't miss a beat.

RKF: Did he find the nonfiction easier to write that fiction?

JML: I think that you could make a strong case, not an iron-clad case, but a strong case, that the books he wrote under pressure with a time limit and a deadline are his best work. *An American Dream, The Armies of the Night, The Executioner's Song.* Arguably his three best books. All written under tremendous pressure. I mean, *Executioner's Song* took eighteen months, 1,000 pages. You could make the case that when he had to do it and was just following his instincts, he wrote his best stuff. When he took his time and tried to figure out his plot—and he didn't have a plot because he didn't have real events he was writing about—in those cases, the books were flawed.

RKF: Do you think that his legacy will be mostly as a novelist or as a writer of nonfiction?

JML: Well, I think we have to call him ambidextrous. He could write fiction and nonfiction with facility, but I guess I have to come down on the side of the nonfiction.

RKF: Now how much did he listen to his editors?

JML: He didn't listen to them at all on strategy. He didn't listen to them on the big picture, on structural elements. He'd listen to anyone on tactical matters. I mean, I corrected mistakes, I pointed out errors. Well, any good writer is going to get tactical advice and take it. But on the big things like, "You got 260 pages on Uruguay in *Harlot's Ghost*, Norman, cut it back," he ignored everybody.

RKF: Might he have been better served if he had listened?

JML: Absolutely. You know, I edited three of Mailer's books for Taschen, and I cut them. And it was with a heavy heart, but as I got into it, I said to myself, "It seems pretty obvious that this needs to be cut back. Cut this back and you can really reveal the great stuff that's inside." I did it for *Marilyn* and *Of A Fire on the Moon* and *The Fight*—I cut less in this one—and I think they read better. Other people can judge whether I am right or wrong. And it's easy for me to say now that Norman isn't alive. You know, I kept looking over my shoulder.

RKF: Why did he leave so many projects unfinished? The sequel to *Harlot's Ghost* is one example.

JML: It was the biggest literary regret of his life that he'd made that promise, "To be continued," and that he could not fulfill it. I think he set the bar so high that he couldn't jump over it. And he was always hearing that train whistle. He wanted to go to new places, do new things. And, therefore, he was unable to finish some projects. He was at his best when he was on the balls of his feet, starting a new project. As he said, "A man in motion always has a chance."

Norman Mailer: Novelist, Journalist, or Historian?

Note: I was invited to write this essay for a special issue of the Journal of Modern Literature *by the issue's editor, John Whalen-Bridge. Along with Robert F. Lucid and Barry Leeds, John and I co-founded the Norman Mailer Society in 2003. The essay is more formal than the rest of the contents of this collection, but steers clear of wooly theory, and presents a cavalcade of Mailer's thoughts on the nature of the novel.*

In *Advertisements for Myself* (1959), Mailer wrote: "I feel that the final purpose of art is to intensify, even, if necessary, to exacerbate the moral consciousness of people. In particular, I think the novel is at its best the most moral of the art forms because it's the most immediate, the most overbearing, if you will. It is the most inescapable." Twenty years later, when Melvyn Bragg asked why he thought fiction was so important, Mailer said, "Oh, because I think it's the place where art and philosophy and adventure finally come together. For me there's nothing more beautiful than a marvelous novel. I love the idea of a novel; to me a novel is better than a reality." In a 1981 interview with Paul Attanasio, later collected in *Pieces and Pontifications* (1982), Mailer hit the same note: "My idea finally is that fiction is a noble pursuit, that ideally it profoundly changes the ways in which people perceive their experience. You know, one Tolstoy, in my mind, is worth maybe 10,000 very good writers."

Journal of Modern Literature 30 (Fall 2006)

Perhaps the most pointed of Mailer's generic comments comes in the preface to his 1976 collection, *Some Honorable Men: Political Conventions, 1960-72*: "Ever since Tom Wolfe began to write those self-serving encomiums to the New Journalism it has been a literary reflex to point to the convention pieces printed here as objects of the new art, and it is possible I received more praise as a new journalist than ever as a novelist. That is an irony that tempts me to spit to the wind: I never worked as a journalist and dislike the profession." After throwing a few more barbs at contemporary journalism, culminating in a comment that his own literary heritage (James T. Farrell, John Steinbeck, John Dos Passos) reminded him "that the world is not supposed to be reassembled by panels of pre-fabricated words," Mailer gives his novelistic credo:

> It was expected of me to see the world with my own eyes and own words. See it by the warp or stance of my character. Which if it could collect into some kind of integrity might be called a style. I was enlisted then on my side of an undeclared war between those modes of perception called journalism and fiction. When it came to accuracy, I was on the side of fiction. I thought fiction could bring us closer to the truth than journalism, which is not to say one should make up facts when writing a story about real people. I would endeavor to get my facts as scrupulously as a reporter. (At least!)

While one can quibble with Mailer's statement that he had never worked as a journalist—he'd written columns and/or assigned articles for a number of popular periodicals, including *Esquire* (over forty) *Village Voice, Life, Parade, Harper's, Commentary*, and *Vanity Fair*—it is true that he'd never worked as a daily deadline journalist. He is, however, one of the leading literary magazinists in American literary history, equal in production to Edmund Wilson, John Updike, and Joan Didion, if not H. L. Mencken. But his comment about receiving more praise for his nonfiction than his fiction has become, in the decades since he made it, even more true.

There is less praise for his fiction by journalists than academic critics, although the proportions are not much different. My survey ranking 416 reviews (1-5, negative to positive) of Mailer's major books (1948-98) in a total of 25 publications—*New York Times, New York Times Book Review, New York Review of Books, New York, Esquire, Village Voice, Time, Nation, Commonweal, Newsweek, New Yorker, Christian Science Monitor, Commentary, National Review, New Leader, New Republic, Saturday Review, Atlantic, Harper's, Boston Globe, Washington Post, Chicago Tribune, Wall Street Journal, Los Angeles Times, San Francisco Chronicle*—bears out the disparity. Of the twenty-seven major books published by Mailer during this period, nine are novels: *The Naked and the Dead* (1948), *Barbary Shore* (1951), *The Deer Park* (1955), *An American Dream* (1965), *Why Are We in Vietnam?* (1967), *Ancient Evenings* (1983), *Tough Guys Don't Dance* (1984), *Harlot's Ghost* (1991), and *The Gospel According to the Son* (1997). Only one of these made the top third of the 25 rankings: *The Naked and the Dead*, has the second highest ranking. It follows Mailer's immensely successful (Pulitzer Prize, Polk Award, National Book Award) first-hand, third-person-personal narrative on the 1967 March on the Pentagon, *The Armies of the Night* (1968), subtitled *History as a Novel, The Novel as History*. The bottom third of the list of twenty-seven books contains six novels, and the middle third has only two: *Why Are We in Vietnam?* in the number thirteen spot, and *Harlot's Ghost* at number fifteen. The record of the literary marketplace, its passing enthusiasms and short-sightedness notwithstanding, over a half-century, 1948-1998, is clear: with the exception of *The Naked and the Dead*, reviewers and, *mutatis mutandis*, readers, have admired Mailer's nonfiction more than his fiction, at least in the period close to publication date. The same is true, for the most part, of academic literary critics, although their opinions would be difficult if not impossible to quantify.

Additional reservations immediately come to the fore. First, the book-buying public is notoriously fickle. Today's bestseller is tomorrow's throwaway. We might ask when the last time Nobel laureate John Galsworthy's *The Forsyte Saga* was taught in an American university, or take note of how much enthusiasm for the works of another Nobel laureate, Sinclair Lewis, has shriveled. We might also remember the poor initial showing of such canonical texts as F. Scott Fitzgerald's *The Great Gatsby*, James Joyce's *Dubliners*, and Virginia Woolf's *Mrs. Dalloway*. Mailer's *An American Dream*, his fourth novel, was generally poorly reviewed, although perceptive critics such as Joan Didion, John W. Aldridge, Tony Tanner, and Barry H. Leeds, rate it as one of his finest narratives; Didion, for instance, compares it favorably to *The Great Gatsby* as a classic New York City novel. *An American Dream*, which was written initially in installments under deadline pressure for *Esquire*, and then revised for book publication, displays Mailer's rich evocative style at its energetic peak, while *The Deer Park* vies with Fitzgerald's *The Last Tycoon* in its depiction of morality in Hollywood Babylon. Mailer's sixth novel, *Why Are We in Vietnam?* is a critical favorite, more for its linguistic inventiveness than for its narrative line. When it appeared in 1967, two years after *An American Dream*, it seemed that Mailer had retrieved the novelistic thread; he was now was ready to re-commence his project, announced in *Advertisements for Myself*, "to hit the longest ball ever to go up into the accelerated hurricane air of our American letters," with a novel that would rank with the best of Hemingway, Theodore Dreiser, and John Dos Passos, whose 1936 novel, *U.S.A.*, Mailer has called "the most successful portrait of America in the first half of the twentieth century." Implicit in Mailer's encomium is his ambition to match Dos Passos's portrait of America with his own portrait of the nation's second half. Mailer wanted to be the sort of major novelist, as he said of these three writers in a 1983 interview with James Campbell, "who puts you through a wringer, changes your life."

But then, unexpectedly, Mailer turned from the novel. From 1968 to 1982, in an astoundingly long sprint, he published twenty books, none of them novels. Some of these were just sparks from the wheel, long essays like *The King of the Hill* (1971), *The Faith of Graffiti* (1974), or collections of previous work: *The Idol and the Octopus* (1968), *The Long Patrol* (1971) and *Pieces and Pontifications* (1982). But eleven of his twenty-seven major works came during this period, including the genre-busting masterpiece, *The Armies of the Night*, as well as his bravura depictions of the 1968 political conventions, the Apollo 11 flight to the Moon, and the Women's Liberation Movement in, respectively, *Miami and the Siege of Chicago* (1968), *Of a Fire on the Moon* (1971), and *The Prisoner of Sex* (1971). In 1979 he produced another masterpiece, *The Executioner's Song*, his western epic about the life and death of Gary Gilmore, which he subtitled "a true life novel." The point bears repeating: excepting *The Executioner's Song*— which in Mailer's view is essentially a novel— he published not one novel from 1968 until 1983 when *Ancient Evenings*, his novel of ancient Egypt, appeared. What happened?

Mailer gave a variety of explanations. He said in 1979, "I'm not sure the Great American Novel can be done anymore. Everything's gotten so complicated, and you have to know so much by now. I think John Dos Passos came as close as anyone with *U.S.A.* He continued, saying that Dos Passos's "method's fine so long as people are more the prey of social forces than the active element that changes society." His method "won't work for books where you really have to create the consciousness of terribly complicated people." In his 1979 interview with Bragg, he says that America in the sixties "was beyond our imaginations, it was more dramatic, more surrealistic, more fanciful, more incredible, more vivid, than anything we would have dared to write about," a remark that recalls what a number of writers—Philip Roth and Tom Wolfe come to mind—said about the dampening of the novelistic impulse induced by the near-apocalyptic events of that decade.

Not only was the material unbelievably good, Mailer found, it also put less strain on narrative faculties. In 1981 he told James McElroy that during that period journalism "was a marvelous way for me to work":

> It was vastly easier than trying to write novels, and I was discouraged with the difficulty of writing them at that point. I had run into this business (in novel writing) of trying to tell a good story and yet say wonderful things about the nature of the world and society, touch all the ultimates, and yet at the same time, have it read like speed. There are so many pitfalls to this. I always had a terrible time with the story. My stories were always ending up begrounded. There I'd be, in the middle of the dunes, no gas in the tank. I loved journalism because it gave me the story, which I'd always been weakest in. Then I discovered the horror of it. Audiences liked it better. They'd all been seeing the same story you'd been seeing and they wanted interpretation. It was those critical faculties that were being called for, rather than one's novelistic gifts. Under all those temptations, I must say I succumbed, and I spent a good many years working at the edge of journalism, because it was so much easier.

In his 1983 interview with Campbell, Mailer explained that he got into journalism by accident when Clay Felker of *Esquire* asked him to cover the 1960 political conventions. "I discovered," he said, "that I had a flair for this kind of thing, and lo-and-behold I was now in journalism. I think I react to situations rather than make decisions . . . I've always found it comfortable to do journalism, but I've also always felt that it was not the high road." Despite his long-held distaste for journalism, it should be noted that of his five books nominated for the National Book Award, only one, *Why Are We in Vietnam?* is a novel. Both of his Pulitzers have been for non-fiction:

The Armies of the Night, as noted earlier, and *The Executioner's Song*, although the Pulitzer for *The Executioner's Song* was awarded in the fictional category, a surprising development given that Mailer has stated over and over again that he never deviated from the known facts of the Gilmore saga, and that the book's real-life plot was a gift. His novelistic impulse when writing it, as he noted in a 1985 interview with Brian Peterson, was to speed up narration, improve dialogue here and there, "until," he said, "it dawned on me that the story was as good as it could be. I realized that God is a much better novelist than the novelist."

Mailer insists there are other factors beside the factuality of a narrative that determine its proper genre. During a 1979 panel discussion on the topic, he reaffirmed his independence on this issue: "I think a writer has the right to call his work whatever he wants to call it. You might say I'm being confusing, but a writer has certain inalienable rights, and one is the right to create confusion." You try to write, he told Karen Jaehne in 1987, "something that defies—no, not defies—that straddles categories. Categories are just critics' attempts to bring order to a complex aesthetic universe . . . These are all forms to be explored, not obeyed," a remark that echoes Bakhtin's statement: "After all, the boundaries between fiction and nonfiction, between literature and nonliterature and so forth are not laid up in heaven."

Before laying out a provisional taxonomy (drawing on Mailer's utterances and Bakhtin's ideas) to further interrogate why Mailer the novelist has devoted so much of his time to what is usually called journalism or narrative history or creative nonfiction, it is worth considering three of Mailer's metaphors for the relationship of the novel and factual narratives. The first came in a 1979 interview with William Buckley Jr. and Jeff Greenfield. Buckley asks a simple question: why did Mailer call *The Executioner's Song* "a true life novel" (a subtitle, it is worth noting, dropped from later editions). Mailer says:

I think of nonfiction as living on two stomachs, like the cow. In other words, the material is eaten, it's partially digested, it's regurgitated and then it's digested again. In other words, in a book of nonfiction, there is a tendency . . . to present the author's conclusions to the reader, and while this is not true for all works of nonfiction, I think it's true for most of them—most serious works of nonfiction . . . (the author) literally digests the material and when he does present a scene, it's as illustrative material to make a difficult passage more simple. And the one thing that nonfiction calls for is understanding—clear understanding of what's being said. It's hard to think of a good book of nonfiction whose waters are not clear. Whereas I think in fiction, what we want to do is we want to create life. We want to give our readers the feeling that they are participating in the life of the characters they're reading about. And to the degree that they're participating in it, they shouldn't necessarily understand everything that's going on any more than we do in life. The moment we understand everything in a book, it can't possibly be fiction . . . not the way I'm defining it.

Mailer's emphasis here is on how the reader works through a novel's surprises with the novelist, a joint operation he endorses. The novels he most admires are compounded of evocations, confusions, possibilities, and mystery. Mailer dislikes novels that are schematic, and prefers suggestiveness to objective description.

In a 1980 *Washington Post* interview with Kevin Bezner, Mailer further developed his metaphor, again in response to a question on the distinction between fiction and nonfiction. He says he wanted *The Executioner's Song* to "read like a novel, to feel like a novel, to smell like a novel." He continued, saying that most nonfiction "bears the same relationship to life as vitamin pills bear to food. In nonfiction, there's a tendency to digest the material, absorb it, and return it to you as vitamin pills. The essence is gotten out of the various experiences, compressed and delivered to the reader. The reader can then digest the nonfiction and convert it back to living reality."

He then makes what at first seems to be a puzzling remark: "Fiction can have two modes, imagined and real. Ideally, fiction gives you the feeling that life is going on, that we are encountering life as we are living it. Nonfiction treats life as if the vividness of the experience is over, and now the meaning of it will be presented to you." It is not immediately clear from this dichotomy whether Mailer favors the "imagined" or the "real" mode of fiction. But in his 1981 interview on this topic with Attansio he makes the matter knottier, while presenting perhaps his sharpest criticism of historians. Attanasio asks him if he thinks the fact/fiction debate is useful:

> I think it's a dumb debate. If a novelist can take someone who's a legendary character and invent episodes for them that seem believable, then they've done something wonderful. There's that meeting between J. P. Morgan and Henry Ford in (E. L. Doctorow's) Ragtime—I think it's one of the best chapters in American literature. It told me an awful lot about Morgan and an awful lot about Henry Ford, and the fact that it obviously never took place made it even more delicious. When you know the kind of bias and warp with which historians write their history—they're dealing with 10,000 facts and they select 300 very careful ones to make their case, and call that stuff history when we all know it's fiction. The mark of a great historian is that he's a great fiction writer. Very few novels are ever true works of the imagination—I mean how many Kafkas have there been?

Mailer, it appears from this statement, believes that "real" novels have recognizable historical settings. The characters of these novels, some imaginary, some real—Morgan and Ford in *Ragtime*, as well as J. Edgar Hoover, Castro, and JFK in *Harlot's Ghost*—live in places one can find on a map, whereas Kafka's beetle lives in a garden of the imagination.

In the same 1981 interview with Attanasio, Mailer says that one of the reasons for the success of *The Executioner's Song* is that it does not have the "paranoid perfection" of writers who don't know how the world works. *The Executioner's Song* succeeded, he says, because "it had all the rough edges of reality. If I had conceived that book in my imagination, it would have been much more perfect and much less good." Coleridge's notion of the imagination as the power that transcends reason and unifies all the faculties is not one that Mailer subscribes to, apparently, although we should remember that from the Renaissance on the definition of the imagination has changed as often as the definition of the novel. When Attanasio brings up Tom Wolfe and his claim that journalism has usurped the place of the novel as the main event in our cultural life, Mailer presents his most acute metaphor on the dichotomy:

> I've said a hundred times that I think journalism is easier than novel writing because you know the story . . . The difficulty of writing a truly impressive novel is equal to asking a singer of the stature of Pavarotti to compose his own music. Journalism makes opera singers of novelists. We've got the story, now all we've got to do is go in and show our vocal cords.

Where does this leave us? I believe Mailer's many comments form a rough-hewn taxonomy, one resting on a fundamental division between the novel on one hand, and all forms of narrative nonfiction, history, and journalism (especially), on the other. For

Mailer the novel is spontaneous, resonant, and intended to illumine questions. History and journalism are pre-digested, concrete, and intended to provide answers to questions they raise. Novels are open, immediate and overbearing; they intensify consciousness and the difficulties of moral choice. History and journalism are lucid and organized; their outcomes are usually predetermined by selected evidence; they deliver buttressed conclusions. In the novel everything is somewhat murky and provisional and when meaning does emerge, it does so in a flash of unexpected but fulfilling brilliance, often a dramatic scene. Conversely, history and journalism are courts where evidence is presented systematically; at the end of the trial, the accretion of linked fact is overwhelming and indisputable. Fiction for Mailer is the high road and its plots are complex and often open-ended. History and journalism are the low road, and their plots are ordered and predictable. Time in the novel accelerates and then dawdles; it moves at no certain speed. In history and journalism, time has been bought, bottled, and labeled. It should be said that this opposition parallels the American romance-British novel dichotomy proposed by Richard Chase in *The American Novel and Its Tradition* (1957).

But there are further divisions, subtler and less remarked on by Mailer. These are the divisions within the genres of both the novel and history/journalism, the minority within each form, which make the dichotomy, in effect, a reversible dualism. Mailer holds that there are two kinds of novel: those based on historical events that take place in recognizable settings, and those that do not and are imagined. Dos Passos, Tolstoy, and Dreiser vs. Kafka, Borges, and Calvino. He calls the former the panoramic novel; the latter, the kind with "paranoid perfection," are fables, fantasies, allegorical tales. The first type, although grounded in historical reality, is indeterminate in structure and plot; the latter, although unfettered from the everyday, is polished and closed, a jeweled box. Mailer favors the first type, but does so in part because history has provided him with the scaffolding of plot. Each of Mailer's first nine novels is precisely set in clearly identified historical moments.

Yet even though Mailer favors the historically based novel, he has reservations about historical narrative because he believes it to be neither unbiased nor comprehensive. Historians marshal their evidence selectively, Mailer feels, thus fictionalizing it. What all this suggests is an oblique, if unintended, contradiction in Mailer's position. On the one hand, he endorses novels stretched on historical frames, using well-known events, for example, the Battle of Kadesh (1200 BCE) in *Ancient Evenings*; the 1962 Cuban Missile Crisis in *Harlot's Ghost*; the Hollywood blacklists of the early 1950s in *The Deer Park*. Only Mailer's murder mystery, *Tough Guys Don't Dance* does not depend on a specific historical event or context—unless it is the cocaine wars of the early 1980s. On the other hand, he states that most historians don't write history at all. In a 1980 interview with me collected in *Pieces and Pontifications* he made this point emphatically. Most people learn, he said, that

> somewhere between high school and college—or is it between graduate school and life? —that history is not history, but a series of immensely sober novels written by men who often don't have large literary talents, and have less to say about the real world than novelists. That's a disturbing discovery. That historians are not dealing with fact, but with the hypothesis they developed in relation to a series of isolated data. The desire to make these facts glow as facets in a mosaic that will enable us to perceive the past is not often done. Once we come to realize that no historians do it more closely than novelists, then all history becomes a novel.

Mailer's reversible dualism derives from his understandable unwillingness to fully or formally endorse any prescriptive definitions of narrative forms. He is an enthusiast for whatever form is closest to hand and like a good street debater can score points at will when arguing for its merits and weaknesses. When he wrote an introduction to his collected short stories in early 1967, he had not yet begun *Why Are We in Vietnam?* Readers of the introduction must have been puzzled by his deprecation of the short story, but Mailer, at this point, needed to throttle any residual interest he might have in it so that he could get back to "the high road": the novel. Speaking of himself in the third person personal, as he soon would in *The Armies of the Night*, he demeans the very stories he introduces:

> The short story bores him a little. He will admit he rarely reads them. He is, in secret, not fond of writers who work at short stories. Nor are they often, he suspects, fond of him. He has a private sneer for the reputations they have amassed. There is a terrible confession to make: he thinks the short story is relatively easy to write. You only have to be good for a day or a week—there is none of that arduous collaboration between character and passion, inspiration and asceticism, which goes into keeping one's balance on the teeter-totter of a novel where work goes on day after day through many a season into the years. Anyone can be good for a week, but who can be good for a year, or two, or three?

Mailer does not certify any narrative form—excepting Platonic notions of the novel—with finality. As a connoisseur of narrative forms, he does not willingly jettison anything from the tool kit he has assembled over fifty years, and he has surprised readers for decades with his narrative inventions, bringing out new variants every few years. To the frustration of some critics, he has refused to confine himself to one room in the house of narrative.

When assembling his mammoth retrospective anthology, *The Time of our Time* (1998), Mailer struggled with the order of the book.

He had selected separate excerpts from all of his major works as well as nearly forgotten items from magazines and literary anthologies, 136 all told. As he reports in the anthology's "Acknowledgments and Appreciations," he told his editor, Jason Epstein, that he wanted the volume "to offer some hint at a social and cultural history over these last fifty years." But he found that the two obvious ways of arranging the excerpts, both to be unsatisfactory. The first was topical: "Should one put together an anthology of excerpts from one's novels, a file of essays on politics and philosophy, some poetry and set-pieces full of place, plus journalism, action, drama, speculation, fulmination, theology?" The "final effect" of this method, he concluded, would be "equal to a row of potted plants." The other obvious course would be to assemble it "in the order published—a useful presentation for a biographer." But doing so would undercut Mailer's desire, as he put it, "to keep some emphasis on what was written rather than on how one had lived while managing, incidentally, to be a writer." Sensitive, no doubt, to the perception that Mailer the man often eclipsed Mailer the writer, he wanted to avoid tracing, year by year, the tumultuous line of his career. "It would be wise," therefore, "to keep to the background." As he still had a lot of writing to do, he also wanted to avoid any hint that the volume was the final consolidation of his life's work, thus a tombstone. Finally, he hit on a solution:

> I would not have to attach each episode to the year in which it was written, no, it would be better to connect it to the year I was writing about. If in 1990 I wrote about 1951, why, then, place the piece back in 1951. The perceptions of a man no longer young could be posed against insights the writer had once set down decades earlier.

Although Mailer violated his own principle by including excerpts from two novels set in the distant past—*Ancient Evenings* and

The Gospel According to the Son—the scheme is intact for the greater part of the collection. In "Acknowledgments and Appreciations" he notes that his unusual—and perhaps unprecedented—solution made *The Time of Our Time* "an out-of-category volume influenced by one of the most monumental works of American Literature, nothing less than *U.S.A.*, by John Dos Passos." He does not explicitly claim that his book does for the second half of the twentieth century what *U.S.A.* does for the first, but the volume stakes his claim.

No careful comparison/contrast of these two exemplars of the novel as super-genre is possible in this essay, but it is a job worth undertaking. A few points can be made. The two texts are of a size: Mailer's at 1286 pages and Dos Passos's at 1449 pages. Both use every story-telling mode available and worry not at all about rapid shifts in narrative focus. Film techniques are adapted by both writers, most notably by Dos Passos who uses the movie newsreel and "camera eye," and the front page of newspapers, as well as capsule biographies of the great figures of the age—J. P. Morgan, FDR, John Reed, and Samuel Insull, to name a few—interspersed with fictional characters. He employs a variety of points of view, and ranges freely in time and space, although generally following a forward chronology.

The Time of Our Time begins with an excerpt from his review of Morley Callaghan's *That Summer in Paris*, an account of Hemingway, Fitzgerald, and other expatriates during the year 1929 (whether planned by Mailer or not, this date precedes by a few years the closing years covered in *U.S.A.*, thus linking the chronologies of the two books). Mailer then turns to a memoir of his Harvard years, moves to excerpts from *The Naked and the Dead* and *An American Dream* that describe World War II combat, followed by an autobiographical account of his difficulties with the fame brought by his first novel. Then comes a comic portrait of Dorothy Parker, excerpts from *Barbary Shore*, *The Deer Park*, and *Harlot's Ghost* dealing with the Cold War, which segue into a fragment describing his experience watching early live broadcasts of the *Steve Allen Show*, and a biographical sketch of a Mexican matador whom Mailer saw perform in 1954. The entire collection goes on just like this, with the exception of the two removals to the distant past mentioned earlier. Book reviews morph into character sketches that dissolve into periodical columns, sports reportage, interviews, public debates, profiles of writers and polemical essays—"The White Negro" (1957) being the most prominent. There is a speech against the Vietnam War given at Berkeley in 1965, long excerpts from the great nonfiction narratives of 1968-1975, a passionate debate with Kate Millet about Henry Miller and D. H. Lawrence (his finest piece of literary criticism), and open letters to Fidel Castro and Salman Rushdie. Several major political figures—JFK, Bobby Kennedy, LBJ, Eugene McCarthy, Nixon, Henry Kissinger, John Ehrlichman, McGovern, Dole, and Clinton—are profiled, as are Marilyn Monroe and Muhammad Ali. The reader soon forgets what form is being essayed in the delight of the unfolding historical cavalcade, one that very much recalls Dos Passos's novel. Mailer's primary purpose here is not to blur genre so much as to "engulf and ingest" (to borrow Bakhtin's verbs) whatever form, stance, or rhetoric needed to carry the story forward to the century's end. If it is also his implicit purpose to demonstrate that, for a novelist in the time of our time, there is no real difference between fact and fiction, he succeeds.

Works Cited:

M. M. Bakhtin. *The Dialogic Imagination. Four Essays*. Trans. Caryl Emerson and Michael Holquist. Austin: University of Texas Press, 1981.

Bloom, Harold. "Norman Mailer's Testament." Review of *The Time of Our Time*. *Washington Post*, May 24, 1988.

Doctorow, E.L. *Ragtime*. NY: Random House, 1975.

Dos Passos, John. *U.S.A.* Edited by Townsend Ludington. NY: Library of America, 1996.

Jaehne, Karen. "Tough Guys' Two Left Feet." *Film Comment* 23, July-August, 1987, 11-17.

"John Dos Passos: A Centennial Commemoration." *Dictionary of Literary Biography Yearbook, 1996.* Detroit: Gale, 1996, 173.

Mailer, Norman. *Advertisements for Myself.* NY: Putnam's, 1959.

___. Interview with Paul Attanasio. *Pieces and Pontifications.* Edited by J. Michael Lennon. Boston: Little, Brown, 1982, 129-36.

___. Interview with Robert Begiebing. *Conversations with Norman Mailer.* Edited by J. Michael Lennon. Jackson: University Press of Mississippi, 1988, 306-29.

___. Interview with Melvyn Bragg. *Conversations with Norman Mailer,* 193-206.

___. Interview with William Buckley Jr. and Jeff Greenfield. *Conversations with Norman Mailer,* 228-51.

___. Interview with J. Michael Lennon. *Pieces and Pontifications,* 163-71.

___. Interview with James McElroy. *Pieces and Pontifications,* 172-82.

___. "Mailer Admits Someone's Better." Interview with Brian Peterson. *Grand Forks* (North Dakota) *Herald,* March 22, 1985, A1, A8.

___. "Making Ends Meet." Interview with James Campbell. *Literary Review,* July 1983, 28-31.

___. *The Short Fiction of Norman Mailer.* NY: Dell, 1967.

___. *Some Honorable Men: Political Conventions, 1960-1972.* Boston: Little, Brown, 1976.

___. "Talking with Mailer." Interview with Paul Attanasio. *Harvard Crimson* (Fall Book Supplement), October 1979, 1, 8, 22-23.

___. *The Time of Our Time.* NY: Random House, 1998.

Schwartz, Tony. "Is New Mailer Book Fiction, in Fact?" *New York Times,* October 26 1979, C24.

Mailer's Last Days

Note: The following are excerpts, lightly edited, from a journal I kept from June 2005 to shortly after Mailer's death on November 10, 2007. Most of the italic entries are followed by my later thoughts in Roman.

Heart Surgery, July 12-15, 2005

Tomorrow Norman goes to Mass General for tests on his heart. No mention lately of the possibility of an operation. On the dining room table was an email from someone telling him of the advantages of a nitroglycerin patch: "six hours of regular heart rate." The patch, I assume, would replace the nitro pills he pops all the time. I don't like this patch thing at all, but understand why he would consider it: to avoid dying on an operating table. He'd rather take the chance with the patch...

Spoke to Norris last night and she said the doctors told Norman that he needs operations on his heart and his two knees. His response: "After I finish the novel." We joked that the only way she could get him to have the operations would be if she encouraged him not to have them. My theology interviews with him convince me that there is another, perhaps the deciding, factor. He feels his after-death status will be enhanced significantly if he is lucid and sane and sharp when he gets on the bus, to use his metaphor. Dying with his eyes open, so to speak, will affect his reincarnation. His avidity for another life will influence the monitoring angels who oversee the process. These angels are overworked bureaucrats and he needs to make his presence, his desires, known to them.

(2020)

We got on the subject of Norman's clothes: Norris said that when he finds a piece of clothing he likes, "he wears it until it falls off his back." He is not the slightest bit interested in how he looks to others (Has he ever used a comb; does he own one?). Last year he became attached to a pair of black, shin-high, pigskin boots, Uggs. He wears them without socks and, he told me, they never stink. All through the past winter and fall his invariable costume was these boots, a sweat suit, and a black felt vest given to him by Russell Crowe. I rarely saw him in anything else when he was home, and assume that Norris had to wrestle his clothes away from him to wash them. As the weather grew warmer, he started wearing shorts and a short-sleeved shirt, but stuck with the boots. One day a few weeks ago he had on a pink shirt, blue jean shorts worn high over his belly, and the Uggs, now sporting a piece of duct tape to heal a split at the back seams. His sons, Matt and John, had a good laugh describing this costume to a visitor. Norman doesn't give a shit. When he travels to do a talk, he usually wears a blue blazer, but hardly ever a tie, although he brings one. He jams everything in his bag like a college kid and worries not at all about wrinkles. When he was younger, he regularly wore a pinstripe suit with a vest, like a banker. His explanation for this choice, given in some interview, is that if one could not distinguish oneself in matters of dress, the best course is to wear something fairly conservative, thus the pinstripes.

Because of *The Fight*, Mailer's account of the 1974 Muhammad Ali-George Foreman heavyweight championship match in Zaire, and a much-celebrated earlier essay, "Ten Thousand Words a Minute," Mailer was well established as a shrewd commentator on the chess-like strategies of "the sweet science," and over the years got to know a lot of boxers, including Sonny Liston and Jake LaMotta, on whom he based the character of Romeo in *An American Dream* (1965). He also appeared on talk shows several times with Muhammad Ali and José Torres. In 2004 Russell Crowe was cast in a Ron Howard film, "Cinderella Man," as James J. Braddock, heavyweight champ

Provincetown, 2005. *Photo by Christina Pabst.*

from 1935-37. Howard hired Mailer as a consultant and flew him to Canada where Crowe was learning to comport himself like a professional boxer. Mailer's assignment was to talk about the boxers of the 1930s Braddock fought, including Joe Louis, Max Baer, and Art Lasky, loading Crowe up with boxing lore and legend. Mailer spent an enjoyable week with the film crew and various trainers and coaches talking about Braddock's matches and the styles of the fighters. He told me that his paycheck for the gig—$100K—was the easiest money he'd ever earned. When he left, he was given one of the felt vests all the film crew received. It had the name and dates of Crowe's training camp in white letters on the front. He wore it almost daily for the next three years. When Norris had to pick out his coffin clothes, she selected the vest, an easy decision that the family applauded.

September 4-October 23, 2005
Picked Norman up for breakfast at Chach's in P-Town. He has decided to have the heart operation, probably later in September. He has had heart problems for about ten years. He feels that the novel (The Castle in the Forest, 2007) *is good enough to be published almost as it stands, at about 600 manuscript pages, or "three-fourths of a novel," he says. He gave me a hard copy of the manuscript with instructions about getting it published by Random House if he died on the operation table. His working title is "Hitler's Devil," a reference to the narrator, Dieter, a servant of Satan, who is referred to as E.O., or Evil One. He's not committed to this title, and mentioned other names, including "Satanic Voice." He'll undoubtedly come up with several more. Our interview book* (On God: An Uncommon Conversation) *could follow the novel, he agreed. Why did he decide on having the operation? His heart doctor is pressing him, as is his local physician. He knows that Norris and his kids want him to have it, and that he could die anytime without it. He's not entirely at ease with the decision though. He told me, "Having my blood pumped out of me and sloshing around in a machine, running through loops of plastic is an unhappy prospect..."*

Norman had a successful quadruple by-pass operation on September 8, and he is in the ICU recovering...

Over the last week Norman has continued to improve, and today he is scheduled to move from Mass General to a rehab facility in Sandwich. I spoke to him on the phone on the morning of the 16th, and he said that the operation was the most powerful experience he has had since he was drafted in 1943. I told him he sounded different, wild and orphic. "That's accurate," he answered. "I saw God and the Devil, angels and demons in some definitive way, but now I can't remember a damn thing about it," he said with a chuckle. The operation brought him closer to Norris, although he was troubled by how much she worried, worried about many small things, like her mother and money. Then he rang off. I received a number of calls and emails from friends and Mailer admirers, including E. L. Doctorow, as news of his operation seeped out...

Norman's nephew, Peter Alson, was married on the 17th to his longtime girlfriend, Alice O'Neill, on the low-tide flats behind the Mailer home in P.Town, I officiated (after getting ordained online in the Universal Life Church) in the symbolic ceremony; they were legally married a few days earlier by the town clerk. Norman wasn't there, but all nine Mailer siblings were present, perhaps for the first time. Poems by Cummings, Graves, Lawrence, and a letter from Rilke were read during the ceremony. Stephen Mailer sang a funny, bawdy song he wrote, "Butt Cheeks on the Gesso," about his idea of taking photos of all nine kids imprinting their bare asses on gesso, a kind of plaster of paris used by artists, and then packaging them for sale with the song. There might have been more to it than this; I don't remember all the details. After much spirited discussion, the idea sank when some of the siblings gave it lukewarm support and Norman argued strenuously against it. The situation led to a temporary breach between Stephen and his dad. But Stephen's bravura rendition of the song at the wedding brought great laughter.

Norman's opposition is belied by the fact that he likes to irritate and embarrass his family by singing two crude comic songs he has written, "Bodily Function Blues" (written when he was in college), and "Alimony

Blues," as well as the World War II song about Hitler's single testicle, sung to the tune of the "Colonel Bogey March": "Hitler has only got one ball/Göring has two but very small/Himmler is very sim'lar/but poor old Goebbels has no balls at all." So, objecting to Stephen's butt cheeks song seems unfair. Good for the goose, good for the gander.

About 75 people attended the ceremony, which went off at low tide around six p.m. Neighbors along the beach watched from their porches as Peter McEachern, Danielle's boyfriend, led the crowd out on the flats in a light mist as he played a jazzy number on his trombone. Sasha Lazard, Michael's wife, sang an 18th century Italian love song. I recited the traditional vows and said (as solemnly as I could), "I pronounce you man and wife." Many thought I was a genuine minister of some sort, and congratulated me on my performance. "I am a faux minister," I replied.

Later, we all ate and drank and talked. I sat with Mailer's daughter Betsy for a while and she spoke of how bitter her mom, Adele, still is about Norman and the stabbing. "I think she still loves him though," Betsy said. Shortly after Adele published her memoir, The Last Party, in 1997, Betsy said, she talked with her father about the book, the stabbing, and his feelings. She said that Norman cried and said, "I let God down." Betsy said Adele was still seeking some kind of formal apology. I told her that he made a formal statement in his 1998 collection, The Time of Our Time, a statement she said she has never read. Indeed, she did not know of its existence, nor did her sister Danielle, according to Betsy. The Mailer children are not necessarily aware of what their father has written. If Danielle and Betsy knew of the statement ("The Shadow of the Crime"), it might have assuaged some of the pain of "The Trouble," as Norman's friends refer to the stabbing. But then, who would tell them about the statement? Norman usually gives them a copy of his books, but I know from conversations with them over the years that they have a spotty knowledge of his work. My sons have not read all of my books, so I should not be surprised. When you are related to a writer, reading his or her books is something on the back burner...

Big news today: Norman will be given a lifetime achievement award by the National Book Foundation on November 17th. It was announced in *the Times and Reuters. I called Norman in Sandwich to congratulate him. He sounded more like himself, but is still wired. He said he thought it was coming at the appropriate time, that is, after Roth and Updike had received the same award. Well, he is probably correct. Norman rankles people. He is always out there talking a blue streak at the end of a limb, as someone once said, and making as many friends as enemies on a given day. It's likely that there was opposition to him at first, while Roth and Updike sailed through. He released the following yesterday, September 22: "I have always believed in good writers accepting awards. I therefore admit to being pleased at the National Book Foundation Award. At the moment my head is still coming together around the open-heart surgery, so I would rather wait a few weeks before commenting further. The function of the novelist is not well understood as yet. I believe the state of the novel is affected by the minds of the best novelists. I would love to talk about that at a press conference at a future date."*

When Jean-Paul Sartre turned down the Nobel Prize for Literature in 1964, saying that he did not want to be "institutionalized," Mailer surprised me by criticizing his decision. After all, he had long esteemed Sartre, and like him, despised being seen as an ornament of the Establishment. He explained his disagreement with Sartre's decision in a speech after he received the National Book Award in 1969 for *The Armies of the Night*, which he opened by saying, "Your speaker is here to state that he likes prizes, honors, and awards, and will accept them." Then he shifted to Sartre: "The most bourgeois elements in French society had been speaking of him for years as Jean-Paul Sartre, perverted existentialist, and would continue to do so. How much better for the final subtleties of their brain if they had been obliged to think of him as Jean-Paul Sartre, perverted existentialist *and* Nobel Prize winner. An entrance might have been made into the complexity of his decision." I see now, after writing his biography, that Mailer's disapproval of Sartre's refusal of the Nobel was seated in his belief that choices made for both good and not-so-good, even venal, motives are those most likely not to rankle either God or the Devil. The cosmic balance is maintained. The strategic plans of the Lord and the Evil One are impenetrable, beyond human ken, and hedging one's bets, therefore, is prudent. Who could say if by accepting the National Book Award that I, Norman Mailer, would advance or impair (however infinitesimally) some foray by the Lord of Heaven in the cosmic struggle with the Lord of Hades?

Texas hold 'em, January 21, 2006

Finished reading the final 100 pages of the Castle *manuscript around noon yesterday, and delivered them today to Norman. He asked if there was anything that bothered me. I told him that I was troubled that the American officer (a Jewish psychiatrist, medical officer) had a pistol, and left it in front of him on the table when interrogating D.T., an SS Officer. He resisted this, but I could see that my point had been taken. We chatted about the German word for toilet paper (*Klosettpapier*), and the date that electricity was introduced in Germany (after 1914 for most homes). He liked the changes I had suggested for the first 140 pages of the final section, although I have not seen the corrected Ms. yet. We agreed that I'd come over for pizza at six and then we would go to Jimmy D's in Eastham to play poker. Norris is away.*

On the drive over, Norman went over all the ways the novel might be received. Out of long experience, he is preparing himself for every possibility, and spoke in great detail of what might and might not be admired in the novel. I'm certain that the excremental excesses of the young Hitler will not be loved, but he disagreed. "Excrement," he said, "comes before language and is always with us." He is confident that the character of Hitler's father, Alois, will be appreciated and thinks his mother, Klara, may be the best-drawn "good" character he has ever portrayed. "Of course," he said. "I haven't had that many 'good' women in my novels." I offered Elena in The Deer Park *and he acquiesced. Deborah in* An America Dream, *no saint, may be his most memorably depicted woman character; his nuanced depiction of Marilyn Monroe in* Marilyn *is another contender.*

We got to Jimmy D's around 7:40. Norman was eager to play. The buy-in was $25 and there were 33 players. The top four would get back about 2/3 of the entry $$$. There were four tables, three green and one red and Norman was seated at the red one, which he disliked. We both had only one drink at dinner and were alert. Norman was the second one out; he had difficulty seeing and hearing; the lighting was poor and the jukebox was blaring. I couldn't see the cards very well either, but they were running for me and I advanced well. After getting knocked out, he chatted with the local characters—most of the folks in the bar knew who he was—and kibitzed at my elbow. He was tired but kept sipping his drinks and cheering me on. When we left, he said, "I told myself, Mailer, have some character and don't hope Mike loses so you can get home to bed." We went over the final hands in detail on the drive back around; he kept telling me I played very well (I came in third and won $100), but in truth I played tentatively and won only because the river ran my way. He also gave me his latest hypothesis on why Texas hold 'em is so popular. He said it is because it enables players to exercise both paranoiac and anti-paranoiac tendencies, which are often buried. When we attempt to surmise who is bluffing, the former is put into play; the latter, a counter-force of sober reason, cross-examines such surmises. Going "all in" is akin to using an unused muscle. I helped Norman in, put out the lights, and went home around 12:30.

During Norman's last two years, Norris spent more and more time at the Brooklyn Heights apartment. She wrote to me in an email that she was "tired of rattling around the Provincetown house while Norman rattles around in his head." It was true. Norman spent the better part of every day until a few months before his death in his third-floor study. She also told me that she wanted to put the P-Town house on the market and then perhaps buy a waterfront apartment where he could stay. Donna and I sympathized with her, but knew she felt badly about leaving him alone. He hated it. I recall one gloomy winter day that last year when Norris was leaving for a long stretch, two or three weeks. Norman got irritated about the way Donna was packing the car, but then went in the house. He and Norris had already argued to a stalemate. When he came back out, he sat the front stoop watching in silence, and Donna saw tears on his face as Norris got ready to leave.

Norris loved New York, loved seeing her friends and her sons John and Matt and her grandchildren, and more so in the winter. As Mailer wrote in *Tough Guys Don't Dance*, Provincetown's population shot up daily in summertime from thirty thousand to sixty, but in the winter, "it settled down to its honest sediment, three thousand souls, and on empty weekday afternoons you might have said the true number of inhabitants must be thirty men and women, all hiding." It was a fine time and place to be a writer, or any artist who needed quiet, but depressing for civilians.

Whenever Norris was in New York, I went daily to 627 Commercial, arriving around ten when Norman was finishing his breakfast and doing crossword puzzles. His mood, overall, was medium grim. We'd go over edits on a manuscript or page proof, or deal with some literary query or invitation in the mail. Often, he'd sign copies of his work that my friends had sent to me for that purpose. Over the years, I must have asked him to sign hundreds of books and magazines. Invariably, after he finished, he'd open one of the books and read it for five-ten minutes. He said it was the only time he ever read his books after publication. Book signing always cheered him up.

After his heart operation in the fall of 2005, we spent a lot of time discussing the two books nearing completion: the Hitler novel, still unnamed, and *On God*, our collection of ten conversations about his spiritual beliefs. He had read Elaine Pagels's *The Gnostic Gospels,* and was attracted by the Gnostics' idea of the demiurge as the cosmic artist, the creator, and also their belief in the transmigration of souls. He thoroughly enjoyed speculating on the complexities of karmic reassignment, and would brighten considerably when anticipating the afterlife meeting where he would get his new identity. I must have heard him tell the same joke about this encounter a dozen times. It goes like this: Mailer appears before the monitoring angel at the Pearly Gates, who greets him.

"Oh, Mr. Mailer, we've heard so much about you and have been anticipating your arrival. It's so good to meet you! Please, tell me what you are hoping for in reincarnation." Mailer replies that he wants to come back as a Black athlete. The angel's tone changes.

"Oh, Mr. Mailer, we are terrifically over-subscribed for that identity. Let me see what we have you down for." He checks his assignment log.

"I'm so sorry Mr. Mailer, but we have you down for cockroach." Downcast, Mailer is silent. Then, reading further down, the angel says, "But here's some good news. You'll be the fastest cockroach in the neighborhood."

September 19-24, 2006, Provincetown

Donna and I have had dinner at the Mailers several times the past two weeks, usually followed by a Texas hold 'em game with some local friends and whatever Mailer family members were visiting. But a couple of times a week, we eat out at Norman's favorite restaurant, Michael Shay's, down the road about 100 yards. The Mailers are well known there and have their own table and waitress. Norman always orders a dozen oysters for an appetizer and then studies the shells, looking for a human face. I asked him once as he studied what he saw, and he said, "It seems to be a Greek warrior." He finds a face on at least half of them, and after the meal the waiter boxes them up. The next day he cleans them and then puts them out to bleach on the deck overlooking the harbor. There is a big pile. Later on, Norris highlights the features of the faces with her paints. He is thinking about a small book containing photos of the shells, and his commentary on the transmigration of souls...

There's a flock of pigeons that roosts on the roof of the Mailer home, perhaps 30-40. The flock swoops about the big brick house and uses it as its daylight landing zone. Norman watches them from his porch fronting the beach—hard not to as they are always whirling about. The birds' formation flying has led him to conclude that they embody the spirits of Army Air Force pilots; another proof of reincarnation. Norman is an Emersonian: all natural facts have spiritual correspondences. The difference between him and Emerson is that he sees demonic links as often as angelic or human ones. He lives in a double world: half naturalistic, half super-natural.

The dust jacket proof for his Hitler novel, The Castle in the Forest arrived today; it's finally locked up. He rejected the suggested jacket designs his publisher sent him and produced his own: a sketch of a castle archway with a swastika at the peak. Random House gave it to an artist who put Norman's name and the novel's title in the black space within the arch. It's lugubrious looking, with signs of age and decay about the dank stonework. I love it. He told us at lunch that the Germans will publish the new novel, but the swastika has to go, not only on the German edition, but also on all European editions, in keeping with the anti-Nazi laws over there. He has no idea what the German response to the novel will be.

He's now reading books on Himmler and thinking hard about the next volume, the sequel. With the promotional tour for the novel before him, he knows he can't begin it yet, but he is making notes and researching. He talked today about Göering and Himmler, how the former saw "the world as a pigsty and he wanted to be the king of the pigs," and how the latter was "a wonk, a nerd, and a monster," and also a repressed homosexual. Norman believes that the Nazis were both attracted to homosexuality and also determined to eliminate it. The book he's reading now is about Heinrich Himmler's quasi-scientific search for the roots of Aryan-Nordic peoples. He finds that it supports his depiction of Himmler in The Castle in the Forest. He said that Göering, Himmler, and Goebbels were just as fascinating to him as Hitler, and that he had already blocked out how he would write the second volume. The problem, however, is that it already seems somewhat stale to him. Disaffection with large continuing projects has been a career-long problem, he readily admitted. Generally, he is more enthusiastic about the conception of a book than its execution. His tentative plan now is to start with the rise and fall of Rasputin, whose supervising demon will be a major minion of the Devil, Dieter, or D. T., and then switch back to Hitler's adolescence and carry the story forward to the late 1920s or early 30s. I asked him once what were the proportions of good and evil in Rasputin, and he said, "Fifty-fifty, and that's why I love him as a character."

We talked about the interview I did with him two weeks ago on Castle, and I suggested editing his comment about Melville believing that white is the color of evil—not Melville's point—to say evil is more sinister when it is white. He agreed. We also agreed that we would go together to Bob Lifton's annual symposium in Wellfleet next weekend. Norman said he wanted to read a piece he'd just written for Nation on Sartre to "the assembled atheistic liberals" at the meeting. I said something from the new novel would probably work better . . .

Norman returned from the dentist in New York on the 21st, toothless, and unhappy about it. He said that the loss of one's uppers is a hard thing for one's vanity. It will be six months until he can have the permanent teeth put in again. In the meantime, he will use his old bridge, which is glued in daily. Because he fears the bridge may slip out when he is speaking, he asked me to read from Castle at the Lifton symposium, which begins tomorrow and is scheduled to run for three days . . .

We drove to Wellfleet three days running, beginning after lunch on the 22nd. About 50 people attended, including Jane Fonda and Daniel Ellsberg. Most are academics, mainly from psychology and history, but with some literary types and theologians as well. The theme this year was evil, right up Norman's alley. Papers were given on the Nazis, on Dante, and on the origins of the Geneva Convention. Bush and Cheney were attacked at every turn as the conferees are all anti-war. No one was more passionate than Ellsberg, who is deeply worried about Israel attacking Iran and fomenting a nuclear war. He lectured us, hectored us, more than he took part in a dialogue.

On Sunday morning, Norman gave a brief introduction and then I read ten pages, a chapter in which the narrator, a demon with the human identity of one Dieter, an SS officer, explains his position in the cosmic war between a limited God and a powerful Devil. Norman noted that this was the first public reading of the novel. I went a bit too fast at the outset and Norman slowed me down. It was hard to keep up a good rhythm with him beside me, shifting in his chair and clucking when I mispronounced a word. The chapter he'd selected was dense, and I didn't think his theological ideas would resonate much with this group of (mainly) anti-war non-believers, but they seemed to like it. Jane Fonda clearly did. She gave Norman a big kiss and told him she was "thrilled." He replied, "I wanted to give you a thrill."

October 6, 2006

Donna and I had a fine lunch at the Wellfleet bookstore and seafood restaurant with Norman and Hans Hanitschek, a loud, funny, irrepressible Austrian journalist he'd known for years. We first went into the bookstore and after a few moments the staff—an old lady and a middle-aged guy—recognized Norman and pulled out a copy of the 1969 Life Magazine containing an excerpt from Of a Fire on the Moon. A color photo of him fills the cover. Hans bought it for $20. Then lunch in the restaurant. It was raining fairly hard and Norman and I got soaked coming in. We got a table and ordered a drink as the rain came down on the saltwater lagoon outside. Norman wanted oysters, the famous Wellfleet oysters, so did Hans. We got a table right in the middle of the room, which held about 25 other diners, mainly older Wellfleeters out for a Friday seafood lunch. While we waited for our meals, Norman told a story about his British publisher, George Weidenfeld, and K. K., a beautiful blonde heiress. NM lusted after her, and thought she was attracted to him, he said. But after three hours together, she said, "Goodnight Norman," and went off with Weidenfeld. This was in the early '80s. Hans then informed us that Weidenfeld was famously endowed, and that his member had a valuable twist to it. Norman: "An S-shape?"

Hans: "No, sort of a half moon." Hans went on in his blustery voice to explain that Americans mis-pronounce "penis." "They call it a pee-NUS," he said, and then repeated it three times for emphasis. This got the attention of the other diners. Norman laughed so hard that his false teeth loosened. He took them out, wiped them with his napkin, and pulled out a long tube of dentifrice glue and applied it liberally. He said he usually does this in the restroom, but "What the hell." The Wellfleet locals, most of whom recognized him, enjoyed the whole scene. The sun came out and we all enjoyed our shellfish and chowders. Norman bagged all of his dozen oyster shells for later examination, and those of Hans too. Hans asked Norman if he would ever write a memoir. Norman said no, but if he did, it would be from the point of view of his six wives, with Norris's chapter being the longest and most important. He is always thinking about narrative form and—especially—point of view. What a wonderful book it would make! I must pursue this with him. Perhaps he could dictate it to me.

Hans left for New York in his car and Norman, Donna and I took the long road back and through the Wellfleet and Truro woods near the ocean—a lovely area, bleak and beautiful with scrub oak and pine trees covered with lichen. Norman said that Random House will use the interview I did with him on the Hitler novel, but it will not go to reviewers, only to bookstores and others.

**"Hitler on My Mind: The Roots of *The Castle in the Forest*"
first appeared in *Provincetown Arts* (2008).**

JML: Can you say something about *The Castle in the Forest* as a way of perceiving history? How is it different from other historical novels?

NM: I think the large difference is embodied in the narrator. Off hand, I can't name a serious novel where an Assistant to the Devil is the one to tell the tale, but I found the choice curiously liberating. It allowed me to enter people's minds at will, which is of course one of the strengths of 19th century fiction. You can go into any mind the author chooses to enter, and so are able to live with the characters as they appear on the surface, and also as they feel within. Of course, those novels were corseted by 19th century moral strictures. Sexual lines of inquiry were hardly pursued.

Now, I did use the third-person omniscient in *The Naked and the Dead*. I went into everyone's head without worrying about it unduly. It never occurred to me that this had become an aesthetic problem. The success of *The Naked and the Dead* obliged me, however, to become more sensitive to the improbability of casual omniscience. Obviously if I was going to keep writing fiction, I had to develop a bit. I will say that ever since, I've been preoccupied with the problem. I certainly wrestled with it in *The Deer Park*. How do you inhabit more than one person's mind? How do you avoid the manacles of the first person observer without violating something ineffable in the presentation? So I was delighted when, behold, I had this Assistant to the Devil ready to tell the tale. Because then you could certainly explore your character's minds, not the least of whom would be young Adolf Hitler.

JML: What percentage, roughly, of the figures in *The Castle in the Forest* actually lived?

NM: All of the major figures but one. I don't like to specify who it is because that can affect the reading of a book. It's as if one of the legs of someone walking by has just been shortened. Now, he's limping in some odd fashion. You don't want to do that to a reader. I should answer your question, however. I'll have to face it, after all, in future interviews. The only major character who is wholly imaginary is Der Alte, the beekeeper. Alois Hitler, Adolf's father, did keep bees in Hafeld, and so must have known a few apiarists in the area. I never came across anything in my research that suggested there was or was not such a person, but I felt his presence was necessary. I also became fascinated with the subject—beekeeping soon took over its own portion of the book. While there are certain symbols in a novel that are explained by the author, or just about— Jake Barnes's wound in *The Sun Also Rises* or Ahab's white whale— white, for example, was declared by Melville to be on occasion an essence of evil even more intense than the absence of light. Most symbols are not so clearly delineated. The power of a symbol isn't always to be delineated by language. Sometimes, it is more evocative as an undefined presence.

JML: Is it fair to say that Hitler's father, Alois, is equal in importance to Hitler himself in your novel?

NM: Maybe more so. I'm truly fond of writing about a character when I don't dominate their development. He or she will show a few vices and virtues I wasn't quite prepared for. As my friend, Jean Malaquais, once said, "The only time I know the truth is at the point of my pen." I find that one of the awards of writing. It is as if you are actually encountering reality which will then show you how to make the next move.

JML: Did you do the same kind of research for this novel as you did in the Picasso biography or on *The Gospel According to the Son?*

NM: Or for *Harlot's Ghost...*

JML: Or *Harlot's Ghost.*

NM: I always do as much research as my temperament can digest. Seven years went into *Harlot's Ghost* and eleven years on *Ancient Evenings.* For *Oswald's Tale,* I needed two full years of research. On *Castle,* I spent four years, the last two while writing it. I had already read everything I could find about Hitler's childhood, of which, incidentally, there are not too many books. Not in English at any rate. I also read every major work on his adult life that has been translated and quite a number of minor ones. The bibliography is not brief. If you are going to follow someone through their adolescence, it helps to know how they turned out later.

JML: Was any one book indispensable to your research?

NM: Three or four on his childhood were important. In the bibliography I've given an asterisk to those, and to a few works that had nothing to do with his childhood but did give me a grasp of later events.

JML: One of the strongest episodes in the novel concerns the coronation of Tsar Nicholas II of Russia in 1896. What was the reason for such an inclusion?

NM: I felt that I had to move away from the subject matter, and do it in dramatic fashion. To be fixed entirely on Adolf Hitler's childhood was going to limit the dimensions of the work. Moreover, the narrator, D. T., the Assistant to the Devil, needed his own action. As an invisible participant, he is much more important to the outcome of the coronation of Nicholas II than he is in Hafeld or the other areas of Austria where the novel takes place. Finally, when you've been doing fiction for as long as I have, you are readier to follow your instinct. The coronation of Nicholas II may yet be seen as necessary preparation for the next novel. Now, at the age of 83, I won't make any promises, but if I can keep working for the next few years and complete the second volume, I confess that I would like to have Rasputin in it. D. T.—my Assistant to the Devil—will also work with Rasputin.

JML: The theme of incest is very strong in the novel. Did you emphasize it, or were you just following material?

NM: There is no explanation of Hitler without assuming some very large differences between him and other human beings. One of these possibilities is incestuous roots. I take that to the point of assuming that his mother was the daughter of his father. There is some likelihood of that. Moreover, the occasion on which he was conceived is treated as extraordinary. I have felt for a long time— and this is where a great many people who read our interview will part company with me altogether—but I expect that God and the Devil, or their representatives if you will, are present in any sexual intercourse that is exceptional. So, I propose that the conception of Adolf Hitler did take place with the Devil present, even as Christians believe that Gabriel was there when Mary was impregnated. If any man has ever been a whole opposite to Christ, it was Adolf Hitler.

JML: My last question comes from Donna, my wife. She said, "Norman is Jewish and is writing about Hitler. How much does his Jewish identity have to do with his desire to write this book?"

NM: Everything. Hitler has been in my mind since I was nine years old. By 1932, my mother was already sensitive, and intensely so, to the dangers he presented. After Hitler came to power in 1933, everything that happened in Nazi Germany used to cause my mother pain. It was as if she knew in advance what was going to occur. She'd grown up with a knowledge of the anti-Semitism her father had had to face in Lithuania. Then, as a child going to school in Long Branch, New Jersey, kids on the street would call her "Christ killer"—no surprise, then, if Hitler was immensely real to her. Finally, he took over a portion of my existence. Many people have little comprehension of what it means to lose half of the millions of people who dwell in your fold of humanity. The Irish have some sharp sense of that considering what they suffered in the potato famine. The Armenians have it. But generally speaking, the average Wasp or well-established Catholic in America does not really understand the depth of the effect. In the main, they do feel antipathetic by now to anti-Semitism, and it is true that any prominent politician who uttered an anti-Semitic remark today would probably see his political career seriously injured. Yet, this is not necessarily equal to understanding how deep a negative presence was Hitler to the Jews of my parents' generation and to mine as well. So, this is a book that I've wanted to begin for the last fifty years. I would go so far as to say I've always assumed that sooner or later I would have to write it.

Mailer's mood dampened noticeably after the Wellfleet conference, and got worse after he made the final changes to the novel, published on his birthday, January 31, 2007. He made some appearances through the spring of 2007, but then became listless, sleeping 18 hours a day. His appetite was gone, and on many a day he would eat only a Dove bar and some oysters. Booze was out, except for an occasional 50-50 glass of orange juice and red wine. Dwayne, his assistant, ordered him cans of Mary Kitchen's Roast Beef Hash, which he remembered from his childhood, and he tried that a few times. By the summer, he was down to 130 pounds. All of his family and several old friends visited, and that cheered him, but by September 8 when I married his daughter Maggie to John Wendling on the flats behind 627, it was clear that he needed to be hospitalized. Two days before the wedding, his daughter Susan and Dwayne (who has some Indian blood) and I had a conversation with him about the way elderly Eskimos and Indians wandered into the woods when they saw the end was near. Mailer asked:

"But how would they die?"

"By not eating or drinking," one of us answered.

"Or eaten by a wild beast," Susan said.

"That would be the way to go," he said, "fighting a wild animal. I am whipped by Time."

Mailer's last public appearance, Lincoln Center, July 22, 2007.

October 3-5, 2007: Mt. Sinai Hospital

Norris was making pancakes and I was drinking coffee. Norman was still in bed. It was the morning of the day he would check in to Mt. Sinai for surgery on his collapsed lung. I didn't hear the door open and when I turned, he was standing a few feet away, naked. I may have gasped. "If you could see the look on your face," he said. As I took in his sunken chest with the long scar from his bypass operation, his wild hair and thin limbs, Lear's line, "a poor, bare, forked animal," came to me. Although I had known him for 35 years, I had never seen him completely unclothed, unaccommodated. His blue eyes glared at me as he turned to the bathroom.

He was testy and picked at his breakfast. Soon after, saying he was tired, he took a nap. He'd been like this for weeks, alert and approachable for only a few hours a day. In the late afternoon Jynne Martin, the publicity person from Random House, came by for a discussion of the impending book launch of On God. *From the summer of 2003, when we began recording our discussions about God and the Devil and related topics, the plan had been for the book to come out in the indeterminate future, perhaps posthumously. But when Norman realized the full extent of his ailments— he underwent open heart surgery two years ago—and has major lung and stomach problems, an 80-pound weight loss over the previous year, not to mention macular degeneration, bum knees, hearing loss, and a lesion on his pancreas—he decided the book should come out "before I get on the bus." Random House was eager to have another Mailer book after* The Castle in the Forest *made the* Times *best seller list a few months earlier.*

Jynne was cheerful and upbeat during our discussion of how the new book would be received, and Norman perked up, telling stories, and making obscene cracks—the old Mailer. But he hardly ate a bite of the delicious Chinese food Norris had ordered, and while we ate and chatted, he looked intently out the big windows at the Manhattan skyline across the East River as if memorizing it. John Buffalo, his youngest, arrived and around seven, with John below and me above, Norman lowered himself carefully down four flights of stairs, and the four of us left Brooklyn in two cars for the hospital. Planning to do some writing, Norman brought a bag containing several books on Hitler and Rasputin. When he arrived with John, he was railing about the "soulless" modern architecture of the hospital, one of his long-time exasperations. After check-in, he argued with the nurse about how many sleeping pills he could take. When he autographed an advance copy of On God for my sisters, it occurred to me it might be the only one he would sign. Surgery was scheduled for mid-morning, and he had to be up at 4:30 for prep, so we would not see him until after surgery. Norris was fretful when she kissed him goodbye.

The following day, the surgeon found us, now joined by Schiller, in the hospital cafeteria. She said the operation, which took three hours, went well, and the lung had been re-inflated. She then presented Norris with a color photo of his sundered chest before the procedure: the collapsed lung was bed-sheet white, the other, berry-red. She explained matter of factly that the white was scar or rind tissue that she had cut away. No one spoke. The photo was startling, a bizarre trespass, but we now have a palpable sense of Norman's wheezing and puffing. His heart was strong throughout the operation, the doctor said, and we could see him later that afternoon. Over the next two hours, Norman's sister Barbara and several of Norman's nine children arrived.

Larry and I went in together after the family. We knew each other slightly, and mainly through Norman, whom we met separately in the fall of 1972. The first time I met Schiller was at Mailer's 75th birthday party in the Rainbow Room of Rockefeller Center. I'm from the academic side; Larry is a media entrepreneur. He is a journalistic Zelig, the hustler who won the rights to tell the stories of several famous-infamous figures—O. J. Simpson, Lee Harvey Oswald, the spy Robert Hanssen, and most famously, Gary Gilmore. A world-class interviewer and photographer (with one good eye), Larry's greatest coup, arguably, was producing most of the 18,000 pages of interviews with double murderer Gilmore and his Utah circle of friends and enemies, a trove that Mailer smelted down into his 1979 masterpiece, The Executioner's Song, gaining him his second Pulitzer. Schiller is Mailer's most important collaborator on both book and film projects. I'm his archivist, the editor of a few of his books, and a collection of scholarly essays on his work. We see his writing and reputation from different angles, and are slightly wary of each other.

Norman, still woozy from the drugs, was effusive, although his mouth was full of tubes and it was difficult to understand him. He told us that he'd had a dream when under anesthesia about a coming world crisis. In it, Larry was the Devil. Norman was God, and had entered into a pact with his ancient enemy to rid the world of technology. We laughed as he expanded on the dream. When the nurse, a young woman, came in he began to flirt with her. He told her that she should write a novel, and open it with an account of her meeting with a famous author (as it turned out, the nurse did aspire to write and later gave Norman some of her prose). Then Norris returned, and he told her that the nurse was going to "drain ink from my veins." He was quite merry.

More visitors arrived the following day, including the rest of his children, except Stephen, who was in a play on the West Coast. Norman's pain killers had been reduced, and he was only mildly exhilarated. Prognosis, the docs said, was good. The collapsed lung, they surmised, had lowered the oxygen level in his blood, weakening him and dampening his appetite, which put him in a downward spiral. For months he has been sleeping more, eating less. Now there is hope.

October 10, 2007

Norris called this afternoon from the hospital and she was blue. Norman wants to come home to Provincetown. He asked her to have my nephew, a Cape Cod doctor, to somehow finagle things so he could be transferred to the Hyannis hospital. From there he can sneak home. "He wants to die in P-Town," she said. She told me that he has lymphoma of the stomach (cancer), but that it's treatable with antibiotics, and he also has pneumonia. The odds are not great that he can beat all these problems, especially since he is losing his desire to live. He hasn't turned his face to the wall yet, but can this be far away?

Norman apologized to her for not being more sympathetic when she was ill with cancer. He thought she was being weak; he was peeved with her for *being sick. Now he knows, he said. I'd love to talk to him, but there is no possibility of doing so now.*

People are arriving in P-Town for the Mailer Society conference and the phone has been ringing all day. Ed Setrakian and Sam Coppola arrive on Friday and will act in Norman's one-act play, Earl and Lyndon, *on Saturday night. They have performed it before at Actors Studio. It was Norman's idea to present it not long before he went into Mt. Sinai.*

Everyone wants to know what his condition and chances are, but mum's the word. Best to be vague right now; he could bounce back. He may have a few more rounds in him. But Norris is beat and Norman is a real handful, insisting that she be there at the hospital all the time.

October 17, 2007

The Mailer Society conference went well. A record 105 registered. The debate between Chief Justice Warren (played by Setrakian) and President Lyndon Johnson (played by Coppola) surprised everyone with its mixture of LBJ's barnyard humor and the polite demurrals of Warren, who LBJ is leaning on to head up what would become the Warren Commission. The play's grasp of the eerie Zeitgeist of the period right after the assassination brought it all back. It was a polished reading by two pros.

At breakfast on Sunday, we had a fine recap session and I appointed a committee to research future locations for the conference. But we will return to P-town next October—how could we not, with Norman lying flat on his back in the hospital. We want him to know that we expect to see him back here next year.

*Norris is having a rough time. Norman wants her at his bedside every minute and is upset when she is not. Her mother broke her toe and she had to handle this, as well as running the house, paying the bills and answering a million phone calls and emails. She is going to try to go to Chicago to do a reading from her new novel (*Cheap Diamonds*) later this week; it would be a welcome break for her. The kids are all helping and visiting the old guy. Norris just emailed me to say that there was a story in the New York Post today that quoted (Mailer's fifth wife) Carol Stevens about Norman* being hospitalized, but the reporter never mentioned her, Norris. Norris's centrality in his life is obvious and strong, but it gets overlooked more than a little, and she gets upset, feels marginalized. Everyone wants a piece of Norman; everyone wants to be seen as his intimate friend.

I emailed Norris to say that Donna and I would like to visit with him again next week and she said of course, so we will go into the City on the 24th after the conference on the March on the Pentagon at Georgetown, and a reading from On God in Wilkes-Barre.

First review is in and it is negative. David Ulin in the L.A. Times says the book is not worth reading. His review is quite dismissive. There have been some nice comments in various blogs and on the web site of the Strand Bookstore in New York, but little else. On publication day, October 16, it was listed as being in 2,786th place on Amazon, not a bad start.

Norris emailed me again to forward an email from Norman's agent noting that the God book is going into a second printing. Demand must be strong based on Norman's reputation because there has only been one review. Norman's daughter-in-law, Salina, Matt's wife, emailed to say that AP is calling her and she is tamping down speculation that Norman is in a perilous state. She is also setting up screening for visitors at Mt. Sinai, in the wake of the Post story. Things will be breaking all week, I'm guessing.

October 27, 2007

We returned to Massachusetts yesterday after visiting with Norman on the 24th and 25th. He looked better. But he is despondent and told Norris that he wants to pull all the tubes and wires out and go to P-Town to die. Communication with him is very difficult as he has a tracheostomy and can only mouth words. He is too weak to write legibly, but he was able to ask in writing, while Donna held the pad, when we were going to P-Town. He pointed at the word "P-Town," and then himself, indicating that he wanted to go with us. Norris is disturbed by his condition and tired from the strain of going every day to the hospital and then visiting her mother; she rides in cabs for several hours a day and it is draining. She said they just sit and look at each other, yet he doesn't want her to leave. She fears that he will be in a near-vegetative state with a stomach plug for food and a ventilator for breathing, unable to eat, talk, read, or write. Their close friend, Pat Lawford Kennedy, was in a similar condition for five years before succumbing. Today, however, Norris emailed to say that John Buffalo had a serious talk with the docs and they do believe he will be able to speak and eat and write again.

Roller coaster is the simile everyone has been using to describe the emotional state of family and friends over the past three weeks. Seeing one of the most ferocious, intense communicators of the last 100 years, the man who has written 40 books and been interviewed a thousand times, locked into silence by his ailments, is heart-breaking. The look in his eyes is woeful. He is angry and very frustrated that we can't read his chicken scratches. We spent several hours with him on both days.

His sister Barbara has been there regularly, and his children, and the ever-faithful Larry Schiller. Now there is a guard at the door of his room to keep out the crazies. A holistic healer tried to get in and the guard turned him away, as he did others who arrived with flowers and cards. Norris finally created a list for the guard with names of families and friends who could visit. One friend, whose name was not on the list, tried to get in by saying he was Mailer's brother. The expense for security must be huge. Norman sleeps a great deal, but does look stronger now that they are pumping calories into him via both a feeding tube and intravenously. One doc told me that his stomach lymphoma has kept him from eating. He also has congestive heart disease, edema, and had a touch of pneumonia. What a tough bird. He told his nephew, Peter Alson, "My ass feels like Iraq."

He was hungry for book news, and I gave him all I could: On God is in a second printing; it will be reviewed in the Times Book Review; I gave a reading at the Barnes & Noble in Wilkes-Barre and 50 copies were sold; the Georgetown conference on the March on the Pentagon organized by Maureen Corrigan had gone well and the President of Georgetown University had toasted him at the closing dinner. Everyone cheered. I told him that the Times had cited On God in its on-line *blog about books. TLS has also written it up and the Boston Globe is supposed to do something with it. Norman perked up a bit at all this news.*

October 28, 2007

To properly understand Mailer, you must see him in opposition to something: a trend, movement, person, or party. It need not be something he loathes– George W. Bush, fundamentalism, or plastic–it is often something he admires, but not unreservedly. He is contrarian always, running against the grain, up the stream. When an idea is presented, his immediate instinct is to peck holes in it, undercut, refute, or demolish.

Everyone is anticipating his demise. We are thinking about a special issue of The Mailer Review, *memorial services in New York and P-Town, wills, the tombstone inscription, and posthumous publications. Not in any crass way, but naturally, so as to be prepared. But he may fool us all and bounce back as he has done so many times over his long life. I'd love to see him prancing and fulminating on television once again. His editor, David Ebershoff, said that Norman's inability to do interviews is hurting sales of* On God. *On publication day, it was at 2,786th place on Amazon; today it was in 12,032nd place at mid-day. We need some major reviews, even negative ones, to get the word out.*

Norris and the family agreed on the inscription for his tombstone, his favorite line from *The Deer Park*: "There was that law of life, so cruel and so just, that one must grow or pay more for remaining the same." Norris died three years after Norman, and is buried next to him in the Provincetown Cemetery.

October 29, 2007

The memory of Norman lying in a hospital bed is haunting me. His eyes looked so sad. Unable to communicate, he nevertheless mouths the words, points, gesticulates, uses his hairy eyebrows. But mainly he just stares, locked into silence. Norris emailed twice late last night, the last time at midnight, to say that they had operated on him for an infection in the vein in his groin area where they take blood. They were successful, but are leaving the wound open to heal instead of stitching it up—they don't want to have to go in again. Another insult to the body.

I called Norris around 9:30 to see how he was and offered to help bring him to P-Town, if it comes to that. She said the boys, John and Michael, had romantic ideas about doing this, but that it was out of the question because he would have no one to care for him there. She is right of course. He'll return to P-Town only to be buried. But I am being too gloomy about his chances. The surgeon who operated on his lungs is still involved and still optimistic. She says he can come back. I just don't know if he wants to. And the other docs have not given up, but then each of them has responsibility for only one or two organs. No one is in charge of the full corpus, it seems. Norris has said several times that he has told her that he wants to rip out all the tubes and die.

November 14, 2007

Norman died on November 10, 2007 at 4:30 a.m. after 39 days in the hospital. Until a few days before he got on the bus, the doctors were holding out hope. Norris was not as sanguine; she saw him slipping day by day. His son Stephen was with him when he died and said that his father opened his eyes and smiled brightly before he went over. The cause of death was acute renal failure, but it was probably lymphoma of the stomach that did it, with lung and heart complications. Undiagnosed for months, back to March, the stomach cancer wasted him. One doc told me that his stomach was a churning mess, making swallowing very difficult. Even when his lung was re-inflated and he was fed via a stomach tube, he was not able to bounce back. He knew he was going and tried to pull out the tubes; they had to tie his arms down.

I saw him last on November 8, about 32 hours before he died. I was there with Norris and Barbara Wasserman, and then John came. I told Norman that an excerpt from the God book was the lead article in Playboy. He nodded and his eyes lit up a bit when I told him. Norris read him a page of it. She told him, "You were here before and you will be here again," and later that he was "the bravest man I've ever known." All of his children and many friends visited him in the hospital; some could not bear to come. Norris was there almost every day. It's worn her down to a fine point.

Michael Mailer called me at 6:15 a.m. on the 10th to tell me he was gone, and Norris called a few minutes later. Then Larry Schiller had me certify to the Associated Press that he had died. Larry said he wanted me to be out front so as to inform the media that I was the authorized biographer. Larry has taken over most of the planning for the visitation and the funeral; he hired off-duty cops and a pool reporter; he bought a cell phone and recorded a message I wrote; he was at Norris's side all the time with advice on handling the media.

About 200 paid respects at McHoul's funeral home in P-Town on the 12th, mainly locals. His agent Jeff Posternak, and his editor, David Ebershoff, were there, along with many other friends, and all the family. John Buffalo put the ace of spades in one of father's pockets, and Donna put a white poker chip in another. He was embalmed earlier in New York, and they slicked his hair down, making him look much different. The funeral director fluffed it up a bit.

I had a fierce kidney stone attack after leaving the funeral home and Donna called 911. We arranged for Larry to be the M.C. at the funeral if I couldn't, but the urologist at the Hyannis Hospital blasted it out. One way or another, Norman dislodged that stone from my kidney. Home from the hospital, I had hundreds of emails and phone messages about the funeral. Reporters began arriving in P-Town. I checked Amazon and On God had moved into 426th place. All of his books took big jumps, led by The Naked and the Dead (87th), The Executioner's Song (163rd), and The Armies of the Night (443rd). Norman would have loved this news, I know it.

Speaking at the grave were several of his children: Michael, Danielle, John, and Stephen. Also, his nephew Peter, his lawyer, Ivan Fisher, Dick and Doris Goodwin, Tom Piazza, Doug Brinkley, Congressman Neal Abercrombie, and Larry Schiller. Danielle's husband Peter played J. J. Johnson's "Lament" on his trombone, and Michael's wife, Sasha Lazard, sang an Irish lullaby. We threw handfuls of sand on his coffin. I closed the ceremony by saying, "Earth receive an honored guest; Norman Mailer is laid to rest." Norris was poised and serene throughout. She graciously posed for photos for the flock of reporters who were there, and answered a few questions. After that, she invited everyone back to the house for food and drink, including two former wives, Beverly Bentley and Carol Stevens. Michael, John, and I met again with reporters at the Provincetown Theater and answered more questions. Back at the house, the mood was generally subdued, punctuated with funny stories about Norman. Two of his favorite restaurants, Pepe's and Front Street, provided the food, gratis. Norris sat in the living room and spoke to all who came, one by one, a remarkable performance. I was tired and sick and Donna and I left early.

Larry Schiller called this morning to list all that must be done: a memorial book; a memorial service (Norris wants it at Carnegie Hall on their birthday, January 31st); collecting of all the obits and tributes; discussions about making the house at 627 Commercial a writers' retreat, perhaps run by the Mailer Society. Right now, I'm too tired to deal with any of this. Norris wants to go to dinner with us tonight to talk about selling her home, and other matters. Norman's death was on the front page of most of the newspapers in the world, and there were tributes on all the major networks. Last night Charlie Rose reprised his appearances on his show; he has been on the Rose show 11 times. Everyone is exhausted right now.

November 18, 2007

Norris has agreed that the memorial should not take place until early April, based on the recommendations of Larry Schiller and her agent, Ike Williams. An April event will give us time to plan, line up notables, and put together a media presentation. She has been offered a free theater on Broadway, but prefers to use Carnegie Hall. Random House will underwrite the rental and be deeply involved. Norris wants Schiller and me to produce the event, with help from the family and others. She drove by herself from P-Town to Brooklyn yesterday and asked me to call again today.

Now that Norman is on the bus, it is time to end this Mailer Log. Without him, without his words and presence, his wonderful, meddling, opinionated, generous, carnal, rambunctious self, there seems no point in going on. The armature of my reflections and reports is gone. But Norman will still be felt, towering over us like great Caesar's ghost.

December 7, 2007

We are collecting all the many tributes and essays of homage for a future memorial volume. There a few nasty attacks: Roger Kimball's in New Criterion *was especially mean and I hope he rots in hell for it. There were some memorable insights in the obits, but most were written based on the clip file so the same stories about Norman stabbing his second wife, Adele, and the fight with Gore Vidal were trotted out again and again. But there were some exceptions. Fr. Gene Kennedy wrote a marvelous piece, and there were moving remarks from Joan Didion, Tom Wolfe, and Gay Talese.*

None of the tributes had much purchase on Norman's need to get involved in so many public "stunts," as he called them; there was little recognition of the fact that after The Naked and the Dead *it was nearly impossible for him to be the quiet observer of life he had previously been. His fame prevented such a stance, and he lurched into public life as a celebrity and then observed how others reacted to him. He needed more and more new experience to fuel his creative engine, and so he tried to recreate, again and again, his personality in public. Sitting back and watching the world go by was not really possible given his gambling instincts, his desire to have his say on so many public issues and events, and his insatiable need for new material. His self-exposure and acting out eventually forced him to create new narrative forms and stances, especially describing himself in the third-person personal in that run of books from 1968-75. His celebrity shaped his oeuvre, re-fashioned his personality, even though one part of him despised the gong show world of celebrity life. He needed the action and the action needed him.*

No other important writer of the past 50 years appeared on more talk shows, wrote as many letters to the editor, contributed to more magazines, got in more fights, feuds, and imbroglios and yet was able to return to that third-floor study in P.Town and write productively for long months before sallying forth again. After a while, it became a pattern: finish a book, go on the book tour, accept invitations for all sorts of public adventures, get drunk, get in scrapes, and then go back to the writing desk. It never really stopped, not until the very end, and he was planning in the weeks before he was hospitalized to spend $200K of the income from the sale of his papers to the University of Texas to direct a new version of The Deer Park: A Play, in P-town, with Michael Mailer as the producer. When I told him that I thought we ought to wait to publish On God so as to aid all those who needed it down the road to fathom his work, he instantly demurred and said, "Fuck that; I want it out there because there is a one-in-ten chance that it will change the way people think about the nature of good and evil, God and the Devil." His motives for pushing his ideas into public view were not merely to gain experience; he also wanted to change consciousness. He never gave up on that.

December 8, 2007

I woke up early this morning with thoughts of Mailer, his life, and career. In Armies of the Night, Mailer said his genius was to "mobilize on the instant," and this is so true. Lock him in a room and tell him to come out with a book in a month and he'd do it. He was dynamite when he had a deadline. But give him ten years and he'd extend the narrative endlessly, quitting only when he was physically, psychologically, and financially exhausted. The creation of the canonical figure, Norman Mailer, as Harold Bloom and others have noted, may be his greatest achievement. He never wrote the great American novel, but he came close, assaulting the mountain from a dozen different angles, and enlarging our notions of narrative possibility in every case. Norman was a connoisseur of narrative forms and techniques, a tactical wizard, but not a strategic architect. His theology of a universe divided between God and the Devil made it inevitable that his endings were open-ended and truncated. When he abandoned one project, he quickly immersed himself in another— he was our most accomplished quick-change artist, and always, as he once put it, the loudest street debater.

* * *

Shortly after ending my journal, Donna and I, Norris, and Larry Schiller, began working with the staff at Random House on plans for Mailer's memorial at Carnegie Hall. It went off as scheduled on April 9, 2008. Over 2,000 people attended the program—open to the public—which lasted almost three hours. Several writer friends spoke, including Joan Didion, Don DeLillo, Tina Brown, and William Kennedy. Sean Penn made a surprise appearance and read his tribute from his Blackberry. I spoke about Mailer's core identity of novelist, and Larry Schiller recalled how Norman had diagnosed his dyslexia when they were doing research on Lee Harvey Oswald in Minsk. All of his immediate family members spoke, and his son Stephen, after announcing that he was the family "wild card," stole the show when he channeled his father, falling to the floor as his father's spirit assumed control. There was a murmur in the crowd when Didion, speaking in a husky whisper, said, "I can think of no other writer who risked so much—and brought it home." At the end, "Autumn in New York" played by Sonny Stitt came over the loudspeaker, and most of the crowd remained to hear the end of one of Norman's favorite songs.

Fathers and Sons

. . . who in his own backyard
Has not opened his heart to the smiling
Secret he cannot quote?
Which goes to show that the Bard
Was sober when he wrote
That this world of fact we love
Is unsubstantial stuff;
All the rest is silence
On the other side of the wall;
And the silence ripeness,
And the ripeness all.
            —W. H. Auden, "The Stage Manager to the Critics"

In August 1975, Donna and I spent three days visiting Mailer and his family in Sorrento, Maine, not far from Bar Harbor. They were renting a large house called "Fortune Rock," the former home of Wells Fargo heiress, Clara Fargo Thomas, who died in 1970. One wing of the house hangs over Somes Sound, the fjord that almost bisects Mt. Desert Island. At low tide, you can see the rocks beneath the cantilevered deck. At high tide, there is a 20-foot jump into 10 feet of water. Eventually, most of the Mailers took the leap. The huge tides and the dramatic view of the fjord's entrance seven miles away, coupled with stories about ghosts in Clara's closets, attracted Mailer. He liked to test himself by walking

(2021)

along the deck railings, which horrified his family. Fortune Rock appealed to Mailer in several ways.

Our visit was the first time I met some of his children and Carol Stevens, his future fifth wife, who was standing at the kitchen counter making coleslaw when we arrived. We also met his mother Fan, a formidable presence who, at first, regarded us askance. When, over dinner, a visiting reporter from *People* magazine referred to Carol as Mrs. Mailer, Fan interrupted him: "I am the *only* Mrs. Mailer in this house," she stated with slap of the table. Donna was awed by Fan, by Norman, and by Carol, a stunning Elizabeth Taylor look-alike and a respected jazz singer who'd worked with Bill Evans and the Modern Jazz Quartet, awed to the point of actually losing her voice when we first arrived. We were impressed with the teamwork of three of Mailer's teenage daughters, Danielle, Betsy, and Kate, who did most of the cooking and watched over their two rambunctious brothers, Michael and Stephen, who were 11 and 9, and Maggie, Norman and Carol's daughter, who was 4.

Norman was present sporadically, and kept disappearing into his writing room to conduct business on the phone. We did share several meals and I had an hour-long discussion with him about the burial practices of the pharaohs, which he was researching for his novel-in-progress, *Ancient Evenings*. We also played a game of chess; he beat me easily. And he zoomed off several times in his Porsche to pick up lobsters or go to the post office—or so he said. The following summer I learned that he had snuck off to see Norris, later his sixth wife, who he had stashed in a nearby motel. When we arrived in 1976, Norris was making coleslaw in the same spot where Carol had stood the year before. These visits to chez Mailer were the beginning of my education in how Norman finessed his clashing commitments.

It is quite possible I was anticipating my father's death when I wrote in my thank you note after the 1975 visit: "For Donna the visit was like meeting, *mutatis mutandis*, the father of her husband after nine years of marriage. She gave a lot to me and my dissertation on you over the years and accumulated, I'm sure, eleven varieties of intuition as to what you were like." Not long after writing this note, my real father had an alcoholic relapse after swearing off drink for about 18 months. He was in the habit of telling his doctor, that he, the doctor, was the *real* alcoholic, and that he, John C. Lennon, knew how to handle the sauce.

My younger brother Peter and I flew back to Massachusetts from Illinois in late November. We went immediately to his hospital bedside along with our twin sisters, Kathleen and Maureen, and my mother. Dad could only whisper, and frustrated by our inability to fully understand, began tapping with his fingers on the bedside table. Finally, one of us recognized that he was using Morse code. He assumed, I believe, that I, as a U.S. Navy veteran, could translate, but I'd long forgotten. Dad learned the dots and dashes at Chanute Field's weather observation school during the war, and somehow retained it. It amazed us, and demonstrated that he still had his faculties. He also scribbled notes, and in one asked for some grapes. "Only if they're not fermented," my mother replied. The last thing, I recall him whispering was, "I don't want to die." He went on November 23, 1975, two weeks shy of his 58th birthday.

My mother was angry at being deserted after 34 years of marriage, and said as much at the three-day wake to any number of family members and friends. The turnout was large. Twice a day for three hours, we stood in line to receive commiserations from family and friends. John C. Lennon was a charming man and most of his contemporaries were still alive, including his five younger siblings, Mollie, Helen, Hughie, Angela, and Frank. Dad's mother, Gram Lennon, (neé Grant), then 84, grieved deeply, but she was also roiled that he let the booze get him—the idea that alcoholism was a disease had no purchase in those years. I recall her saying, "He always thought he was smarter than almost everyone else."

He did and he was. Well read, fluent in French and Latin, with a passable knowledge of German and enough Italian to read the librettos of the operas of Verdi and Puccini, he also composed songs on the piano (he copyrighted one). On Saturday mornings, he listened faithfully to the broadcasts of the Metropolitan Opera, anticipating some of the comments of announcer Milton J. Cross, and conducting the overtures before the living room mirror with his ivory baton. On Monday evenings we all watched *Our Hit Parade*, and within a day or two Dad was playing "Mr. Sandman," "Sixteen Tons," "Hernando's Hideaway," and other songs of the day. Although he was only a high school graduate, his vocabulary and knowledge of numerous writers—Fitzgerald, Conrad, and Dickens come to mind—were daunting.

My mother was also a voracious reader, especially of poetry. On many evenings she recited her favorites for me: Yeats's "When You Are Old," Hopkins's "Spring and Fall," Dickinson's "I Died for Beauty." Tennyson's "The Charge of the Light Brigade" was another favorite. When her children balked at performing a chore, Mom's voice rang out with a slight twist on a line from "The Charge": "Yours not to reason why / yours but to do or die." Others include Frost's "Birches," Longfellow's "The Wreck of the Hesperus," and Alfred Lord Noyes's "The Highwayman," which I pretty much had by heart. Under my mother's tutelage, I also memorized Service's "The Shooting of Dan McGrew" and "The House with Nobody in It" by Joyce Kilmer. My siblings and our children were all required by my mother to memorize this lugubrious piece, as were many schoolchildren of her era.

> Whenever I walk to Suffern along the Erie track
> I go by a poor old farmhouse with its shingles broken and black.
> I suppose I've passed it a hundred times, but I always stop for a minute
> And look at the house, the tragic house, the house with nobody in it.
> I never have seen a haunted house, but I hear there are such things;

That they hold the talk of spirits, their mirth and sorrowings.
I know this house isn't haunted, and I wish it were, I do;
For it wouldn't be so lonely if it had a ghost or two.

Somewhere, probably from Gram Lennon, I learned that Dad had an I.Q. of 138, measured when he was an Army officer during WWII. He acted as the family's dictionary, defining and spelling words for us, explaining current events via the large green atlas he treasured, and helping me with my Latin homework. He relished his role as knowledge font. For years, he completed the Sunday *New York Times* crossword puzzle. The *Times Book Review* had canonical status in our house, and from the late 1950s on, I saved every issue, lugging them from house to house. All because of Dad. He was a *litterateur*, a polymath. We knew it and he was happy to remind us if we forgot.

Dad's genius reputation was bolstered in 1950 when he and my mother appeared on the national radio program, *Break the Bank*, hosted by Bert Parks. Mom had sent in a postcard, and it was plucked from a wish bowl. They went to New York City and stayed at the Statler Hotel. Mom knew some of the answers, but Dad knew them all, and they broke the bank, winning $4,350, a sum that every Lennon knew. It paid for a new furnace in our home.

The mystery was why he'd never gone to college. My mother encouraged him, pointing out that two of her brothers went on the GI Bill. He was eligible, but demurred, postponed, joked it away. "What could they teach me?" he'd say with a chuckle. Money was no doubt a factor. When I was five in 1947, Peter was born, and the twins the following year. My mother worked at secretarial jobs, and encouraged him until she didn't. The Irish know how to bury things. By this time Dad was a salesman at the Fall River Electric Light Company. He didn't like the job, and loathed interacting with the hoi polloi, as he called them. I'd join him at work occasionally and help him stuff flyers into envelopes, a task he infinitely preferred to sucking up to customers shopping for stoves and refrigerators. His disdain puzzled me.

After work, he often went for drinks with his two literary pals, Bill McAvoy and Eddie Quirk, both of whom worked as clerks at City Hall. McAvoy was a charming character out of a Joyce short story. A singer and bibulous story-teller, he wore his overcoat over his shoulders, like a cloak, like John Barrymore. I was told this was "artistic." Eddie Quirk, also well-read, wore a vest, had thick glasses and a moustache, and was a student of ancient history. Years later, when I read about the owl-eyed gentleman in the library at Gatsby's mansion, Eddie leaped to mind. As a boy, I'd sit in his lap and he'd tell me about the Druids, the pharaohs, King Arthur and Mordred, and draw pictures of ancient urns and vases, plinths and columns. I believe I began telling people I wanted to be an archeologist because of his stories. The middle finger on one of his hands had been smashed and the digit permanently bent at the outermost joint. He had a way of using the crooked digit to guide his pencil as he sketched. I marveled at this, but couldn't get a clear answer as to how he got the injury. Many nights Dad, Bill, and Eddie careened into the house after dinner. Mom, who liked them both, often warmed up some food while Dad played the piano and they sang. Sometimes my Uncle Allen came by and the four men sang barbershop quartet songs.

Bill McAvoy's brother John was the impresario of the Somerset Playhouse, the local summer theater, and through him, my grandmother Mitchell began renting out her cottage next to our house to the actors. For about four years in the mid-1950s, Gram would make a summer visit to one of her children around the country, and our family got to meet the actors. I recall sitting next to Ethel Waters as she read her Bible under our weeping willow tree. Other guests were Farley Granger, Mollie Goldberg, Menasha Skulnik, Don Hayden (Gale Storm's boyfriend Freddy in the 50s TV series "My Little Margie," who wrecked Gram's kitchen when drunk), and Gypsy Rose Lee, accompanied by her two Siamese cats. Because my grandmother had no telephone, the actors had to come to our house to make calls. This is how in July 1955 I met Sarah Churchill (Winston's daughter), who was appearing in the lead role of *No Time for Comedy*. Buoyant and talkative, she called me "old sport," and borrowed my English bike for rides along the Taunton River. She heard my father playing the piano during one of her visits, and soon she and Dad were drinking highballs and working their way through the American songbook, as well as British favorites like "We'll Meet Again."

One of our neighbors was an old Englishman, James Blackledge, who lived with his wife down the street. Dad knew that he'd fought in the Boer War with Churchill, and invited him to meet Sarah. He declined, saying, "If it were Winnie, I'd pop over." Sarah got a good laugh when she heard this. She was close to her father, who was at that time still going strong. I wondered what my mother thought of Dad's duets with Sarah.

Only once do I recall my mother getting angry after one of Dad's drinking and singing evenings. She was washing dishes while he was sitting at the kitchen table with a drink after McAvoy and Quirk had departed. He sassed her about something and she answered him back. I was standing in the doorway to the living room, watching. When Dad cranked his sarcasm up another notch, Mom, an athletic redhead, whirled and from 15 feet away slung a plate like a discus at his head. He saw it coming and ducked, and then she lit into him amid the broken crockery.

It was many years before I came up with a supposition as to why my father refused to go to college. To explain, I have to go back to another puzzle: Dad's father, Hugh H. Lennon. I wasn't very old when I realized that he was missing, and asked Gram Lennon.

"Gram Mitchell has a husband. Where's yours?"

"He died a long time ago," she said quietly, looking away.

Mary Mitchell Lennon and John C. Lennon, 1966

My father's siblings were similarly vague. At family gatherings, no one ever spoke of Grandpa Lennon's virtues or foibles; there were no funny stories about his eccentricities, but plenty of grim ones about the family's hard times in the Great Depression. Only Aunt Mollie, my maiden aunt, as she was described, seemed to brighten when I asked about him. And ask I did. Something was being withheld, I suspected.

Gram Lennon was a textbook Irish matriarch, and attendance at her home at holidays was obligatory. All sixteen of my Lennon first cousins and their parents showed up, each bearing gifts for Gram and Mollie. We were usually joined by Gram's sister, Della Hinchcliffe, and her seven children and their families. We heard tales of filching coal off freight trains, and "shooting the butts"—scavenging half-smoked cigarettes from the gutters of Main Street in Fall River. When we visited, we often brought coffee cans filled with bacon fat. Gram used it as one the four ingredients in her homemade lard and lye soap, bars of which I still have. Here is her recipe, dictated to Mollie.

> 5 lbs. grease strained through a thin cloth. 1 can of Babbitt's Lye (No other kind). Dissolve the lye in one quart of cold water—let stand until cold. Let the grease get cold then add 1 handful of borax and one handful of sugar. Stir all together then add the lye and stir until it becomes creamy. Don't stir until it is thick. If you do it will become watery. Pour into a shallow pan (we call it a dripping pan). Let stand overnight—in the morning mark it off in squares. I let mine stand a few days before using.

Gram made soap during the Depression to avoid the cost of buying store-bought products like Ivory Soap, which was "99 and 44/100 percent pure," and expensive. But her soap was also functional. Made from grease, it was nonpareil in removing it, a kind of homeopathic cleanser.

Grandpa Lennon was never mentioned, but stories were told about his siblings, especially great-uncles Billy and Eddie, who were still alive and kicking. I learned that when my father was a teenager, he had moved across town to live with Aunt Della and her husband Bill, now deceased. This seemed odd to me.

"Why did he go to Della's"?

"Oh, she had more room."

There were many stories about how Dad was treated like a prince by Della, who had a woodworker make him his own pool cue. Well-fingered memories of Dad's lofty place at the Hinchcliffe home, and his cousins' comic resentments of this favoritism, were regularly retold. But, as bottles of Narragansett Beer were passed about, and piles of sweets were devoured (Gram Lennon became triumphantly fat after her retirement from the city hospital, where she worked in the laundry), not a word was spoken about Grandpa Lennon. Dad's fabulous pool cue was extolled as if it were Excalibur, King Arthur's indestructible sword. But Hugh H., the dead father, went unmentioned, although his specter haunted the family. I was pertinaciously curious—the family joke was that I'd been vaccinated with a phonograph needle—but the only other fact I squeezed out of the clan was that Grandpa's occupation required him to travel about New England opening new stores for the Great Atlantic and Pacific grocery store chain.

So it rested for many years. Gram and Mollie continued living together, eventually joined by Mollie's dear friend, Mac, Dorothy Macdonald, who had served with her in the WACs during WWII. Mac was in terrible shape: massive, bed-ridden, stone-blind. Loyal to the tradition of matriarchal fealty, I, like my siblings and cousins and our children, continued to visit Gram Lennon regularly all through the decades. We kissed Gram Lennon in her hospital bed in the living room, and then kissed Mac in hers on the other side of the house.

Then, in the fall of 1962, came a development. It was my senior year at Stonehill College, in North Easton, Massachusetts, and I was living with two buddies in a cottage near the school. Our landlady, Mrs. Loud, was a handsome woman in her late 50s. I talked to her occasionally, usually when I paid the rent money. One day she asked my last name, and when I told her she said that she had once known someone named Lennon.

"What was his first name?"

"Hugh."

"Where did you meet him"?

"At the racetrack."

When I went home for the weekend, I told my mother about the conversation, and asked if Mrs. Loud's racetrack friend might be Grandpa Lennon. She said nothing, but contacted Grandpa's namesake, Uncle Hughie. A month or so later Hughie reported that he had gone to the Registry of Vital Statistics at Boston City Hall where he learned what had happened to his father.

Over the next few months, the details of Grandpa's desertion came out. It wasn't a sharp break, but a slow, agonizing uncoupling over several months in 1932-33 while he was on the road for A & P. Visits home and support money slowed, and then stopped. His letters were few. Gram, an observant Catholic, never considered divorce. Finally, my father, then 15 or 16, was deputized to meet with him. Where I never learned. It was a hard meeting for both, I heard, but not from my father, and not from his mother. Pride prevented either from speaking of Grandpa. Uncle Hughie told me the bare facts, namely that Hugh H. was told by his eldest child that the family didn't want him to darken their door again.

He never did.

Hughie later learned from Uncle Billy that Grandpa had been fired from A & P for embezzlement, and lived thereafter as a gambler. Billy said that at times there was $10,000 in cash on the tables of the poker games he played. Hugh H. died of cancer a year or so after the end of WWII. He is buried in a Boston cemetery, which Uncle Hughie visited. One of the last messages from Hugh

H. was a birthday card he sent to Mollie on her 13th birthday in 1932. When she died at age 86, we found the card, addressed to Mary Louise Lennon, on her night table, signed, "With love, Dad."

My surmise is that Hugh H.'s desertion, and his eldest son informing him of the cleaving of familial ties, created a deep psychic wound in Dad. He became the man of the house, and went to work in the spinning mills while in high school, and then for the Electric Light Company. He was accorded recognition and sympathy, certainly, but always seemed to have a modestly aggrieved sense of entitlement.

He drank a bit and then, after the war, a lot. There was often a distant and solemn air about him, although it registered more on me than on my siblings. All three had a warm relationship with him, and have fond memories. His coolness toward me was there from the time he returned from the war. I recall my mother's fruitless pleading with him to play catch with me when I was in Little League, or help erect a basketball hoop. His distance increased when I entered college right after my 17th birthday. This was the same age, roughly, that Dad was when he had his fateful 1933 meeting with his father—and the moment when the country's, and his family's economic situation was most parlous. My sister Maureen thinks he was envious of me, and that could be. But it is also the case that Hugh H.'s lengthy absences, and then his disappearance into the gambling dens of Boston, meant that Dad lacked an efficacious role model. He had to figure out how to deal with fatherhood on the fly. Perhaps he concluded that I could, even should, have to do the same. In Dad's mind, one can surmise, his eldest son was a smart bit more prepared for adulthood than he had ever been. What, therefore, was the need to lave Michael in any bath of paternal solicitude? Tough it out.

I didn't fully recognize there was an emotional gap between us until Mailer began to fill it. This didn't happen overnight, and occurred only fleetingly during our annual summer visits to visit the

Mailers, and also when Bob Lucid and I made our regular trips to Brooklyn to pick up cartons of Mailer's papers and deposit them in the Manhattan storage vault. Other hints came from his letters and phone calls. There was one symbolic moment in the spring of 1986 at Elaine's restaurant in Manhattan. Norman and I were sitting at a small table across from the bar, and several people stopped at the table to gab with Mailer. George Plimpton was one of them. As we sipped our drinks, I handed Norman the first copy of a collection of essays about his work that I had edited. He read the first few pages of my introduction, put the book down, and asked me to be one of his literary executors. Norman needed informed comment on his work, and the support and recognition that went with it, and I was happy to provide it. But he also returned it. He read and then sent my writing to his agent, questioned and supported me concerning my ambitions and problems and, over the years, heard and responded thoughtfully to Lennon family history, including my father's sad story. Norman was also generous with our sons, who saw him as an avuncular figure, and engaged them in open-ended table talk.

I don't want to leave a misleading impression of Dad. He was always a good, faithful provider—a couple of orders of magnitude better than Hugh H., obviously—and was also ferociously loyal to his extended family. The bonds of affection with his mother and Aunt Della were especially strong. He worked as a loom fixer, meter reader, appliance salesman, Metropolitan Life insurance man, and other jobs. I recall him leaving early on winter weekends wearing his old army field jacket to do electrical wiring work for $20 a day. He and his employer, Milt, would arrive home in the dark rubbing their red hands, and then drink Caribous, half whiskey and half Flame Tokay. Finally, in his early 40s, he got a good job as an auditor for the Massachusetts National Guard, but retired early due to his declining health. He remained in the Guard for many years, and was ultimately promoted to Lt. Colonel.

As for college, it's possible that Dad may have been uneasy about it, fearing failure, or perhaps he wished to suck on the marrow of his bitterness. Or, more likely, he felt he had suffered enough, given enough, and shouldn't have to exert himself anymore. I know that when I made plans to attend college, he was scornful: "Why does he need to go to college?" he asked my mother. By the late 1960s, when I was in graduate school, he was deep into drink. I was busy teaching and taking classes and only visited a couple of times a month. On days when he knew I was coming, according to my sisters (who sedulously watched over him), he spent hours memorizing obscure words from the dictionary, and then took pains to induce me to define them. He took great delight in criticizing my errors in literary lore and grammar.

Dad, I was told by Hughie, resembled their father. Decades later this was confirmed. In a cache of old newspaper clippings, Mass cards, and obituaries that my sisters had preserved was a photograph on the front of a penny postcard. Postmarked Charlestown Station, Boston, January 1912, it is addressed to 18-year old Della Grant, Gram Lennon's sister. It shows Hugh H. and three other men in white jackets and ties behind the counter of a gas-lit A & P market with a stamped tin ceiling. Black-haired and handsome—like my father—Hugh H. is the tallest, looks to be the oldest (he was 28), and appears to be the manager. He appears to be looking to his left. Canned goods are in numbered shelves behind them, and to the side of the counter is a sign, "Very Best Tea 29¢," and a display from the National Biscuit Company. His note to Della reads: "Although this is rather dark you can tell who we are. Twoomey is at the end rested on a barrel."

Five years after the card was sent, on February 6, 1917, Hugh H. married Mary A. Grant, and by 1924 they were the parents of six children. Their marriage lasted 29 years, but they lived together for only half that span. Gram Lennon was nearly beggared by her husband's desertion, but her later years were less harsh. Her meager

Hugh H. Lennon, second from left, and co-workers, A&P Store, Boston, 1912

washerwoman pension from the City of Fall River was augmented by Mollie and her siblings, and she had endless visits from her children, grandchildren, and their children. After Hughie found his father's grave, he did some further research. He found that as his legal spouse, Gram was eligible for her husband's Social Security pension. The marriage and death certificates were submitted and Gram collected it for the next 37 years. She died in 1990, just a few months short of her 100th birthday.

Seeking to complete the circle of the story, I decided to tell Mrs. Loud about Uncle Hughie's detective work. My pals and I were graduating—it was the end of May 1963—and I had to return the key to the cottage. As I began to lay out the details of Hugh H.'s desertion, she told me that she wasn't interested, took the key and shut the door in my face. When I informed my father of Mrs. Loud's response, he nodded, but said not a word.

FINIS

About The Author

J. Michael Lennon, Professor Emeritus of English at Wilkes University, and Chair of the Editorial Board of the *Mailer Review*, is the author or editor of several books about Norman Mailer, including *Norman Mailer: A Double Life* (2013), *Selected Letters of Norman Mailer* (2014), and *On God: An Uncommon Conversation* (2007, co-authored with Mailer). He teaches in the Maslow Family Graduate Creative Writing Program at Wilkes University, which he co-founded in 2005. His work has appeared in *Paris Review, New Yorker, New York Review of Books, New York, Washington Post, Chicago Tribune, Times Literary Supplement, Provincetown Arts, Hippocampus,* and the *Mailer Review.*

Books from Etruscan Press

Zarathustra Must Die | Dorian Alexander
The Disappearance of Seth | Kazim Ali
The Last Orgasm | Nin Andrews
Drift Ice | Jennifer Atkinson
Crow Man | Tom Bailey
Coronology | Claire Bateman
Reading the Signs and other itinerant essays | Stephen Benz
Topographies | Stephen Benz
What We Ask of Flesh | Remica L. Bingham
The Greatest Jewish-American Lover in Hungarian History | Michael Blumenthal
No Hurry | Michael Blumenthal
Choir of the Wells | Bruce Bond
Cinder | Bruce Bond
The Other Sky | Bruce Bond and Aron Wiesenfeld
Peal | Bruce Bond
Scar | Bruce Bond
Poems and Their Making: A Conversation | Moderated by Philip Brady
Crave: Sojourn of a Hungry Soul | Laurie Jean Cannady
Toucans in the Arctic | Scott Coffel
Sixteen | Auguste Corteau
Wattle & daub | Brian Coughlan
Body of a Dancer | Renée E. D'Aoust
Generations: Lullaby With Incendiary Device, The Nazi Patrol and How It Is That We | Dante Di Stefano, William Heyen, and H. L. Hix
Ill Angels | Dante Di Stefano
Aard-vark to Axolotl: Pictures From my Grandfather's Dictionary | Karen Donovan
Trio: Planet Parable, Run: A Verse-History of Victoria Woodhull, and Endless Body | Karen Donovan, Diane Raptosh, and Daneen Wardrop
Scything Grace | Sean Thomas Dougherty

Etruscan Press Is Proud of Support Received From

Wilkes University

Youngstown State University

Ohio Arts Council

The Stephen & Jeryl Oristaglio Foundation

Community of Literary Magazines and Presses

National Endowment for the Arts

Drs. Barbara Brothers & Gratia Murphy Endowment

The Thendara Foundation

Founded in 2001 with a generous grant from the Oristaglio Foundation, Etruscan Press is a nonprofit cooperative of poets and writers working to produce and promote books that nurture the dialogue among genres, achieve a distinctive voice, and reshape the literary and cultural histories of which we are a part.

etruscan press
www.etruscanpress.org
Etruscan Press books may be ordered from

Consortium Book Sales and Distribution
800.283.3572
www.cbsd.com

Etruscan Press is a 501(c)(3) nonprofit organization.
Contributions to Etruscan Press are tax deductible
as allowed under applicable law.
For more information, a prospectus,
or to order one of our titles,
contact us at books@etruscanpress.org.